HARRY HALL'S
CLASSIC WINNERS

Harry Hall, with his son Ernest

Harry Hall's Classic Winners

Charles Lane

J.A. ALLEN

Published in Great Britain in 1990 by
J. A. Allen & Company Limited
1 Lower Grosvenor Place
London SW1W 0EL

Typeset in 11/12½ pt Goudy Old Style by
Typeset by Setrite Typesetters Ltd, Hong Kong
Printed in Hong Kong by Dah Hua Printing Press Co Ltd
Designed by Nancy Lawrence

British Library Cataloguing in Publication Data
Lane, Charles
 Harry Hall's Classic Winners.
 1. English paintings. Hall, Harry, 1815−1882
 759.2

 ISBN 0−85131−471−6

For Daphne,
in memory of
George

CONTENTS

ILLUSTRATIONS

Monochrome

ACKNOWLEDGEMENTS

I AM IMMENSELY grateful to the many individuals who have responded to my questions about racehorses and their owners, often providing an interesting anecdote of their nineteenth century relatives who are, for the most part, the subjects of this book. Without their help the account of the Classic races would lack colour and be no more than a list of results. I am also particularly grateful to Major David Swannell and Mr David Oldrey who kindly read the book and made many extremely valuable comments and corrections.

The biographical details of the Hall family are drawn from a number of sources, not least of which being the two great-granddaughters of the artist. Dr Joanna Martin and Mrs A. Boulton have made extensive searches on my behalf and I am equally grateful to Miss Joan Bailey who has scoured magazines and newspapers for references to Harry Hall and his work.

The staffs of the London Library, the Devon Library Services at Exeter and the Bournemouth Library patiently dealt with many requests and permitted me to retain rare books for long periods. I am most grateful to them. I wish to record my gratitude to Mrs Rhodes and Miss Eeles whose quick skill allowed me to edit the typescript almost within hours of their receiving the manuscript pages.

Owners in England and America have been very generous in letting me use photographs of their paintings. For obvious reasons the source of many of these must remain anonymous and are shown as from a private collection. The Stewards of the Jockey Club have also kindly allowed me to illustrate their portraits of jockeys painted by Harry Hall for *The Sporting Magazine*. I am indebted to the trustees of a number of museums and galleries for the use of photographs of works from their collections. Without the help of Mr David Fuller of Arthur Ackermann & Son and Mr Byfield of Richard Green my selection of photographs would have been too limited to do justice to Hall. Mr Julian Armytage has come to my aid on many occasions with prints of racehorses. Acknowledgement of all these sources is given with the illustrations.

Lastly, I acknowledge and apologise to the shade of Sir Francis Hastings Doyle whose ballad of a Yorkshire horse winning the Derby I have transformed to use as an introduction to each chapter of this book.

INTRODUCTION

In the Preface to his book *From Gladiateur to Persimmon*, Sydenham Dixon wrote: 'I have devoted myself almost exclusively to horses rather than to men. In the first place, I may frankly confess to regarding the former as infinitely more interesting of the two, and, in the second, it is possible to write perfectly freely and truthfully about them without any serious fear of giving offence. When one is dealing with men the case is altogether different.' I am sure it was the possibility of upsetting his contemporaries more than a real belief that only the characters and performances of horses were worth his attention which led Dixon to approach his story of thirty years of turf history in this way. More than a century has passed since the death of Harry Hall so I feel less constrained in writing about men (and women) rather than horses, finding the former so much more interesting.

Hall learnt first to paint human portraits and invariably where his pictures include owners, trainers and jockeys they are better likenesses than the winning colt or filly. By inference I am disparaging of Harry Hall's ability to paint the horse and this requires some explanation. If one compares contemporary written descriptions of Classic winners in the sporting magazines of the period with Hall's racehorse portraits one is immediately struck by the way they so exactly accord. This is often to the extent that in a painting the 'long neck' or 'short barrel' is represented in caricature. This element is most marked in the portraits he painted for the print publishers Fuller, Moore and Baily from 1842 to 1881. However, even taking into account that an early photograph may

show a past winner as an aged stallion and a painting of the same horse as the three-year-old victor of the 2,000 Guineas, the differences are too great to pretend that Hall painted with the realism of George Stubbs — notwithstanding the criticism of The Druid, Sydenham Dixon's father, that Stubbs's 'chief failing was a lack of anatomical knowledge'!

From the time that J. F. Herring turned to painting farmyard scenes until the introduction of the tinted photograph, Harry Hall was without equal in the business of portraying on panel and canvas the humans and horses comprising the 'turf'. Whether at a race meeting or in his studio in Church Lane, Newmarket, the artist was in the company of the racing fraternity and journalists. They were attracted by his pithy comments and shrewd observations on the shape, fitness and probable performance of a 'sure thing'. At his busiest in the 1850s and 1860s when supplying paintings or sketches for reproduction by print publishers, the proprietors of *The Sporting Magazine*, *The Field*, the *Illustrated London News* and once for *Punch*, he was, in effect, a sporting journalist in paint. As a journalist he had to meet deadlines, which accounts for some of his work being judged as less than perfect. Allowed time and a composition of his own designing, Hall painted many accurate, decorative and appealing pictures recording the best horses of his day and, just as importantly, their attendants.

Most of this book is devoted to the human *dramatis personae* of the Classic races during Hall's working lifetime, illustrated to a large extent by his paintings of racehorses.

CHAPTER 1
1838−1840

The fairest of the land are here
To watch the struggle of the year
The dew of beauty and of mirth
Lies on the living flowers of earth

THE DERBY AT EPSOM (established in 1780) and St Leger at Doncaster (1776) were regarded as the highlights of the Racing Calendar in the late 1830s. However, the importance of the 2,000 Guineas Stakes at Newmarket was well established, since the performance of the horses which ran provided a valuable indicator to their likely success or otherwise in later races, particularly the Derby. Similarly, the running of the fillies in the Newmarket 1,000 Guineas, which took place two days after the 2,000 Guineas, gave a strong indication of their fitness for the Epsom Oaks (1799) run two days after the Derby. These five races, all for three-year-old horses, are described as the 'Classics'. Of almost equal importance in the minds of owners were the Gold Cups at Doncaster (1766), Ascot (1807) and Goodwood (1812) for three-year-old horses or older.

While Newmarket could claim to be the centre of racing in the late 1830s the Jockey Club, whose rooms were in the town, was only just beginning to extend what might loosely be described as the control of racing to other courses across the country. Until this time each meeting had its own stewards sometimes jealously guarding their inadequate local rules; not that those at Newmarket were by any standard perfect. The movement of horses was improving rapidly, making it easier for them to race far from their training stables. All concerned soon saw the advantages of having uniform regulations for flat racing wherever it took place. The local stewards accepted that an aspect of attracting large fields of subscribers to races, with their consequent high value stakes, was to run a well-regulated meeting based on rules tried and tested at Newmarket by the important owners of the day − the stewards and members of the Jockey Club.

An even more pressing reason to regularise the sport was to eradicate its reputation for skulduggery, trickery, fraud, violence, bribery and other devious practices which had been rampant for many years. The standing in society of rich and influential men was undermined by their involvement in the murky world of the turf and the scandals associated with betting, the root cause of every malpractice.

In the eighteenth century gentlemen arranged matches between their horses, agreed the terms between themselves, sometimes with the help of a neutral handicapper, and wagered for a certain sum their own horse would win. If one of the owners wished to call off the match this was accomplished by a pre-determined forfeit being given to the other side. Such arrangements were not impervious to malpractices, particularly when third parties wished to bet on the outcome, but generally there were very few occasions when the match was not run as intended by the horses' owners. With the increase in the number of 'open' races and the cost of maintaining large stables which could not be covered by winning stakes alone (although these were slowly increasing), it was necessary and possible for owners to bet on others' horses as well as their own. This required a knowledge of the performance of potential runners which introduced the employment of touts − euphemistically known as 'gentlemen of observation' − when trials were run before races. Having acquired information on the fitness or failure of a horse it then became necessary either to make a bet oneself or employ a commissioner to arrange favourable wagers with those who had less knowledge of the horse's current form. In turn the commission agents began to offer betting prices on their own account on all the horses in a race. This was known as a betting-round or making a book and, hence, the profession of bookmaker came into being. To defend their own position and interests bookmakers formed a loose collective known as the Ring. A number of the more successful became owners of racehorses as well as bookmakers but were usually of a very different pedigree to those who had made private wagers on matches in the past.

In 1776 the enterprising Richard Tattersall obtained a long lease on some land at Hyde Park Corner, London where he established weekly sales of horses and, later, hounds and carriages. The Corner, as it was known, became a fashionable meeting place. In 1780 Tattersall provided a room where members of the Jockey Club could meet and in 1818 a new Subscription Room was built where individuals could make their bets with each other at their own odds. It was not long before members of the Ring also made themselves available at Tattersalls. Wagers were settled on the Monday morning following the race and it was then that a few, unable to meet their debts, became defaulters. Two years before this account starts, between the Derby and settling day, the Hon. Berkely Craven shot himself — unable to face the disgrace of defaulting by £800 — but this was an exceptional occurrence.

The greed of bookmakers and gamblers led them to devise ways of 'making the opposition safe' by tampering with horses, bribing trainers and jockeys (who were allowed to bet in the nineteenth century) and other acts of corruption. At the same time a few owners from older, aristocratic families were not beyond misleading others about the performance of their horses in trials to influence the betting odds in their favour, scratching horses at the last moment usually because they were pre-empted in the betting and could not obtain the long odds they wanted, and other practices which sailed close to the wind of dishonesty.

Charles Greville, an impecunious manager and owner of racehorses (with two Classic winners to his name: Preserve in the 1835 1,000 Guineas and Mango in the 1837 St Leger), declared his ambivalent feelings for racing in his Memoirs when he wrote: 'my life is spent in the alternations of excitement from the amusement and speculation of the turf and of remorse and shame at the pursuit itself'. Again in 1846, when his horse Alarm won the Emperor's Cup (which took the place of the Ascot Gold Cup from 1845 to 1853), he reflects upon the 'moment of excitement and enjoyment when I won this fine piece of plate; but that past, there returned the undying consciousness of the unworthiness of the pursuit'. He was always hoping for a successful betting coup, although he could rarely afford to lay out a large sum to realise one, to make him

independent, 'enable me to relinquish my office when I pleased [Clerk to the Privy Council] and be my own man, and giving me the power of doing many an act of kindness, and assisting those I care for'. He finally disentangled himself as an owner of racehorses in 1855 after forty years of enjoyment and disgust.

For a time Charles Greville was the intimate friend and racing confederate of his cousin Lord George Bentinck, the third son of the fourth Duke of Portland. The Duke was a modest, generous and enlightened man with an interest in racing which did not include betting. Lord George had a far more complex personality. Among his few friends he could be good-natured, charming, even fun, although his sense of humour was unpredictable. He was ambitious for success in politics and racing at almost any cost, demonstrating the darker side to his character as domineering, ruthless, meddlesome and sometimes vindictive to those who showed opposition to his plans.

Born in 1802, Bentinck was introduced to racing in 1824 shortly before succeeding his brother the Marquis of Titchfield as Member of Parliament for Lyme Regis and becoming Private Secretary to George Canning. Previously he had been a quarrelsome officer in the 9th Lancers and later the 2nd Life Guards. He quickly became obsessed with the turf, betting large sums and owning a long string of racehorses. Both these activities he hid from his father whom he knew would disapprove, particularly of his betting. His horses ran in the names of Greville, Lord Lichfield, the Duke of Richmond and some others of less repute with whom he seemed content to associate at that time. After a disastrous betting loss his father discovered what his son was doing and tried to divert him to other fields. In this he was unsuccessful and within a year Bentinck was again making his mark on the turf. From 1830 he was imposing his strong will on every aspect of racing aimed at ensuring his own success. He indulged in practices which could be described as within the letter but not always the spirit of the admittedly ill-defined and few laws of racing at the time. He also introduced improvements in the organisation of meetings which eradicated some of the tricks which could be practised between the saddling of a racehorse and when it passed the judge's eye — to whom the winner was previously expected to give a present! Later, he became the detective of the turf declaring war on the blackguard owners, trainers and jockeys with whom he had previously been happy to consort. His aristocratic bearing, tall and upright stature, good looks and individual yet perfect dress obtained for him the grudging admiration of friend and foe alike in politics and on the turf. From his immense energy and determination there were great expectations that the 'dictator' of the turf might also become the Prime Minister of England.

In 1838 Bentinck was racing his horses in his own name. They were trained by John Barham Day and his sons at Danebury in Wiltshire, from where Grey Momus came to Newmarket in the late spring to win the 2,000 Guineas Stakes and become the favourite for the Derby. The four 2,000 Guineas from 1834 to 1837 had been won by horses owned by Lord Jersey and, although Bentinck won this race again in 1840, the general tendency from the late 1830s onwards was for the Classics to be less dominated by a small number of men. The field of owners expanded enormously and while a few were successful in consecutive years in one race or another, this became exceptional. Sir Gilbert Heathcote's Amato won the 1838 Derby and Lord Chesterfield carried off the Oaks with Industry and the St Leger with Don John in the same year.

Sir Gilbert and the sixth Earl of Chesterfield had very different natures to that of Bentinck and, in their individual ways, personified those characteristics and virtues which were lacking among many turfites. In some respects it was surprising that they were associated with this 'shameful pursuit', but without their interest and that of others like them, racing might not have survived through the years when its reputation sank so low, from 1800 to 1860.

The little Amato was raised in a paddock close both to the Epsom course and his owner's home. Having performed well in trials the colt ridden by James Chapple (Plate 41) ran first time out in the Derby, broke down shortly afterwards and never raced again. Amato was the only Classic winner of this munificent and unselfish man who, as well as generously rewarding his trainers and jockeys, usually gave whatever stakes he won to the poor of the neighbourhood.

Lord Chesterfield was equally generous, good-natured and extremely popular in every level of society. He came to racing as a young man in 1827 when he too was a confederate of Charles Greville. Money being no object at first, he quickly came to prominence although he owned no Classic winners before Industry and Don John; both were trained by the successful northern trainer John Scott and ridden by his brother, Bill, then in his prime. Chesterfield was an excellent judge of horses and racing was not his only involvement with them. He was master of the Royal Buckhounds and later the Pytchley, and handled the team of his own drag and other coaches with great skill. He sought the best in everything, enjoying life to the full, but it was the London gaming tables which made deep inroads into his personal fortune, rather than racing. Realising he could not sustain

the early pace, he set about reducing his stud (although he again won the Oaks in 1849), selling some of his property and living quietly. In this way he managed to keep his interest in the turf, but on a much more modest scale. He remained a popular figure but withdrew into a strange world of living in lodgings when in London; there he slept for most of the day, was driven in a cab to his club for dinner and left in the early hours of the morning to return to bed. In the country, at Bretby Park, his regime was similar to that for London except that he spent many hours gazing at the stars through a telescope adjusted by his butler. Resulting as it did from a drastic change of circumstances, this behaviour was no more eccentric than that of Mr Fulwar Craven who for many years consorted with the liveliest and lowest of the racing world before becoming a paragon of religious rectitude. In the 1830s and 1840s sudden changes of fortune among racing men were quite common and their consequences were not yet the subject of Victorian moral condemnation or praise.

— 1839 —

The Derby of 1839 was won by Bloomsbury raced in the name of Mr William Ridsdale, the brother of the professional better and owner, Robert Ridsdale. It is said that Robert started life as a gentleman's servant, was successful in backing horses, joined forces with John Gully (whose life is described later), was a fine horseman and, on the one hand considered moderately honest, but on the other known as a 'most dangerous and dexterous manipulator of jockeys'. The apogee of his success was winning the 1832 Derby with St Giles. Robert then quarrelled with his erstwhile confederate and despite successfully sueing Gully and winning damages, his downfall quickly followed and he was forced to sell his horses. His brother William, who at the time was acting as trainer for Lord Chesterfield, took over a foal whom no one else would buy and named him Bloomsbury. There was some doubt as to who owned the colt, Lord Chesterfield or William Ridsdale, which started a succession of unsatisfactory events and possible irregularities.

Bloomsbury, like Amato the year before, had not run before the Derby and consequently started as an outsider, although the Ridsdale brothers knew his quality. The race took place in miserable conditions for mid May with an icy east wind and a snow flurry. Simeon Templeman (Plate 41), Bloomsbury's rider, was one of the fraternity of north-country jockeys who were beginning to invade the south with increasing

1 *Harry Hall, a self-portrait as a young man* Private collection

success. A taciturn and honest sportsman, 'Castor' in *The Sporting Magazine* describes him as one who:

> might be bold enough to let Mr Hall take or steal a sketch of him; but when you come to ask for something to associate with this — where he was born? which were the best horses he ever rode? and so forth — then will he draw up and consider, deliberately enough, whether he had not better follow his usual tactics, and hold his tongue.

Bloomsbury was his first Derby winner, and he was as ignorant as the public of the colt's ability, not betting a shilling on the outcome. Mr Fulwar Craven's Deception, with Trenn up, made the running and once in the straight built up a lead by being driven on by her jockey at a pace she could not sustain. Simeon Templeman held Bloomsbury until the last furlong when he made his effort and beat Deception by a length. There were those who thought Trenn never intended to win with the horse he trained and rode. Two days after the race, (when Deception had won the Oaks, ridden by J. B. Day), Lord George Bentinck in one of his meddlesome moods persuaded the eccentric Fulwar Craven to object to Bloomsbury's Derby victory on the grounds that his entry description did not tally with the Stud Book. The stewards at Epsom overruled this objection when Craven failed to produce any evidence in time. Bloomsbury went on to win at Ascot. On this occasion Lord Lichfield owned the runner-up and, in turn, he was pressed by

Bentinck to object and place the matter before the Jockey Club. Again, insufficient evidence could be found and the case was withdrawn by Lichfield. In the meantime, Bentinck had persuaded Weatherby's, the Derby stake holders, not to pay Ridsdale. The unfortunate William then had to take the case to court where, on the evidence available, the jury quite rightly found in his favour. William Ridsdale was one of the first to win the Derby who was neither an aristocrat nor rich nor landed. I cannot help wondering, base as the thought may be, if this was the reason for those who so determinedly tried to deny him success. There was certainly some cause to doubt the complete probity of Bloomsbury's age and antecedents, but the efforts to have him disqualified verged on the vindictive.

In the autumn Bloomsbury was defeated in the St Leger. Had he won, it is possible that Robert Ridsdale might have recovered from his earlier crash, but he died a few years later in desperate poverty. Bloomsbury was placed in a number of races in 1840 and was exported to Germany at the end of the following season. A redeeming feature of the story was a commission for Harry Hall to paint Bloomsbury with his jockey, owner and lad, (Plate 9).

Harry Hall was born in Cambridge on 18 August 1815, the first son of Henry Atherton Hall, yeoman and later butler at St John's College, and Maria Mann (Prior). From an early age he showed considerable talent with the pencil as the self-portrait (Plate 1)

2 *Mr Edward Weatherby, attributed to Harry Hall* Private collection

shows. For a short time he was sent to London to study painting with a Mr Pavis, and it is probable that he was instructed in painting horses by Abraham Cooper. The first record that I have of Harry Hall's work comes from an advertisement in the *Suffolk Chronicle* for Saturday 30 December 1837:

To be Published by Subscription
a Portrait
of
FRANCIS KING EAGLE, ESQ.,
from a Drawing
(made expressly for the purpose)
by Mr Henry Hall
The Drawing may be seen at Mr Newby's, Bookseller, Angel Hill, Bury St Edmund's, where names of Subscribers are received. Prints 5s; Proofs on India Paper, 10s

Whether Newby found enough subscribers for this venture, I do not know.

By 1838 Hall was living at The Star Family and Commercial Inn at the corner of Sun Lane and the High Street, Newmarket. He was already painting those connected with the town and the turf. He first exhibited at the Royal Academy in this year showing a portrait of Mr Edward Weatherby, Keeper of the Match Book (Plate 2). Another portrait of the period is that of Christopher Wilson, a Yorkshireman who was a staunch supporter of racing. He was a senior member of the Jockey Club, respected for his honesty and straight dealing during a period when these qualities were uncommon among turfites. Among his racing successes were Champion, the first horse to win the Derby and St Leger, in 1800; Wizard who won the first 2,000 Guineas in 1809 and Charlotte who won the first 1,000 Guineas in 1814. The portrait of this 'father of the turf' was engraved by F. C. Lewis (Plate 3).

Hall's portrait of Bloomsbury (Plate 9) is extremely fine. In composition there are echoes of Abraham Cooper and in the figures a little of Ben Marshall, Cooper's tutor. The lack of landscape detail and almost cloudless sky give Bloomsbury, William Ridsdale and his pony a statuesque air offset by the casualness of the lad who folds the rug. Perhaps Sim Templeman is a shade too small on Bloomsbury's back, but contemporary descriptions of the long-

3 *Mr Christopher Wilson, by Harry Hall. Engraved by F.C. Lewis*
Courtesy of the Trustees of the British Museum

necked colt are faithfully recorded in paint by Hall. The picture was completed in early 1840 and shown at the Royal Society of British Artists' annual exhibition later that year.

— 1840 —

Undoubtedly 1840 was Crucifix's year. She won the 2,000 Guineas, 1,000 Guineas and Oaks for Lord George Bentinck. She had been bought at Lord Chesterfield's sale with her dam for a very small sum, but her potential was soon recognised by Bentinck and the Days who trained her. John Day Snr rode her in all three Classics, but the race over the hard Epsom ground was her last. At stud she bore Surplice, whom Bentinck sold as a yearling with his complete stables in 1846. To his chagrin, the colt won the Derby two years later.

Harry Hall painted two large portraits of Crucifix composed in much the same manner as that of Bloomsbury, with John Day Jnr standing by his hack

in a similar position to that of William Ridsdale in the earlier picture. The sky and ground are dealt with a little more fully than previously, in the same Newmarket setting (Plate 10). Crucifix's small head and long, thin neck reflect the style which Herring had been pursuing for a quarter of the century, but which Marshall had partly avoided and Stubbs, with his anatomical honesty, had never employed. In the painting of racehorses Hall somewhat overdid these features, but in his paintings of mares and stallions the head and neck are more realistically proportioned. The two versions of this scene are identical in composition. One is in the Paul Mellon Collection at the Yale Center for British Art and the other in private hands, the latter showing more landscape detail than the former. Hall also painted Crucifix in a loosebox. This smaller picture may have been commissioned by the proprietors of *the Sporting Magazine* or bought by them, for it was engraved and appeared in the periodical in September 1840.

The Queen and the Prince Consort visited the Derby this year. It was a fine, early June day but their presence was received without enthusiasm by the crowd who had come out of London for some fresh air, away from the hard times and unsettled atmosphere which prevailed in the city. Charles Greville records that when the Queen had visited Ascot two years previously there were: 'few hats taken off. This remark of respect has quite gone out of use, and neither her station nor her sex procures it; we are not the nearer a revolution for this, but it is ugly.' On both occasions the Queen was charming, speaking to everyone she could, but Derby Day was then less of a social occasion than a few years later which, with the cool reception, may account for her not repeating the visit.

The runners in the Derby were a moderate lot. The winner, Little Wonder, who, unknown to his owner, a Mr Robertson of Berwick-on-Tweed, may have had a year in hand on the day of the race. Forth, his trainer, knew very well and won a considerable fortune on the horse which was skilfully ridden by Macdonald, defeating the wily Bill Scott on Lord Westminster's favourite, Launcelot. However, Scott won the St Leger with Launcelot. The Marquis of Westminster ran two horses in the race, Launcelot and Maroon; the latter was ridden by Holmes. At the finish Holmes had to pull Maroon since the bay colt looked like passing the judge's eye first. By his Lordship declaring for Launcelot to win before the start, he had the right to have Maroon 'pulled' so that his horses finished in the order he wished. This rather strange procedure (to the layman) continued for many years. This was Scott's third, if rather hollow, successive win at Doncaster, further reinforcing his domination of the race (Scott rode the winner in 1821, 1825, 1828, 1829, 1838, 1839, 1840, 1841 and lastly in 1846).

As far as I am aware, Hall was not commissioned to paint Launcelot or Little Wonder. As yet he had to step across the threshold of being asked regularly to supply designs for the print publishers. These aquatint plates of the Classic winners of the day were both very fine reproductions and extremely popular. While the fee paid to the artist was not generous, the advertisement of his name at the foot of the print was far more valuable. For some months of 1840 and 1841 J. F. Herring was in France completing a commission of the Duke of Orleans to paint a number of his horses. Some of these pictures were engraved and published in London by John Moore ('Printseller by Appointment to HRH the Duke of Orleans') of Upper St Martin's Lane. This may have annoyed S. and J. Fuller to whom Herring was engaged to provide the originals for their two outstanding series of St Leger and Derby winners dating from 1815 and 1827 respectively. Whatever the reason, there seems to have been a break in the Fuller—Herring relationship which soon provided an opening for Hall, albeit for only a few years with this publisher.

At the end of 1840 Hall was twenty-five years old and his pictures of Bloomsbury and Crucifix show him to be a mature and gifted painter of both human and horse portraits. The exhibited canvas of Bloomsbury, let alone the commission to paint Crucifix, must have done much to establish his name as the most promising successor to Herring whose enthusiasm for painting racehorses was apparently on the wane.

CHAPTER 2

1841–1845

Snorting and prancing — sidling by
With arching neck, and glancing eye,
In every shape of strength and grace,
The horses gather for the race.

A MISLEADING PICTURE of the extent of the turf in the 1840s might be deduced by considering, as I do here, only the horses, their owners, trainers and jockeys who were successful in the Classic races. These winners, both equine and human, formed a very small proportion of the total numbers involved in this sport, now called an 'industry' — but an unlikely description one hundred and fifty years ago. The horses which won the Classic races were among the best of their age in the country but there were others of similar quality perhaps only lacking their top form on the vital day. The 'also ran' of the Classics were often the winners of considerable stakes both on the three courses of these five races and elsewhere in the country. In 1841 over 300 owners had their colours shown in the Racing Calendar and there were more than 1,200 racehorses under training excluding those at stud. On the one hand there were some of modest means who may have had one or two horses with a public trainer, while on the other, in 1845, Lord George Bentinck kept sixty thoroughbreds in training of which thirty-six started in 195 races. This cost him, with stakes and forfeits, over £20,000. Horses had to be entered well in advance of the race itself so that while there were 103 subscribers for the Oaks of 1840, only fifteen fillies ran on the day. In 1841, twenty-nine runners comprised the largest field in the history of the Derby to that year, drawn from 154 subscribers. The smallest Derby field was four in 1794. These statistics may provide an indication of the scope of the turf of the period. While the Classic races were for three-year-olds only, their prestige was rightly acknowledged and based on the obvious fact that their winners were the 'pick of the bunch'. At the same time, nothing is certain in racing and luck played a major part for the winners of at least two out of the five Classics every year.

Lord Albermarle's Ralph won the 2,000 Guineas of 1841. This chestnut colt was ridden by John Barham Day. He was forty-six years old and approaching his prime as a trainer while coming to the end of his race riding career which had started, in Classic winning terms, in 1826. The Duke of Grafton was his patron and friend and it was in 1826 that he rode the winners of the 2,000 and 1,000 Guineas for him. As a jockey, the Derby eluded him, but he rode three more 2,000 and four more 1,000 Guineas winners as well as five Oaks and two St Legers, which was a remarkable score in the years that Jem Robinson dominated the scales.

John Day had also long been the Duke of Portland's favourite jockey and when the latter's son, Lord George Bentinck, took up racing in earnest it was natural that he too should call on Day from time to time, and it was to his stables at Danebury that Bentinck brought some of his horses in 1836. Lord George spent a considerable sum on the Danebury gallops and paddocks, reportedly joining in the physical task of spreading bone meal to improve the soil. A return for this investment came with Grey Momus winning the 2,000 Guineas in 1838 and, as we have seen, Crucifix's remarkable performance in the 2,000 Guineas, 1,000 Guineas and Oaks of 1840. With the patronage of the Dukes of Grafton and Portland, Bentinck and other leading owners of the day, the stables flourished under the austere and vigorous direction of John Day; 'Honest John', as Bentinck named him. However, there was a trait in Day's character which indirectly led to his undoing, and that was betting. As a jockey he often bet on the horses he rode but also sometimes on those who were ridden against him, which was unwise; and, as a public trainer, he sometimes found it difficult to do his best with a horse for one owner when, in the same race and from his own stables, there was a chance of

4 *Mr John Barham Day, with his sons John and William Day, by Harry Hall, 1841*
Courtesy of the Trustees of the Tate Gallery

making a good wager by backing another's. In 1841, suspecting that training was being conducted more for the convenience of the Days' betting arrangements than his own, Lord George Bentinck left Danebury and moved all his horses to Goodwood. This was a bitter blow to John Day Snr and his older sons who were by then assisting him. Perhaps Lord George was being unfair, but it was typical of the man to brook no opposition, imagined or real. From later incidents and because of the company which the Days kept, it is not difficult to believe that part of Bentinck's suspicions were justified.

John Day had twelve children. Among them were John Day Jnr, a more than adequate jockey and later trainer; Sam, a potentially outstanding rider who rode Greville's Mango in the 1837 St Leger but died a year later after a hunting accident, aged nineteen; William, a good jockey but a better (if not very straight) trainer; and Alfred Day, an outstanding jockey.

Another jockey in the family was Day's younger brother Samuel whom, for the sake of clarity, I describe as 'Sam Day Snr'. John Barham Day and his sons John and William were portrayed by Harry Hall in 1841 (Plate 4). It is difficult to relate the old but sprightly figure in Crucifix's saddle in 1840 (Plate 10) to the grumpy and hunched John Day Snr on his pony in this picture. Perhaps he was still smarting at the loss of Bentinck's patronage!

Jem Robinson (Plate 11), born in the same year as J. B. Day, 1793, rode Potentia to win the 1,000 Guineas for Mr Stanlake Batson in 1841. Mr Batson was as highly respected a member of the Jockey Club as Jem Robinson was among all Turfites. Younger than Frank Buckle and a contemporary of Sam Chifney Jnr, Robinson was a better jockey than both of them. As a rider his record of winning the Derby on six occasions (1817, 1824, 1825, 1827, 1828 and 1836) stood until the beginning of this century when it was

5 *Mr John Gully, by Harry Hall*   Private collection

equalled by Steve Donoghue (two races were wartime substitutes run at Newmarket); but not beaten until Lester Pigott rode his seventh of nine Derby winners in 1976.

At odds of 33 to 1, Potentia was not well thought of for the Derby so Jem Robinson rode a colt by Plenipotentiary for a Mr Rush. Plenipotentiary was Mr Batson's Derby winner of 1834, but neither his offspring nor Potentia came anywhere in the 1841 race although the latter made the running for a time. Coronation was the eventual winner, and Ralph, the 2,000 Guineas winner and second favourite, came fifth. Although Mr Rawlinson's Coronation was the favourite, the bookmakers had disregarded his claims for consideration. They lost heavily, which balanced the account for the public who had suffered through outsiders winning the previous four Derby Stakes. Coronation was ridden by P. Connolly whose only other Derby success had been on Plenipotentiary,

providing a tenuous but typical thread between horses, owners and jockeys over a period of years.

Lord Westminster's Van Amburgh was second in the Derby and two days later he won the Oaks with his filly Ghuznee. The name was given to the horse when a yearling, recalling the capture of a fort of this name on 23 July 1839 during the first Afghan War. It was a strange choice for a filly foal. However, events were often commemorated by naming horses after them. A more obvious connection was that of Coronation foaled in 1838 in the year of the crowning of the young Queen Victoria. In the early autumn Lord Westminster was again successful, this time when his Satirist won the St Leger. Coronation was second, ridden on this occasion by John Day.

The Grosvenors were among the leading Turfites for many years both as breeders and owners. Richard Grosvenor, the eldest son of Sir Robert Grosvenor, the sixth Baronet, was raised to the peerage as Baron

6 '*Marking the Covey*', *by Harry Hall, from the Illustrated London News, 1854*

Grosvenor of Eaton (in Cheshire) in 1761 for parliamentary services. He was further created Earl Grosvenor in 1784 by which time he had won three consecutive Oaks Stakes from 1781 to 1783, but I do not suggest these two achievements were connected! He was also the victor of the Derby on three occasions while his nephew, General Thomas Grosvenor, won the Oaks in 1807 and 1825. Richard Grosvenor's third and only surviving son, Robert, raced as Lord Grosvenor until created the Marquess of Westminster in 1831. Lord Westminster owned Touchstone, the St Leger winner of 1834, who developed into a highly successful stallion at stud with immediate progeny winning twelve Classic races. The second Marquess's 1841 victories in the Oaks and St Leger temporarily brought an end to the family Classic successes until 1880 when the then Duke of Westminster started his run.

Disliking fuss and show, the Grosvenors were sometimes considered secretive and cold. This is an unfair criticism of a family of vast wealth with, at this period, an unusual and strong dislike of ostentation of any kind. The first and second Marquesses were, according to their wives, a little dull. In fact they were intelligent men of taste, generous and with a keen sensibility of the duties their wealth and position imposed. They were both MPs for Chester and later Cheshire, and philanthropic in their work for that county and Flintshire of which they owned over 30,000 acres. They were equally enlightened in the development of their 600 acres of London. The very successful northern trainer John Scott looked after their horses until 1841 when Lord Westminster removed them from Malton in Yorkshire. He felt that Scott did not always give him a true report of their individual form. This led to his declaring one of a number of his horses in a certain race as the best of his entries, only to see one of the others win. It made him appear to be giving deliberately false information to the public and his friends on which they promptly lost

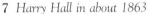

7 *Harry Hall in about 1863*

8 *Ellen Hall in about 1863*

their money. The alternative was that Scott, knowing the true performance of each horse, obtained good odds on the winner because he had not recommended his owner to back the colt or filly. This conflict came to a head with Satirist's surprising win in the St Leger. Despite Scott's reputation as an outstanding and honest trainer, Lord Westminster was entitled to dispense with his services to avoid any suggestion that he was party to malpractices which were quite foreign to his nature, and to avoid notoriety of any kind.

Harry Hall was still painting more human than equine portraits in 1841, and perhaps some of his time was occupied that year in paying attention to an Ellen Payne, the second of three daughters of Solomon and Elizabeth Payne. Solomon is described variously as a plumber or glazier. The Paynes lived in Newmarket where they had been for some years having come from Shipham in Norfolk. By the size of the household, Solomon Payne was obviously successful and equally Harry Hall felt sufficiently well established to support his daughter. They were married at All Saints Church on 16 September 1841.

At this time Newmarket High Street was a wide thoroughfare between mainly Georgian houses, some

with projecting bay-windows from which the occupants could observe an almost constant stream of equestrian traffic, much of it walking to and from the training grounds on the Heath to the north and west of the town. Part of the north side of the High Street was destroyed by a fire in 1683 which accounts for there being few buildings of earlier interest, but this does not mean there is nothing of note to see today. There are houses of distinction which were bought or leased by owners, trainers and the more successful jockeys of the day. For those less well off, there were a large number of inns prospering from the visitors to the races. On a wall at the east end of the High Street, by an archway leading to the courtyard behind the Rutland Arms, the names of local jockeys and stable-lads are carved in the brickwork providing a perpetual roll of honour of the humbler actors of the Newmarket scene. It was not long before Hall's portraits could be found on the walls of the elegant houses, the prints after his pictures of racehorses decorated the parlours of the inns, and the characters associated with racing and the town might be seen peering inquisitively into Hall's little studio in Church Lane just off the High Street.

41 *Jockeys: Nat Flatman (top left), James Chapple (top right), Luke Snowden (bottom left), Sim Templeman (bottom right)*
Courtesy of the Stewards of the Jockey Club

— 1842 —

By 1842 John Bowes was already well known on the turf, not least as the owner of Mundig (meaning: 'of age', being born in the year of Bowes's majority), the winner of the Derby in 1835; the first 'northern' horse to do so. His trainer was John Scott, whose brother Bill steered Bowes's three Classic winners to victory in 1842 and 1843. Ten years later, in 1852 and 1853, four more Classic victories were secured by Bowes's horses ridden by Frank Butler.

The Earl of Strathmore married a local girl, Mary Millner, shortly before his death, by which date their son John was nine years old. John Bowes inherited a racing establishment at Streatlam in Durham and a further estate in Northumberland. The late peer's Scottish title passed to a brother and the English title of Lord Bowes of Streatlam became extinct. Tall, handsome, intelligent and reserved, John Bowes registered his colours, black with black cap in 1833, a year after his majority. He was then MP for South Durham, but his interest was in the breeding of racehorses and, unlike so many other owners, very few of his successful animals had been purchased as yearlings. He was also a keen but sensible betting man and invariably backed his horses either on his own initiative or, more often, with the advice and encouragement of John Scott. He and Scott were on the friendliest terms admiring each other's role as a judge of a good prospect and as a trainer who could bring a horse to the post in the best condition.

Scott's ability in this last respect was demonstrated when Bowes's Meteor won the 2,000 Guineas in 1842. Meteor, one of the few horses which Bowes had bought, was highly strung and infirm, but Bill Scott succeeded in coaxing him first past the judge, ahead of seven other runners. A painting of Meteor by Harry Hall was engraved in aquatint by George Hunt and published by John Moore on 20 June, a month after the race.

The 1,000 Guineas was won by Lord George Bentinck's filly Firebrand, ridden by Sam Rogers and trained by John Kent at Goodwood. Since Bentinck had just removed his horses from Danebury, the Days felt they knew the strengths and weaknesses of those which were so recently in their stables. The rivalry between Danebury and Goodwood became intense with some irrational betting by the Days which Bentinck countered with predictable enthusiasm and success, although Firebrand was his last Classic winner. As at Danebury, Lord George improved the existing stables, gallops and paddocks at Goodwood with the agreement of their owner, his friend the Duke of Richmond, who himself raced but on a modest scale compared with Bentinck. John Kent was a trainer of a very different stamp to John Day whose rough and ready treatment of horses sometimes lacked the thought and care which was practised at Goodwood. Bentinck won a great many races with horses of all ages and there was little doubt that, in the end, a man of his determination and resources would succeed even in the face of the skill, skulduggery and cunning of the Days and their confederates.

As a young Guards officer, Colonel Anson fought at Waterloo before taking up soldiering in England with the attendant possibilities of spending almost as much time as he liked on the turf. He was a man of great politeness and charm who was soon looked upon as an outstanding diplomat in sorting out the quarrels of turfites whose volatile temperaments led them into one scrape or another. He married the sister of the Countess of Chesterfield which brought him even more closely into that circle of the aristocracy which patronised racing despite its continuing dubious reputation. Owners with wagers in mind also turned to him as a handicapper for their matches because of his astute knowledge of racehorses and their form. Anson's own horses were trained by John Scott and his first Classic win was the Derby of 1842. He bought Attila cheaply as a yearling. The brown colt ran well as a two-year-old and won a sweepstake at Newmarket in the spring. A month later he was second favourite for the Derby.

As usual there was an immense crowd at Epsom out from London for the day. The practice of the mounted spectators was to gallop from the betting ring to see the jockeys mount, from there canter to witness the start, back to the finishing post and finally to hear the announcement of the winner. In 1842 this rushing hither and thither was punctuated by the start taking an hour to accomplish. The year before it had taken an hour and a half with the contestants coming under orders at half-past two but not being off until 4 p.m.! The term 'jockeying for position' fails to describe the aim of many which was to jockey their opponents out of the line. If the favourite was known to be fractious then the longer the time spent at the post the greater the probability that the colt or filly would become unmanageable or exhaust itself before running a yard of the course. The role of the starter was an unenviable one particularly when there was a large field. If the mounted spectators were also shouting gratuitous advice his chances of achieving a satisfactory and fair line-up were further reduced. No doubt the experienced Bill Scott on Attila, so long as he was sufficiently sober, did his best to unnerve the favourite, Coldrenick, at the outset. The race, once under way, was not a fast one. Coming through with a sharp burst

42 *Jockeys: Job Marson (top left), John Osborne (top right), Charles Marlow (bottom left), Sam Rogers (bottom right)* Courtesy of the Stewards of the Jockey Club

from the distance, Attila won with ease, beating Lord Verulam's Robert de Gorham by two lengths, thus avoiding the need for a further stampede of spectators to hear the result from the judge's mouth. Colonel Anson, Lord Chesterfield and all those betting owners connected with Scott's Malton stables made handsome coups on the race.

The Oaks was won by the endearingly named Our Nell. She ran in the colours of her trainer George Dawson who, at this distance in time, is probably best known as the father of a brood of four trainer sons: Thomas, Mathew, Joseph, and John. George Dawson trained at Gullane in the Lothians and his was a considerable feat in producing the winner at Epsom from sixteen starters. Our Nell was ridden by Tommy Lye who, in the autumn, rode the St Leger winner Blue Bonnet first past the post but also into the ground.

Blue Bonnet was Lord Eglington's first Classic winner, trained at Middleham in Yorkshire by George Dawson's son Tom, the eldest of his seventeen children. Blue Bonnet had a sorry history of lameness and failed to win a race before going to Doncaster where she started at 8 to 1 against. The day before the St Leger Lord Eglinton came down from Scotland not knowing that Tom Dawson had worked wonders on the filly who suddenly came into form. With her dismal past record she was a rank outsider. The only good thing which the bookmakers might have thought of her was that she was a daughter of Touchstone; however, she was this stallion's first Classic-winning foal and his prowess as a sire was not yet recognised. Accepting Tom Dawson's confident prediction that she was bound to win the following day, Lord Eglinton had no difficulty in laying a bet of £10,000 to £150, another of £10,000 to £200 and a third of £10,000 to £300 on her winning. Attila, the favourite, was soon in difficulties and about two hundred yards from home Blue Bonnet took the lead. Tommy Lye, riding Blue Bonnet, had also made a great wager on her and in his determination to collect a small fortune he drove the poor filly so viciously that at the finish her flanks were raw from his attentions. Dawson swore that Lye would not ride for him again, but the damage was done and Blue Bonnet never regained her St Leger form. The value of the race was £3,600 to which Lord Eglinton was able to add £30,000 (a Bentinckian win) laying the foundations for a much greater future commitment to the turf.

Harry Hall painted both the Derby winner Attila (Plate 13) and Blue Bonnet (Plate 43), the latter for the publishers S. and J. Fuller, continuing their two series of prints which had previously been painted by J. F. Herring. The portraits of Attila and Blue Bonnet are similar in style with the smallness of heads and narrowness of necks slightly more pronounced than in the earlier pictures of Bloomsbury and Crucifix. It is a pity that these distortions which have so little anatomical realism were acceptable to, and probably welcomed by those who commissioned such paintings. Herring and Abraham Cooper led the way and Hall followed them with, if anything, a greater degree of caricature. It distanced him further from any comparison with Stubbs or Marshall, and even from his successor, Emil Adam, whose smooth and sometimes lifeless portraits are at least honest likenesses of their subjects. Although, as on this occasion, Hall often added 'Newmarket' to his signature on the canvas, the landscape backgrounds for his horses were usually of the site of their victories. The Downs at Epsom provide an extremely sparse and simple back-cloth for Attila, and Blue Bonnet stands on the Town Moor at Doncaster. Harry Hall undertook similar commissions for the Fullers until they stopped publication in 1846.

Harry and Ellen Hall's first child was born on 18 October 1842. He was baptised Sidney Prior, Prior being the maiden name of Hall's mother. Sidney Hall was educated at Merchant Taylors and Pembroke College, Oxford where he obtained a First Class degree in Greats before turning to a successful career as a portrait painter. He was also for many years an illustrator for *The Graphic*, covering the Franco–German War of 1870/71 and a number of royal tours for the periodical. He married twice. His only son was by his first marriage to Emma Holland. Harry Reginald Holland Hall distinguished himself in the First World War before becoming Keeper of Egyptian and Assyrian Antiquities in the British Museum. Emma Hall died in 1894 and in 1903 Sidney married Mary Gow, a woman artist of note. He died in 1922 and his son, who did not marry, survived him by only eight years.

— 1843 —

John Bowes was so disappointed with a two-year-old colt which he bred and named Cotherstone after a local Durham village, that he tried unsuccessfully to dispose of him. Cotherstone should have shown more promise for while he was by Touchstone, his dam was Emma, the mother of Mundig, Bowes's 1835 Derby winner. During the winter of 1842/43 Cotherstone improved enormously and, when he was given a trial in the early spring, he went so well that Bill Scott held him in to deceive the attendant touts. John Bowes was told of the colt's apparent potential and immediately bet heavily on him, obtaining long odds since the ring was as yet unaware of the three-year-old's improvement. Bowes's confidence was fully

43 *Lord Eglinton's Blue Bonnet, Tommy Lye up (St Leger, 1842)* The Baltimore Museum of Art, USA

justified when Scott rode Cotherstone to victory in the 2,000 Guineas. Lord George Bentinck was very hopeful for his Gaper entered for the Derby and placed a great deal of money on him; the Days laid as heavily against him, continuing the Danebury—Goodwood feud. However, Bentinck also had the wisdom to realise after the 2,000 Guineas that Cotherstone (Plate 14) was an outstanding horse and managed to hedge his possible losses on Gaper by backing Bowes's colt who stood as favourite as the day of the race approached.

Because of the difficulties at the start of the Derby in previous years the jockeys were warned that if they attempted any delaying tactics they would face stiff penalties. No doubt Bentinck had a say in this matter since he was at the time examining a number of systems to improve starting. In the event they were off at the first attempt with Gaper making the early running. However, he soon shot his bolt, or had been ridden too hard too soon by Sam Rogers, and Bill Scott took Cotherstone to an easy win by two lengths in front of Colonel Charrettie's little-thought-of Gorhambury. This was John Scott's third successive

Derby victory. John Bowes won more than £20,000 on the race and Lord George, despite his considerable losses on Gaper, came away from settling with £30,000 in his long black wallet.

The 1,000 Guineas was won by Mr T. Thornhill's Extempore. She was the last Classic winner for the immensely fat and good natured Squire Thornhill of Riddlesworth in Norfolk, and also for the 57-year-old jockey Sam Chifney Jnr. Sam was known on the turf and by its many followers for his skill in understanding exactly what strength the horse beneath him had left towards the close of a race, how to husband that effort and when to produce it with a sudden and surprising rush from behind the leader to be first past the judge's post. Thornhill's first Classic win with Chifney in the saddle was with Sam (named after the jockey) in 1818. The long and friendly partnership which embraced four Classic victories was broken when Thornhill died the following year (1844), leaving Sam his Newmarket house and stables.

Frank Butler (Plate 11) was given an excellent education as a boy. With the Duke of York's trainer for his father and Sam Chifney's sister for his mother, it was not unexpected that he became a jockey, and an immensely successful one at that. He was taught to ride by Sam and William Chifney. Initially Butler's patrons were few but his successes as a novice at the more important meetings in the Calendar of 1842 ensured him offers of an increasing number of rides thereafter. He rode a good race on Lord Chesterfield's unexceptional Parthian in the 1843 Derby and two days later achieved his first Classic victory riding Mr Ford's Poison in the Oaks. At about this time the brothers Scott (John, the trainer and Bill, the jockey) fell out due mainly to Bill's increasing problem of failing to stay sober in the saddle. On John Scott's advice, Frank Butler partnered Bowes's Cotherstone, the favourite for the St Leger. Although there was some comment on Butler's riding in this race he succeeded Bill Scott as John Bowes's first jockey.

The St Leger was won by Mr Wrather's Nutwith (a comparative outsider at 100 to 6 against) ridden by the northcountryman, Job Marson (Plate 15). Marson was making steady headway in terms of recognition when he was given the opportunity to ride the little bay colt. The form of Nutwith, Cotherstone and a third horse, Lord Chesterfield's Prizefighter, had been shown to be very close earlier in the year. In the St Leger Prizefighter jumped off well at a smart pace. He led for a time until the apparently struggling Cotherstone gradually overhauled him. Nutwith was lying about fourth throughout until Marson slipped him between the two leaders to win in masterly fashion in the last twenty yards. Cotherstone was second and Prizefighter third. This was Marson's first victory.

In 1843 Lord George Bentinck expelled all settling day defaulters from racecourses which were under the control of the Jockey Club, starting at Goodwood which was the private property of his friend the Duke of Richmond. In revenge, two brothers named Russell served writs on Bentinck and many of the leading turfites for contravening a Statute of Queen Anne which forbade winning more than £10 when betting on a racehorse. The first case against Bentinck was heard at Guildford Assizes in August 1844, at which the Russells sought to show that Lord George had won £3,000 from John Day Snr on the Derby winner the year before. John Gully, Bentinck's betting commissioner, said he took the wager on his own account and on this technicality the case foundered. Bentinck and the Duke of Richmond quickly introduced their 'Manly Sports Bill' to Parliament which effectively repealed the ancient statute. Helpful as it was to improve the reputation of racing by banning defaulters, 1844 saw one of the most devious and notorious cases of fraud experienced on the turf.

— 1844 —

The 2,000 Guineas of 1844 was won by J. B. Day's The Ugly Buck (in whom John Gully held an interest), ridden by John Day Jnr. By virtue of this bright bay colt beating Bentinck's moderate The Devil to Pay by only a neck, Lord George thought nothing of the Buck's chances in the Derby. Notwithstanding this view, the Buck was favourite at Epsom but, being deliberately interfered with during the race, came nowhere. Ratan, the second favourite, backed to win an enormous stake by his owner, the gambler and bookmaker William Crockford, was nobbled in his loosebox the night before the race. To make quite sure of Ratan's defeat, Sam Rogers rode him atrociously. It was subsequently discovered by a Stewards' inquiry that Rogers had placed a sizeable bet against Ratan winning. He was warned off the turf for a number of years. Another horse, Leander, to whom objection was made before the start on account of his suspect age, was knocked down and broke a leg a furlong from the start. He had to be destroyed and the Stewards ordered an examination of his lower jaw, sawn off by veterinary surgeons. Leander was found to be at least a four-year-old and his owners, two German brothers named Lichtwald, were banned from the English turf for life. All these malpractices were of little significance when compared to the fraud surrounding the 'winner' of the 1844 Derby.

A horse owned by Mr A. Wood called Running Rein was three-quarters of a length in front of the runner up, Colonel Peel's Orlando, with Ionian (also belonging to Peel) two lengths behind Orlando. Running Rein was in reality a four-year-old colt named Maccabeus. It is unlikely that Wood, an Epsom corn merchant, knew of the switch of horses made two years previously by an unscrupulous gambler Abraham Goodman Levy. The year before the Derby, Running Rein (Maccabeus) had won a two-year-old race on which occasion there was widespread doubt about his age. The Duke of Rutland, owner of the second horse in this race, was supported by Lord George Bentinck in objecting to Running Rein. The Stewards of the Jockey Club held an inquiry. The real Running Rein was bred by a Mr Cobb of Malton and one of his stable lads who was present when the colt was born came down from Yorkshire to Newmarket. To the astonishment of all, the man unhesitatingly said Running Rein (Maccabeus) was the genuine Malton foal. The Duke's case collapsed and Goodman Levy pocketing his substantial stake embarked on the next stage of the fraud. However he misappreciated Bentinck's tenacity once he was on the scent of a villain of this

44 *Mr G. Osbaldeston's Sorrella, owner up (1,000 Guineas, 1844, ridden by J. Robinson)*   The Leger Galleries Ltd.

ilk. Running Rein was not entered for the 2,000 Guineas but by the time of the Derby Bentinck considered he had sufficient evidence to petition the Epsom Stewards to investigate Running Rein's identity and age before the race. In this he was supported by John Bowes of Streatlam and the trainer John Scott. Surprisingly, the Stewards decided that Running Rein could run but if he should win, the stakes would be withheld until an inquiry had been carried out. Running Rein won. He was also the horse which ran into Leander leading to the latter's destruction and disclosure, although there is no reason to believe this was anything but an accident. Colonel Peel immediately claimed the stakes and all was confusion as the Stewards sent for the unfortunate Mr Wood who could not be found. Eventually a case of *Wood v. Peel* came to court and a combination of the evidence obtained through Bentinck's zealous detective work and the fact that Running Rein had disappeared led to Wood withdrawing his claim. Goodman Levy, whose role became public knowledge during the hearing, went abroad in haste, without the £50,000 he might have won. The notoriety of the case and the views of

many not connected with the turf were uncomfortably summed up by the Judge, Baron Alderson, who pointed out that 'if gentlemen condescend to race with blackguards, they must condescend to expect to be cheated'.

George Osbaldeston's filly Sorrella (Plate 44) ridden by Robinson won the 1,000 Guineas shortly after 'The Squire', as the peppery owner was known, had fought a duel with Bentinck. Both men were not above attempting to deceive the public over the form of their horses, but when Bentinck lost a small bet to Osbaldeston and described its payment as robbery, the Squire challenged Lord George. To duel with pistols was quite foreign to Bentinck's nature. He had refused to satisfy a fellow officer in this way when he was a young cavalryman. On this occasion he again refused at first, but on the advice of Colonel Anson, the peacemaker, he finally agreed. One early spring morning Bentinck presented himself on Wormwood Scrubs, dressed from head to foot in black, to give Osbaldeston his satisfaction but no aiming mark. The Squire was a very fine shot; Lord George had allegedly never previously handled a pistol. Anson officiated and gave them the order to fire when he called 'Three'. He shouted 'One' followed by a long pause, and then 'Two, Three' in quick succession. Bentinck fired in the air and Osbaldeston's hurried shot after the unexpectedly quick 'Three' passed through his enemy's hat. Osbaldeston was furious at Anson's trick to save his friend's life, but in time his attitude mellowed and he and Bentinck, without becoming friends, treated each other with respectful politeness.

Colonel Anson's The Princess won the Oaks with Frank Butler up, his second successive win in the race. This was Anson's last Classic victory. He continued to race, to act as a go-between in many difficult situations and was a very popular turfite. He rose steadily to the rank of Major-General and then, to everyone's surprise, accepted the command of a division in Bengal, later took over the Madras army and in 1856 became the Commander-in-Chief in India. When elements of the Bengal army mutinied, Anson marched with a strong force against Delhi but he was stricken with cholera en route and died at Karnal on 27 May 1857 — Derby day in England. The news was received with great sadness, not least among his many turf friends.

The Town Moor course at Doncaster and the organisation of the races were in the hands of the Corporation and in the early 1840s in a deplorable state. After the 1841 St Leger a deputation from the Corporation met with some members of the Jockey Club to discuss improvements. The Corporation offered to add a cup valued at 200 Guineas to the £500 subscription they already made. Cordially accepting the cup, Bentinck then demanded a £1,000 subscription in his usual hectoring way:

> We know we have the power to destroy and annihilate your races, and we are determined to do so unless you are disposed to make annually so liberal a contribution as we think in justice and fairness you ought.

— which they did! This and other measures resulted in some success. On 17 September 1844 the course was far better attended than previously, although the St Leger itself comprised only nine runners and the jockey Jem Robinson described the pace as paltry. All the runners were together in the final straight until Mr E. H. Irwin's Foig a Ballagh drew ahead to win by a length from The Cure. Colonel Anson's The Princess was a good third.

As well as painting all the Classic winners of 1844 and many other horses, Harry Hall also had a portrait of William Pigott of Dullingham, Newmarket exhibited at the Royal Academy, and portraits of John Fairlie of Cheveley Park, Newmarket, and his late wife shown at the Royal Society of British Artists.

Hall's second son, Arthur Henry Pitt Hall, was born in May. Like his older brother he received an excellent education and became an artist. He died of pneumonia when thirty-two years old before really succeeding in his chosen career.

— 1845 —

From 4 December 1844 until 23 March 1845 the weather was very severe. The opportunity for training racehorses in preparation for the 2,000 Guineas on Tuesday 29 April 1845 was limited. Lord Stradbroke's Idas, ridden by Elnathan ('Nat') Flatman, won an unremarkable race.

The Rous family had lived at Henham Hall in Suffolk since the time of Henry VIII, but it was not until the Coronation of George IV in 1821 that the then Baron Rous was elevated to the Earldom of Stradbroke. The Stradbrokes were not as wealthy as many of their turfite contemporaries but the first Earl kept a small stable of horses which he raced at Newmarket, often in private Matches. The second Earl, on the death of his father in 1827, continued the racing tradition, but Idas was his only Classic success. More importantly, so far as this account is concerned, Henry John Rous, the younger brother of the second Earl, shared with him the boyhood delights of involvement with the turf. In 1808, aged 13, young Rous sailed as a midshipman in His Majesty's Royal William. He was at sea intermittently for the next twenty-eight years, but when at home continued the racing partnership with his older brother who had left the Guards in 1818 after distinguished service during the Peninsular War and in the Netherlands. As young men they were both elected to membership of the Jockey Club. Rous's last command was of the Pique in 1834. She was a 36-gun frigate doing duty off the coastline of Canada. In 1835 the ship was badly damaged striking uncharted rocks off Labrador. By a remarkable feat of seamanship and courage, Rous brought her safely back to England for which, after a court martial where he and his Master were fully acquitted, he received the muted thanks of the Admiralty. In January 1836 Rous left the Navy and devoted himself to a full-time occupation on the turf, to employing his considerable talents as a handicapper and, most of all, to becoming the expert to whom everyone turned for the interpretation and improvement of the rules of racing.

Two years after midshipman Rous first went to sea, Nat Flatman (Plate 41) was born at Halton in Suffolk. At an early age he joined the stables of a trainer near Newmarket progressing from exercise riding to trials until his first appearance in Lord Exeter's racing colours in 1829. He soon proved himself to be an extremely able jockey and subsequently rode in the jackets and caps of a great many owners. Nat had three important assets. The first was his weight which was under seven stone in his early career, and he always kept below seven stone seven pounds; the second was that he rode scrupulously to orders; and the third was that he never disclosed the results of riding trials, for which he was consequently in great demand. His reputation was based more on good conduct and sensible riding than brilliance or spectacular achievements, although his performance in the early 1840s at Ascot, Goodwood and Newmarket was outstanding by any standard.

Lord Stradbroke's Idas (ridden by George Edwards) was favourite for the Derby and Charles Greville's Alarm was well enough thought of for his owner to back him as heavily as he could afford. Whether by the design of some of the jockeys or inefficiency of the starter the large field of thirty-one runners failed to come into line quickly. Alarm, ridden by Nat, became agitated and kicked the third favourite, The Libel. The Libel reared up striking Flatman, who fell off. Alarm bolted. Lord George Bentinck, who had quarrelled with his cousin Greville two years before, observed the incident through his glass from the Stewards' stand and provided a scornful commentary for the benefit of those around him. Alarm was finally caught and Nat Flatman remounted, the race starting an hour late. Idas was soon beaten and Alarm ran surprisingly well, but the winner by a length was Mr W. Gratwicke's unquoted The Merry Monarch ridden by F. Bell (Plate 16). Mr Gratwicke's interest in the turf lasted for many years. He had won the Derby previously in 1829 with Frederick, the brother of The Merry Monarch's dam, and he had further Classic successes in 1858. His horses were trained at Goodwood before being moved to Newmarket. A slightly uncomfortable character, Gratwicke was perhaps known best for his suspicious nature. The Merry Monarch's success among a moderate lot was not repeated and at stud he was undistinguished. Charles Greville's Alarm, although injured during his Derby escapade, went on to win the Cambridgeshire at the end of the 1845 season and the Emperor's Cup the following year. This last success made Greville feel even more cheated of the 1845 Derby.

John Kent Snr and Jnr trained the Duke of Richmond's horses at Goodwood where Bentinck's racing activities were at their height. I cannot help wondering whether the Duke, congenial and generous host that he was, was not particularly pleased that two fillies from his small string, Pic-nic and Refraction, won the 1845 1,000 Guineas and Oaks respectively in the face of Lord George's somewhat overpowering scale of racing. Pic-nic was ridden by W. Abdale and Refraction by Henry Bell, the better-known brother of The Merry Monarch's jockey.

The Baron was bred in Ireland by a Mr George Watts. John Scott, the trainer, saw the colt as a two-year-old and suggested that he should send him to Malton where Scott would train him to win the St Leger, which he did. The Merry Monarch was scratched from the race at the last moment which caused some anger among those who had backed him. The race was scheduled for three o'clock but they were not off until 3.45 p.m. According to a contemporary account Bentinck was the cause of the delay when he directed the start:

> This was in some degree brought about by the extensively dramatic way in which Lord George Bentinck organised it, for the behoof of the spectators as well as the fair play of those interested. Having drawn the fifteen, which constituted the field, together, at the St Leger post, and marched them in two lines, settled by lots, past the Stand, and nearly to the distance; then wheeling them, they were led slowly back to the post, and the flag being dashed to the ground by the noble Lord, off flew the eager phalanx.

The Baron, ridden by Frank Butler, started badly and was last away, but in a tremendous run on the outside won by a length in one of the finest St Legers ever seen.

By the end of 1845 Harry Hall was fully established. He lived in the High Street and his father-in-law bought a small stable in Church Lane which became his studio and the meeting place for trainers, jockeys and the rest of the racing world interested in watching him at work. A picture of a Suffolk Cob belonging to the Reverend Martin Lloyd of Branches Park, Newmarket was exhibited at the Royal Academy, and Hall received commissions from the Duke of Richmond, Lord Albermarle and other owners to paint their winners. He was also providing similar portraits for the print publishers Fuller and Moore. Other work included a large study of the mare named Perhaps with her foal in the more pastoral setting of a rustic yard.

Hall had made a good start to a career which gathered pace as he received more and more commissions. Whether the artist realised it at the time, it can now be seen that from the mid 1840s Hall was the only painter of racehorses in the country. J. F. Herring, Abraham Cooper and Charles Hancock were turning to different fields of inspiration leaving a gap which Harry Hall quickly filled.

CHAPTER 3
1846–1850

Soothed for a moment all, they stand
together, like a sculptured band;
Each quivering eyelid flutters thick,
Each face is flushed, each heart beats quick.

JOHN GULLY (PLATE 5) was a quite remarkable man. Born near Bath, the son of a publican who later became a butcher, Gully's upbringing promised little of his future as champion pugilist of England, betting commissioner, successful racehorse owner, Member of Parliament, coal magnate and country gentleman.

His father died young and Gully took over the butchery but soon found himself in financial difficulties and, at the age of twenty-one, in London's Fleet Prison for debt. Whether Henry ('Hen') Pearce, the champion boxer of England, knew Gully in Bath from whence he also came is not clear, but he visited him in The Fleet. He may have been curious to discover if Gully could fight as well as rumour suggested. Nick-named the Game Chicken, Pearce was a gallant and chivalrous man, and also very kind. After sparring with him at the prison, Pearce quickly realised that Gully could box and might be a worthy opponent. He hit upon a plan of setting up a match between the two of them as a way of releasing Gully from the Fleet. Pearce found backers to promote the fight for 1,000 guineas and Colonel Mellish, a notorious gambler, paid Gully's debt so that he could train and prepare himself for the coming contest.

The match took place at Hailsham in Sussex in the autumn of 1805. Every aristocratic sportsman was present led by the Duke of Clarence, later William IV. Gully was taller than the Game Chicken and had the advantage of out-reaching him. Although the Champion started and ended well, Gully fought tremendously and with effect for seventy minutes before Colonel Mellish persuaded him to retire. The battered Pearce congratulated Gully on being the best man he had ever fought so ensuring the latter's popularity in a field into which he had been so rapidly propelled.

When Hen Pearce retired due to ill-health shortly after this battle, Gully informally assumed his title. Two years later he twice defended it against Bob Gregson of Lancashire. On the first occasion in October 1807 at Six Mile Bottom between Cambridge and Newmarket, Gully was the victor after thirty-six rounds of a desperate and evenly contested slogging match. Gregson's backers were sure that a return bout would reverse the October decision so they fought again the following May. However, on this second occasion, and despite another long fight, Gully proved considerably superior to Gregson.

Gully married the pretty daughter of a London inn-keeper and he took a small public house in Lincoln's Inn Field. Quickly tiring of this employment he turned to the turf. He had no pretensions to be thought the equal of those gentlemen who had so warmly applauded his courage when facing the Game Chicken and who attended his retiring benefit bout at the Tennis Court with the old professional Tom Cribb, but he was ambitious to be among them.

As his apparently astute judgement of a horse's quality and reputation for hard but straight dealing spread, Gully quickly became a busy and respected betting commissioner for Bentinck, Chesterfield and other leading turfites of the day. He progressed steadily from buying his first racehorse, Cardenio, in 1812 to 'arriving' as a fully fledged leading owner in 1827 when he bought the Derby winner, Marmeluke, from Lord Jersey for £4,000. Before the sale became generally known, Gully had laid £10,000 to £1,000 on Marmeluke winning the St Leger, and a further bet of £20,000 to £1,000 with William Crockford. Marmeluke was a bad-tempered horse and at a protracted start, probably arranged by Crockford, he was left at the post. Sam Chifney Jnr recovered the seventy yards lead of the rest of the field and in a strong finish only just failed to beat Matilda by half a length. Gully knew he was the victim of an almost certain conspiracy but was able to pay all claims immediately.

A year or so later he became a friend and confederate of Robert Ridsdale. Their most fruitful betting year was 1832 when St Giles in Ridsdale's colours won the Derby and Margrave in Gully's violet jacket and white cap was first in the St Leger. However, the division of the spoils of Margrave's victory resulted in Ridsdale accusing Gully of dishonesty. Some time later this quarrel led to Gully foolishly losing his temper in the hunting field where he publicly horsewhipped the diminutive Ridsdale. Despite doubts about the scourged man's probity, Gully's action was considered that of a bully. Ridsdale successfully sued Gully and was awarded damages of £500; a result received with popular acclaim.

Part of John Gully's wealth was based on coal mining, an infant industry in which he shrewdly invested in Yorkshire, where he lived in quiet but comfortable style at Ackworth Park. In late 1832 he was elected unopposed as Member for Pontefract in the first Reformed Parliament. Charles Greville, having included Gully in a list of the worst of bad characters who entered politics at this time, continues with an interesting portrait:

> In person he is tall and finely formed, full of strength and grace, with delicate hands and feet, his face coarse and with a bad expression, his head set well on his shoulders, and remarkably graceful and even dignified in his actions and manners; totally without education, he has strong sense, discretion, reserve, and a species of good taste which has prevented, in the height of his fortunes, his behaviour ever transgressing the bounds of modesty and respect, and he has gradually separated himself from the rabble of betters and blackguards of whom he was once the most conspicuous, steadily asserted his own independence and acquired gentility without ever presuming towards those whom he had been accustomed to regard with deference.

Gully's lack of education did not prevent him from taking part in debates in Parliament but his comments were usually short, caustic and to the point. He made few long speeches, unlike Bentinck who would often hold forth on a subject in the greatest detail for two hours on end. Gully gave up his short Parliamentary career in 1837 (he stood in 1840 but was defeated) and again devoted all his energy to racing.

Shortly before Lord George Bentinck took his horses away from Danebury in 1841, Gully sent his to the Days for training. The Days and Messrs Gully, Thomas Pedley (Gully's son-in-law), Henry Hill (he was

known as Harry Hill but to avoid confusion with Harry Hall, I call him 'Henry' throughout), Henry Padwick, Arnold and Turner (all bookmaker-owners) became known as 'The Danebury Confederacy', forming a powerful team of professionals whose combined strength on the turf was feared by all but Bentinck, and whose honesty was doubted by everyone. The confederacy was not without its problems. In 1845 John Gully was confident that his colt, Old England, would win the Derby and was surprised to find the bookmakers' odds against his horse stayed long. He became suspicious that there was a plot to make Old England safe. Falling on Danebury in a fury he confronted John Day Snr and his sons. Questioning them with such anger and force of character it was not long before he knew what was wrong. A man named Hargreaves, who had previously been involved with Sam Rogers when Crockford's Ratan was 'got at' in the 1844 Derby, had persuaded William and probably John Day Jnr to make sure that Old England would be tampered with in a most vicious way. Gully went straight to Tattersalls where he publicly denounced Hargreave's activities describing the scoundrel as 'a lucky, screaming gentleman with a large face and pink eyes'. The Jockey Club investigated the affair and although there was insufficient evidence to indict Hargreaves, William Day was warned off the turf for a time with two others who were to have fixed Gully's colt. In the event, a sound Old England came third ridden by Sam Day Snr who was to serve Gully so well the following year.

The Classic races of 1846 fell to Gully and Bill Scott in the proportion of three to two. If Scott had been less drunk when riding in the Derby the share of races would certainly have been the other way about. Bill Scott found a promising young horse named Tibthorpe whom he sent to be trained with William Oates since the quarrel with his brother John continued. He renamed the colt Sir Tatton Sykes after the revered Yorkshire sportsman who once employed him. Sir Tatton, the man, was primarily an agriculturist whose kindness, honesty and sober ways were legendary. Born in 1772, his name first appears as an owner in the Racing Calendar in 1803. He inherited a small stud from his older brother, Sir Mark Masterman Sykes, who died in 1832, and immediately expanded it so that at times there were as many as one hundred and twenty brood mares in hand. Despite the immense outlay and effort which he put into breeding, he was not successful. This was due in part to there being so many horses at Sledmere that the majority had to live hard out of doors and partly due to his moderate stallions having to cover a great many mares. Sir Tatton was also interested in breeding sheep, and revelled in the physical exercise of lending a hand to his labourers on his farms. Sir Tatton, the horse, won the 2,000 Guineas comfortably, ridden by his owner.

John Gully bought the filly Mendicant (a Touchstone daughter) from a Mr Whitworth in 1844. She was trained at Danebury by John Day Jnr and won the 1846 1,000 Guineas with Sam Day Snr up. The same combination were the victors of the Oaks, on which race Gully won a considerable sum having appreciated Mendicant's quality when he could obtain long odds about her.

Pyrrhus the First was also bought as a yearling and sent to the Days for training. Gully shared the cost (£300) and ownership of the colt and his dam with John Day Snr. The latter falling temporarily short of funds sold his share to Gully for £100 early in 1846. Pyrrhus was second favourite for the Derby to Mr Meiklam's Fancy Boy. Sir Tatton Sykes was marvellously fit but the bookmakers did not favour him, perhaps expecting, or possibly ensuring, that Bill Scott would be far from sober for the race. At the post Scott was abusive to the starter who warned him of his conduct before exercising his revenge by dropping the flag when Sir Tatton was not ready. The splendid horse quickly caught the field, was through them in a flash and well in the lead when still two furlongs from the finish. Unfortunately Scott was now almost insensible and Sir Tatton, lacking any form of guidance, veered across the course. Sam Day on Pyrrhus the First immediately saw his chance and riding the colt furiously along the now empty rails won by a neck. As a sole owner, this was John Gully's first Derby victory.

Although without Classic winners in 1845 and 1846, Lord George Bentinck's successes in other important races were formidable. As with his political life, everything was conducted in great detail. He wrote daily, and sometimes as often as three times a day, to John Kent his Goodwood trainer. The loyal Kent was expected to reply, point by tedious point, to every one of these missives! Bentinck's betting coups were enormous, giving him a profit of £100,000 in 1845. The following year at Newmarket, Ascot and Goodwood he was well on his way to exceeding this figure and his commitment to racing seemed stronger than ever.

At the 1846 Goodwood meeting in July, Lord George was staying as usual with the Duke of Richmond and a house-party of gentlemen connected with the turf. Among them was Mr George Payne. Payne was then aged forty-two and at the height of his popularity in a world comprising hunting, the turf and playing cards. At one time he managed Lord Glasgow's stud, was a brilliant master of the Pytchley Hunt, a moderately successful owner of racehorses and lifelong friend and confederate of Charles Greville. He

was an intelligent man of considerable inherited wealth which fortune he lost and won again on a number of occasions in a lifetime enjoyed to the full. Payne was a close friend of Rous and his advice was often taken by the then Captain when faced with a difficult problem about the rules of racing or a handicap. A young man, Mr Edward Lloyd-Mostyn (later Lord Mostyn) was also staying at Goodwood House. He too owned a small stud and was a moderate better, but not in any way in the same class as Payne or Bentinck.

One evening after dinner when Bentinck had taken his customary doze, his mind perhaps concerned with some political issue of the day, he offered to those sitting with him, without any preamble, his complete stud, every horse, lock, stock, engagement, cart and accoutrement to the person who would give him £10,000 for the lot. The astonished guests were still considering this extraordinary proposal when George Payne asked if he could think over the offer and would pay a forfeit of £300 the following noon if he did not take it up. Bentinck agreed and went straight to bed. The following morning Payne asked John Kent (who was also the Duke of Richmond's trainer) if he would move to Michel Grove where Payne's horses were trained. Kent declined and George Payne paid his forfeit to Bentinck. A group of bookmakers headed by Henry Padwick of the Danebury Confederacy hearing of this attractive proposition then offered to buy the stud but Lord George refused to sell to 'blackguards'. A little later Edward Lloyd-Mostyn gave Lord George a cheque for £10,000 and the deal was made. Mostyn took possession of over 200 thoroughbreds, which were many more than he could manage. He sold a number recouping his outlay within a few days. It is probable that the value of the whole establishment was more than six or seven times the amount he paid for it. Bentinck was Senior Steward of the Jockey Club and continued his interest in racing and betting, following the fortunes of his 'old' horses by attending the principal meetings of the Calendar. At the same time he devoted even greater energy to his Parliamentary duties.

As joint favourite at 3 to 1 with General Shubrick's Brocardo, Bill Scott knew that he had a more than ordinary chance of riding Sir Tatton Sykes to victory in the St Leger. Mindful of the outcome of the Derby he had limited his liquid intake on the morning of the Doncaster race. However, he was still sufficiently inebriated to shout and swear at anyone nearby as he mounted and made his uncertain way onto the course. Sir Tatton Sykes, the man, seeing Scott ride out reproved him for cursing so much, promising that if he won he would act as groom and lead them in. Bill Scott's fondness for the old baronet was no less than

45 *Sir Tatton Sykes, ridden by his owner Bill Scott, being led in by Sir Tatton Sykes (St Leger, 1846). Engraving by Charles Hunt Julian Armytage*

that of everyone else, so he pulled himself together as well as he could. In a fast and memorable race Sir Tatton Sykes comfortably beat Colonel Anson's Iago ridden by Frank Butler. There are a number of paintings of Sir Tatton at his namesake's head, the exhausted Scott in an alcoholic daze and a cheering crowd around them as they make their way to unsaddling. Hall painted at least two versions of the scene, one of which was engraved by Charles Hunt and published by John Moore the following November (Plate 45). This was Bill Scott's last St Leger victory (of nine). Within two years he was dead, pickled but in his sober moments proud of his reputation as one of the foremost northern jockeys.

A week or so after this St Leger, a horse and a rider of quite different natures were described in all the journals of the period. Wyatt's monumental equestrian statue of the Duke of Wellington was slowly hoisted to the top of the Green Park Arch in London. This triumph of engineering was conducted by a Mr McCullam, the boatswain of Woolwich Dockyard, who did not consider the feat more than an ordinary task!

— 1847 —

In 1847, Sir Robert Pigot's Conyngham, ridden beautifully by the 52-year-old Jem Robinson, won the 2,000 Guineas, defeating Edward Lloyd-Mostyn's Planet (Nat Flatman). The year before, Planet belonged to Bentinck, and Mostyn had recently refused an offer of £5,000 for the colt and a filly, Slander. Had he accepted he would have recouped half his original outlay. As it was, he had another place with Slander who came second in the 1,000 Guineas to George Payne's only Classic success Clementina, a clever winner in a race of only five horses.

Conyngham's form in the 2,000 Guineas made the colt the Derby favourite, but he came nowhere. The race was won easily by Mr Pedley's Cossack. Cossack was trained at Danebury where Pedley was one of the confederacy of bookmaker-owners which, with the disappearance of the previous competition from Bentinck and Goodwood, was enjoying considerable success at the time. Harry Hall painted Cossack (for The Sporting Magazine) as well as the second horse, War Eagle (exhibited at the Royal Society of British Artists' Exhibition in 1848) and Van Tromp placed third. The Sporting Magazine's engraving of Cossack was the second of what became a long line of small sketches made by Hall for the proprietors. They were painted on board, approximately ten inches high by thirteen wide, with little detail except the prominent markings of the horse clearly depicted. For this reason

a collection of the hundred or so racehorse engravings from The Sporting Magazine is useful in identifying other unnamed portraits by Harry Hall. In July 1847 the Magazine comments briefly on Cossack and has this to say about Hall:

> Of Mr Hall our say must be short, for deeds not words are the touchstone of the painter, even as of his subjects; and these in either instance we believe to be sufficiently good to speak for themselves. If not yet at the top of the tree as an animal painter, Mr Hall is rapidly advancing; and having made Newmarket his home, he, of course, enjoys every advantage of studying the proportions and catching the characteristics of the English racehorse.

Sim Templeman rode Cossack and two days later was up on Miami to win the Oaks, giving Sir Joseph Hawley his first of eight Classic victories.

After the Derby there were suspicions that Job Marson's riding was not all that it should have been. Somewhat inevitably Lord George Bentinck was involved since he had bet heavily on the idle and bad-tempered Van Tromp. Allegedly, Marson gave Bentinck and Lady Eglinton such different reasons for Van Tromp's Derby failure that they tried to persuade Lord Eglinton not to give Marson another ride. The following September Eglinton had two runners in the St Leger: Eryx and Van Tromp. Of the pair he preferred Eryx and put Charles Marlow on him, giving Van Tromp to Marson since they knew each other. Van Tromp had improved immensely since May. On a glorious day in front of an enormous crowd Marson took his revenge on Cossack and a little on Eglinton by easily winning the St Leger. Eryx was third. Notwithstanding this success, Lord Eglinton dispensed with Marson's services at the end of the season and Marlow was made his first jockey. Predictably Marson was upset and for a time 'took to that foolish means of consolation' which robbed the turf of many of its best performers. However, a few years later, in Lord Zetland's jacket, Marson proved he was a more than able jockey which pointed to his dismissal by Lord Eglinton as possibly unjustified.

— 1848 —

As in 1846, Touchstone was the sire of two Classic winners in 1848. The first was Flatcatcher, winner of the 2,000 Guineas ridden by Robinson. This bay colt was owned by a Mr Green, a bookmaker and partner of the unsavoury William Stebbings, the brother of Henry Stebbings who was to have been the instrument in making John Gully's Old England 'safe' before the 1845 Derby. Henry Stebbings trained thirty or so

46 *Lord Stanley's Canezou, Frank Butler up (1,000 Guineas, 1848)* Christie's

horses for his brother and Green at Hambleton in Yorkshire. Apart from this one Classic win the little confederacy was not successful.

The 1,000 Guineas was won by Lord Stanley's brown filly Canezou ridden by Frank Butler and trained by John Scott. On the death of his father, Stanley became the fourteenth Earl of Derby. Unlike the thirteenth Earl who took no interest in the turf, his successor was as fond of racing as his grandfather had been, combining this passion with a full political life with consummate ease. In both houses of Parliament and later as Premier on two occasions, his occupation of high office was based on intelligence, charm and, above all, spell-binding oratory. On the turf, politics were never mentioned and he was happiest when walking in his paddocks at his home, Knowsley. Canezou was successful in the following year by winning the Goodwood Cup, repeating the feat in 1850 and adding the Doncaster Cup in the same season. She was one of Lord Derby's most successful horses, all of whose characteristics and performances were discussed endlessly and with fondness by Derby and

Scott who were firm friends throughout the twenty-one years of their association.

When Bentinck sold his stud to Lloyd-Mostyn he asked that a colt named Surplice, a son of Touchstone and his favourite Crucifix, should continue to be trained at Goodwood by John Kent. This was done, but Mostyn sold a half-share of Surplice to Lord Clifden, an awkward man with an unattractive manner whose horses were managed by an equally difficult and foolish young man named Francis Villiers. Surplice was entered for the Derby, as was Lord Clifden's Loadstone, trained at Newmarket with his other horses. After some successes as a two-year-old, John Kent was sure of Surplice's quality although he was not raced as a three-year-old before going to Epsom. Villiers thought he knew better, backing Loadstone heavily at the same time as laying against Surplice. An azure day, cloudless with a faint breeze, made 24 May 1848 ideal for the most important Classic race of the year, and for Queen Victoria's birthday. Sim Templeman rode Surplice sensibly taking the lead some way from home and just holding off a strong challenge from John Bowes's Springy Jack to win by a neck. Clifden, Mostyn and Bentinck won handsomely and Villiers was in difficulties when it came to settling. However Bentinck's betting success did little to compensate for failing to fulfil his long cherished aim of being the owner of a Derby winner. A few days later in the library of the House of Commons, Disraeli, who admired Bentinck's political zeal, tried to console him. Making 'a sort of superb groan' Lord George attempted to shrug off his bad luck, questioning the significance of the race. Disraeli suggested the Derby was the 'Blue Riband of the turf', driving a despondent Bentinck back into a tome of statistics he was consulting in preparation for some weighty debate.

Bentinck commissioned Harry Hall to paint a portrait of Surplice (Plate 19) with John Kent and Sim Templeman in 1848. To overcome the problem of not painting the jockey in Lord Clifden's colours, Templeman is shown in his travelling clothes on a hack, looking almost as a passer-by might, pausing to stare at some interesting spectacle with which he is not connected. This fine, large painting was exhibited at the Royal Society of British Artists the following year, by which time Bentinck was dead.

Cymba won the Oaks in the colours of Mr Henry Hill (purple and yellow stripe, purple cap); he owned her jointly with John Gully. Henry Hill was a bookmaker with a great deal of common sense, adequate numeracy for his profession but without many other attractive characteristics. For many years he was Lord George Bentinck's principal betting commissioner, being one of a very small number allowed into his Lordship's bedroom to conduct business. He also assisted Bentinck in his discovery of the true identity of Running Rein. When Hill took to owning racehorses he trained for a short time with John Scott. However, after a disagreement he moved to John Day and became a leading member of the Danebury Confederacy. Henry Hill did not have much money on Cymba since she had gone off her feed following a trial shortly before the race. On the day, she won comfortably.

After the improvements made at Doncaster in the previous two years, the 1848 meeting was disappointing. The correspondent of *The Times*, while not directing his remarks to the St Leger day, had this to say:

> The racing was below zero in the matter of interest. The Flying Dutchman flew away with the Champagne (Stakes) in a canter. The great Four-Year-Old Sweepstake was a walk over; there was a match, which Lord Glasgow lost of course; two other wretched apologies for sport — and that ended it.

The St Leger itself was a fast race but from 132 subscribers there were only nine runners 'and not half of these with a friend in the world who would give a macaroon for their prospects'. Surplice, with Nat Flatman up on this occasion won by a neck from Lord Stanley's Canezou. The colt became the first horse to win the Derby and St Leger since Christopher Wilson's Champion inaugurated this double in 1800.

During the Doncaster races, Bentinck stayed with his father at Welbeck and the day after the meeting was due to visit Lord Manvers who lived close by at Thoresby. Sending his valet with his luggage by cart, Bentinck decided to walk to his friend's house. In the evening the valet became alarmed when his master did not arrive at Thoresby. He returned to Welbeck where a small search party was sent along the likely route taken by Bentinck. He was found laying dead beside a path having suffered a catastrophic heart attack some hours before.

Although the first quarrel between Bentinck and his cousin Charles Greville had been patched up, it was not long before they had irreconcilably fallen out again. In these circumstances it is surprising that in his memoirs Greville writes so well of Bentinck; but this is typical of Greville's obituaries — they are all unquestionably fair. Lord George Bentinck wrought many reforms of the turf which, when he first became interested, was in a poor state with a reputation to match. Being self-willed and sometimes arrogant, he brooked no opposition in what he set out to do, naturally making enemies in the process. The improvements which he imposed with such zeal and stamina were for the most part successful in dealing with the skulduggery and its blackguard authors. Some of his own practices were close to those he was determined to stamp out. 'His tricks and stratagems he regarded as the tactics and manoeuvres by which success was achieved. He desired to win money, not so much for the money, as because it was the test and trophy of success; he counted the thousands he won after a great race as a general would count his prisoners and his cannon after a great victory.' He was however liberal with his friends and generous with those whom he employed. Greville goes on to wonder whether Bentinck did not regret some of his earlier 'tricks and stratagems', pointing to the paradox of being obsessed with making money and yet selling his entire stud for a small fraction of its value. With the turf, politics was an equal passion, but his inability sometimes to recognise the wood for the trees was the reason why only his friends saw him as a future Premier. To both fields he devoted his time and enormous energy. In early life he admitted to Greville his love for an unobtainable lady, and perhaps a wife with a gentle

47 *Mr P.P. Rolfe's Collingwood, Nat Flatman up*   Arthur Ackermann & Son Ltd.

character might have mellowed the man. As it was, this bachelor's austere personal regime and immense appetite for work probably took their toll and cut life short when he was at the height of his undoubted powers.

In 1848 Harry Hall was engaged by Baily Brothers of Cornhill, London, to paint Derby and St Leger winners for the plates they published in succession to Messrs Fuller and John Moore. He continued to provide these paintings until his death thirty-four years later. Somewhat disappointingly, the first plate, engraved by Charles Hunt, is of Surplice in a loosebox without his jockey, trainer or even groom. It was published on 15 June and reprinted after the St Leger with the detail of that victory added to the description below the scene. Also in 1848, *The Sporting Magazine* published small steel engravings after Hall of Van Tromp (St Leger, 1847), Surplice, Cymba and The Hero (Goodwood Cup, 1848). In January 1849 there is an engraving of the finish of the previous year's St Leger with Surplice and Canezou fighting it out, with the following comment:

Being disappointed in our promised portrait of the Leger winner [but Surplice had been published in July 1848 as the Derby winner] we engaged Mr Hall to illustrate the finish of this memorable event — a scene which we think he has put on with singular success. The Set To has a rare merit of looking like a race, as well as embodying the portraits of those engaged in it. Of Harry Hall's racehorses we have often had occasion to speak in terms of well-earned approval, and we may here make especial mention of his jockeys. We have seldom seen anything more characteristic than the resolute, but still elegant attitude of Frank Butler. Who will but recognise the manner of the man, as it comes to a near thing, sitting so well back on his horse, and lifting him at every stride, with a fearful effort, from head to heel, as he feels that mere 'Threatening' won't serve them? Flatman's figure, if not so inviting when at work, is equally after the original — quite earnest and telling in action as his accomplished opponent, but Nat in no way qualifies his punishment with grace in administering it that Butler displays.

48 *Lord Rivers's Mounseer, Dockery up (Chester Cup, 1850)* O. & P. Johnson Ltd.

This wordy 'puff' of Hall's painting is perhaps exaggerated but of interest since it describes one of his few action pictures. The writer continues with a self-important caution:

> We hope Mr Hall will not be spoilt by the praise we have felt is his due and our duty to give him, but continue a close study of that art in which he can lack no encouragement while he shows such ability.

In 1848 Harry Hall was again given an opportunity to paint portraits when he was asked by one Charles Phelips to paint himself with his great friend, the Reverend Philip Honywood. Honywood owned a pack of beagles, hunting in Essex and Hertfordshire. Pride of place in The Merry Beaglers (Plate 20) is given to the huntsman Tom Pitts, which is right and proper except that Tom somewhat let down this position in later life. Pitts was also Honywood's manservant and the Rector of Marks Hall was often to be seen patrolling the local inns trying to discover the whereabouts of his man. Like so many at the end of a very active life with nothing much to show for it but memories,

the huntsman turned to the bottle for solace. As usual, the portraits are good and a descendant of Phelips is teased today for looking so like his relation in the painting.

— 1849 —

The spring of 1849 was very late in arriving. On 24 April Mr Nichol's Nunnykirk (by Touchstone) with Frank Butler up won the 2,000 Guineas by half a length from Lord Clifden's Honeycomb. Two days later The Flea (owned by Mr F. Clarke) gave the eighteen-year-old jockey Alfred Day (Plate 12) his first Classic win in the 1,000 Guineas. Young Alfred was J. B. Day's fourth son and up to slightly fewer tricks than some of his brothers. He was well mannered, which placed him much in demand, and his riding was stylish. On this occasion he beat Nat Flatman on Clarissa and outrode some of the best jockeys of the day including Frank Butler, James

49 *Lord Zetland's Voltigeur, with trainer Robert Hill and Job Marson (Derby and St Leger, 1850), Engraving by Charles Hunt   Julian Armytage*

Chapple, Jem Robinson, Sam Rogers (back on the turf) and Sim Templeman.

Lord Eglinton has been mentioned in passing as the owner of Blue Bonnet (St Leger, 1842) and Van Tromp (a disappointing third in the Derby but winner of the St Leger in 1847). It is now time to fill out the portrait of this Scottish Earl, whose horse The Flying Dutchman dominated the turf in 1849 and played a conspicuous part in the racing annals of the following two years. The thirteenth Earl of Eglinton was born in 1812 and while still at Eton succeeded to the Scottish title on the death of his grandfather (his father had died when he was not two years old). He was a man of immense charm, high ideals, open-hearted, with a great deal of money but not so much brain; a talented sportsman whom everyone loved, not only in his native country and England, but in Ireland as well where he was Lord Lieutenant during both of Lord Derby's Administrations. He came to prominence in 1839 when he spent two years and nearly £50,000 in arranging the Eglinton Tournament at his home in Ayrshire. His aim was to demonstrate that the chivalry, colour and romance of the Middle Ages was still alive in the hearts of Britons if only it could be aroused. Enormous crowds descended on Eglinton Castle from the farthest corners of Europe and even America to witness jousting and other ancient sports — all free. What was also in abundance was incessant rain which sadly ruined all but the last day of the event which had been produced with such care and enthusiasm. However, despite the atrocious weather, the tournament increased Lord Eglinton's popularity hugely, not least because of his genuine concern for all those who were thoroughly soaked! From this point in his life he was cajoled into politics, but this did not interfere with his interest in the turf, which was just one of his numerous pastimes. Like many generous people he was lucky. His involvement in racing seemed a little half-hearted at times since he rarely visited his trainers, first Tom Dawson, the public trainer, and then privately John Fobert, both at Middleham. He would go to Newmarket, Epsom or Doncaster the day before the meeting started largely unaware of which of his horses were running during the following days.

After his 1847 St Leger success, Eglinton made a bargain with a Mr Vansittart, the owner of Van Tromp's dam Barbelle, that he would buy the mare's successive good foals for £1,000 each. The first of these was a bay colt, The Flying Dutchman, by Bay Middleton, born in 1846. As a two-year-old The Flying Dutchman won all his races and came to the Derby in 1849 as the joint favourite with Colonel Peel's Tadmor. The 2,000 Guineas winner, Nunnykirk, was third favourite at 6 to 1. At the close

of the race The Dutchman party was given a nasty fright by a rank outsider, Hotspur, who was only half a length behind at the finish with Tadmor third, a further half-length away. Charles Marlow was The Flying Dutchman's jockey (Plate 21). He was as congenial as his new master and while accepting the privilege of becoming Lord Eglinton's first jockey in succession to Job Marson, he too felt his predecessor was not treated fairly after his successes with Van Tromp. Lord Eglinton won a considerable sum on the Derby as did many others at the expense of the bookmakers who never enjoy a favourite winning. William Davis, the 'Leviathan' of this trade had to pay out £40,000 on settling day. Although there was a large crowd for the St Leger it lacked the patronage of the titled and fashionable set who were not prepared to travel north to see some moderate racing in a badly organised meeting, for Doncaster was again in decline. Marlow and The Flying Dutchman won the race comfortably in front of Nunnykirk ridden by Alfred Day. Eglinton's Montgomerie tartan, yellow sleeves and cap can be seen on the neat figure of Marlow in a number of pictures which Harry Hall was commissioned to paint for the owner, the trainer Fobert and the print publishers (Plate 42). The association between Eglinton, Marlow and The Dutchman was to continue for a further two years with even greater éclat than in 1849.

Between the Derby and the St Leger, the nocturnal Lord Chesterfield's little brown filly, Lady Evelyn, won the Oaks giving Frank Butler the first of his four successive wins in the race.

— 1850 —

Reports of the 2,000 Guineas of 1850 describe the field as both lacking in numbers and quality — 'not one in it even second-rate'. There was a large crowd but 'the provision for their entertainment was low'. In a race not without some excitement, Henry Hill's Pitsford ridden by Alfred Day won by a neck. Two days later, on Thursday 2 May, an unnamed filly, by Slane out of Exotic belonging to Lord Orford, won the 1,000 Guineas with Frank Butler up. Again the field was a moderate lot perhaps presaging a dull flat-racing season, but this did not prove to be the case. The breeder of Voltigeur, a Mr Robert Stephenson of Hartlepool, was unable to sell the colt as a yearling at Tattersalls although Robert Hill, Lord Zetland's trainer, clearly saw something in him. Six months later Zetland was persuaded to change his mind and with some reluctance bought Voltigeur for £1,000 with a contingency of a further £500 should he win the Derby. Hill trained Voltigeur at Lord Zetland's

50 *Lord Albermarle's Bolingbroke, held by his trainer W. Edwards* Christie's

home, Aske in Yorkshire. In the autumn of 1849 the colt ran a trial which demonstrated that he was a very good horse indeed and all Yorkshire backed 'Volti' for the Blue Riband the following year. After the trial Voltigeur won a single race at Richmond but did not run again before the Derby. Despite the Yorkshire enthusiasm and the weight of countrywide bets by Masons, since Zetland was the head of English Free-masonry, the southern turf pundits were not impressed. Voltigeur started sixth favourite for the race at 16 to 1 against. At the last moment it was discovered that there were some outstanding forfeits on Voltigeur which, unless paid, would bar the colt from running. Zetland, irritated at being slightly caught out, decided to scratch his horse — to the utter dismay of all his backers, not least every estate worker at Aske who had laid his last shilling on the colt. When the effect of his Lordship's intention was pointed out to him, he immediately relented, the forfeits were paid and Voltigeur ran. In the race Job Marson steered the colt to an easy victory in front of Pitsford. The bookmaker, William Davis, had a second successive disastrous Derby but Lord Zetland's interest in betting was such that he won only £600, just covering the forfeits he had to pay before the race.

Voltigeur was odds-on favourite for the St Leger. In a somewhat rough start before an immense crowd, Marson had to take the lead earlier than intended to avoid any further trouble. To the horror of the Yorkshire spectators an Irish horse, Russborough, started to close with Voltigeur in the last furlong. The Set To over the last few yards resulted in a dead heat. The owners agreed on a deciding heat immediately. Voltigeur was kept moving and warm and Russborough had his teeth examined since there was a suspicion about his age. In the run-off the wildly enthusiastic crowd all but enveloped the contestants as they were driven on by their jockeys fired by the cheering and excitement around them. Lord Zetland's horse won after another terrific struggle. Forty-eight hours later Voltigeur was turned out again for the Doncaster Cup.

This was no ordinary Cup race, more a match between the Derby and St Leger winners of 1849 and 1850. The Flying Dutchman's four-year-old perform-ance in winning the Emperor's Plate at Ascot and other races was as brilliant as that of his Classic victories the year before. He was unbeaten. With Charles Marlow still his jockey, there was no reason to question the fact the bookmakers made The Dutch-man the favourite but he had to give nineteen pounds to the younger horse, Voltigeur. Job Marson was having difficulty in keeping his weight down and on this occasion the outstanding match rider, Nat Flatman, wore Lord Zetland's distinctive jacket of white with red spots and cap. As might be expected, an even greater crowd than the one which witnessed the St Leger turned out to see the duel between the unbeaten champions. Both jockeys were instructed to play a waiting game but Marlow, who may have misinterpreted his master's orders and undoubtedly had found it necessary to fortify his courage with spirits before the start, set off at a fast gallop opening up a considerable lead. Nat on Voltigeur bided his time while remaining in contact. With three furlongs to go, he brought 'Volti' up to The Dutchman and despite Marlow's every effort won the race by half a length. The crowd was astounded; Lord Eglinton briefly lost his charm and Marlow was to be seen sobbing gin and water tears.

Eglinton decided to take The Flying Dutchman out of training but was subsequently persuaded that a further contest between his colt and the unbeaten Voltigeur was essential to prove beyond doubt which was the better horse. Lord Zetland agreed and a match was arranged at York the following spring. Captain Rous was asked to decide the weights which he did by giving the standard weight-for-age penalty of eight and a half pounds to the older horse, The Flying Dutchman.

On Tuesday 13 May 1851 The Great Match, as it became known, was run over two miles of the Knavesmire course at York. A special train was run from London leaving at 7 a.m. to swell the local crowd. Interest in the event was intense. The stake was £1,000 and there was heavy betting on both runners with the older horse at marginally shorter odds. The Flying Dutchman was prepared by John Fobert and, despite his foolishness at Doncaster, Charles Marlow was his jockey. Voltigeur was again ridden by Nat Flatman. Volti took a lead of three lengths making light of the deep going. Marlow did not attempt to take The Dutchman up to him until after the last turn, when steadily reducing the gap he came level half-way up the distance. Voltigeur faltered and The Flying Dutchman won by a length. 'The train which left York at 6 o'clock on Tuesday evening arrived in London at 25 past 12 carrying at least 400 persons, drawn by a single locomotive.'

The Flying Dutchman was immediately retired to stud but was not particularly successful in England. In 1858 he was sold for £4,000 and exported to France where he sired a number of winners. Voltigeur con-tinued his four and five-year-old seasons but with few good results and was sent to stud in 1853.

Harry Hall painted a delightful picture of the Set To in the Doncaster Cup (Plate 22) which, with different jockeys, was similar to that described in *The Sporting Magazine* of Surplice and Canezou. He also painted a number of portraits of Voltigeur (as he had the year before of The Dutchman) for the publisher Baily, and a large group of The Great Match, also used by Baily in 1854. After the 1850 Derby, Baily Brothers published a plate of Voltigeur saddled in a stable (Plate 49) with Robert Hill and Job Marson in attendance, engraved by Charles Hunt. This plate was reprinted with the St Leger result added to the title. After the Doncaster Cup Baily published a second aquatint, this time engraved by John Harris, showing an unsaddled Voltigeur on Doncaster racecourse with Hill and Marson again by him. The legend includes: 'Winner of the Derby Stakes at Epsom, the Doncaster Great St Leger and the Doncaster Cup, 1850.'

Lord Zetland commissioned Hall to paint The Great Match which is a *tour de force* of human portraiture rather than of the horses in the race (Plate 23). The slightly stiff figures are, from left to right: Lord Zetland, Flatman up, Robert Hill, Captain Rous, George Payne, Marlow, Lord Eglinton, and John Fobert. In the distance, across the Knavesmire, the racecourse grandstand and York Minster can be seen. The picture was engraved by Charles Hunt, who was soon to turn to painting as well as engraving, and published by Baily Brothers in May 1854. The painting may be nearer to this date than to the event itself.

CHAPTER 4
1851–1855

Look how the mass, which rushed away
As full of spirits as the day,
So close compacted for a while,
Is lengthening into single file.

THE UNTIMELY DEATH OF Lord George Bentinck in 1848 deprived racing of not only a turf reformer but an individual whose management of his horses was marked by its meticulous attention to detail, and whose betting was on a scale which not many could afford and to which few aspired. Sir Joseph Hawley went some way to matching Lord George in these last two traits. For a time he was also interested in changing a number of racing practices, rather than cleaning the Augean stables. Hawley inherited his title when aged seventeen. He served for a short time in the Army and his friends hoped he would enter politics, for which he appeared well suited. The young Sir Joseph had no intention of acceding to their wishes. Temporarily leaving his home, Leybourne Grange in Kent, he sailed slowly through the Mediterranean in his yacht, The Mischief. Settling in Italy he cultivated the fine arts in which pursuit his considerable intellect served him well. Striking up a friendship with the more dilettante J. Massey Stanley, the pair found time to import a few moderate racehorses from England and raced them on the somewhat haphazard turf of Florence.

Sir Joseph returned to England when aged twenty-six, and began to build up a small stable, first with a public trainer, Beresford, at Newmarket and then buying an establishment of his own at Fyfield in Wiltshire, installing there his private trainer, Alec Taylor. Although not immediately successful in his 'cherry and black cap' he won a number of minor races and bought Mendicant (1,000 Guineas and Oaks, 1846) from John Gully for £3,500. At the time this purchase was considered pure folly by the experts of breeding but within a few years they were proved wrong. In 1847 Miami, ridden by Sim Templeman, gave Hawley his first Classic victory (the Oaks) and from this time the still young baronet took the bit

between his teeth in the first of the two phases of his turf career. The 1851 2,000 Guineas was won by Lord Enfield's Hernandez ridden by Nat Flatman ahead of George Osbaldeston's Mountain Deer. Two days later Sir Joseph Hawley's Aphrodite, with Job Marson up, won the 1,000 Guineas. The filly was later runner-up in the St Leger.

Hawley bought Teddington as a foal in 1848 and his friend Massey Stanley also had an interest in him. As a two-year-old the colt was not very successful but in the following spring ran an excellent trial with another of Sir Joseph's horses, the five-year-old Vatican. The result of the trial became generally known and Teddington was soon favourite for the Derby. A week before the race the colt had sore shins and, on the morning of the Classic, Teddington was off his feed. Hawley and his trainer must have kept these problems to themselves since the horse remained at short odds. The world and his wife were in England for the Great Exhibition and on 21 May they drove down to Epsom for a change of entertainment from gazing at the exhibits in the Crystal Palace. The field of thirty-three runners was the largest yet and the weather was obligingly perfect. Teddington lay in waiting for the first part of the race but took the lead at the mile post and was hardly challenged thereafter, beating the second favourite Marlborough Buck by two lengths. Teddington did not run in the St Leger but won a good match for £1,000 against Osbaldeston's Mountain Deer in the autumn. He was successful as a four-year-old (Doncaster Cup) and the following year won the last of the Emperor's Plates, (which reverted to the Ascot Gold Cup in 1854). He was unremarkable at stud.

Teddington's victory gave Job Marson his second successive win in the Derby and he and Alec Taylor were well rewarded by Sir Joseph; too generously for

51 *Mr A. Nichol's Newminster, Sim Templeman up, with the trainer John Scott (St Leger, 1851)* Arthur Ackermann & Son Ltd.

Captain Rous's liking. Hawley won £80,000 on the race which was equally distasteful to the Captain. Notwithstanding Rous's dislike of Hawley, he flew to his aid in the autumn when Sir Joseph's motives were questioned when selling Vatican just prior to the Doncaster Cup which he won with The Ban. However, Rous's efforts were to no avail for Hawley felt his honour was doubted and he immediately sold his horses in training keeping a few mares only, including Mendicant, for breeding at Leybourne Grange. At the same time Hawley's partnership with John Massey Stanley foundered, although the latter continued to keep horses with Alec Taylor at Fyfield until 1856 when the former ran into financial difficulties. So ended Hawley's first excursion into racing.

Frank Butler completed the hat-trick in the Oaks riding Iris. Iris belonged to Lord Stanley whose devotion to the turf continued despite his new political duties as First Lord of the Treasury. Lord Stanley also succeeded his father in 1851 as the Earl of Derby.

The small, long, wiry Newminster was bred by a Mr Orde of Nunnykirk. Nunnykirk, the horse (2,000 Guineas 1849) was Newminster's brother. Newminster was a son of Touchstone and his dam was the wonderful staying mare Beeswing (Ascot Gold Cup, Doncaster Cup on four occasions, and the Chester Cup). Mr Nichol bought the colt as a yearling and he was sent to John Scott. He proved difficult to train and did not run well in the Derby, but starting at 12 to 1 against in the St Leger he flew over the ground to win convincingly with Sim Templeman up. A pair of paintings by Harry Hall of Newminster and Beeswing were sold a few years ago from the collection of E. R. Templeman, and a painting of Newminster (Plate 51) shows John Scott standing by his grey hack admiring the little Classic winner who was hardly more than fifteen hands high.

— 1852 —

In 1852 Rous was promoted to Rear Admiral of the Blue and it is as Admiral Rous that he is so well known as the nineteenth-century expert on the rules of racing, many of which he created, refined or reformed with a singular dedication. He was also the person to whom owners turned whenever a handicap was required. His calculation of weights for age were universally respected, (in the Great Match between The Flying Dutchman and Voltigeur he introduced the use of a ½ lb for the first time), and his knowledge of horses or access to information on their performance gave him the means fairly to apply handicaps to animals of different abilities. Obviously there were occasions when he was misled and also times when he

misjudged a horse's fitness, but these were few and far between. At Newmarket his word was almost law throughout his life regardless of his contemporary position in the Jockey Club. The Admiral would ride out on the Heath each morning during meetings with his friends, Colonel Peel (the younger brother of the statesman, Sir Robert), Lord Glasgow and Lord Exeter; they were inseparable companions.

Colonel Peel was born in 1799 and commissioned into the Army three days before the battle of Waterloo. He saw no active service but steadily climbed the promotion ladder by purchase. As a young man he turned to the turf for entertainment and after a good many years gained some success, not least with Orlando in the Running Rein Derby. However, he sold his stud in 1851 but, as Bentinck had done before him, maintained his keen interest in racing. He was promoted Major-General in 1854 and sought permission from the Secretary for War, Lord Panmure, to join the Army then besieging Sebastopol in the Crimea. He was fifty-five years old, hale and hearty, but to his dismay was peremptorily told he was too old to serve abroad.

Lord Glasgow was a true eccentric in dress, habits and actions. He wore Nankeen trousers which were too short for him, a badly cut waistcoat of the same material, a dark blue coat with plain brass buttons and a very tall hat. He never wore a top-coat whatever the weather. He was short-tempered, used strong language freely and yet was warm-hearted and generous to his friends whatever their station in life. He had little success with his large stable of horses and equally long string of trainers and jockeys whom he engaged and dismissed at the rate of one or two a season. As *The Times* correspondent reported of a match at Doncaster: 'Lord Glasgow lost of course.' He was as loathe to give his horses names as he was ready to shoot those showing little promise — the last an act of kindness to prevent their falling into bad hands if sold, and also of necessity to make room in his stables for fresh drafts of yearlings. His only Classic success was in the 2,000 Guineas with a colt he was unexpectedly ready to name after his friend, General Peel. When Lord Glasgow died in 1869, he left half his horses to Peel with instructions that they must be raced, so again involving the General as an owner of thoroughbreds.

Lord Exeter was born in the same year as Rous. When he came to Newmarket each spring he lived at Foley House from which a long carriage drive ran to Exeter House where his trainer, James Harlock, lived. In wet and frosty weather his racehorses were trained along this sheltered driveway. Lord Exeter was perpetually trying his horses, often against the wishes of his trainer, and even if they were to race the same day. According to William Day, he was a rather small

52 *Lord Exeter's Stockwell, J. Norman up (2,000 Guineas and St Leger, 1852)*
Engraving by John Harris Julian Armytage

man, always dressed in black, with an unfashionable shirt collar around which a long, stiffly starched tie was wound several times. This prevented the Marquis from turning his head without moving his whole body, resulting in even his friends receiving no acknowledgement as they saluted him in Newmarket High Street. He bred most of his own horses, starting racing in about 1817 and won seven Classics between 1821 and 1832, but not the Derby or St Leger. In 1850 Lord Exeter bought a chestnut named Stockwell for £150 from a Mr Theobald of Stockwell. He was entered for the 2,000 Guineas, Derby and St Leger of 1852. On 27 April the going at Newmarket for the 2,000 Guineas was heavy, which suited the exceptionally strong Stockwell. Ridden by J. Norman, nicknamed The Post-Boy, the colt led almost from the off and won by half a length ahead of the Duke of Richmond's Homebrewed. An unexceptional filly named Kate, owned by Mr Sargent and ridden by Alfred Day won the 1,000 Guineas two days later.

Shortly before the Derby, Stockwell was afflicted by a septic boil on his leg which was cut open. He was

therefore out of form resulting in odds of 16 to 1 being laid against him. The colt was also in trouble during the race when Norman tried to put him through too narrow a gap against the rails. John Bowes's Daniel O'Rourke turned out the winner of a race in which a number of suspicious incidents took their toll of at least three other hopefuls. There was some criticism of Frank Butler when he rode Springy Jack to second place behind Surplice in the 1848 Derby. It is possible he made his 'rush' a shade too late on that occasion, but in 1852 he took the tiny Daniel O'Rourke to the front in masterly style at just the right moment. Hall painted the colt a number of times and in Plate 24 he is shown with Butler up accompanied by an unidentified figure. It has been suggested that this is John Scott, Daniel O'Rourke's trainer, but from a comparison with Plate 53 this is plainly not so. For some years John Bowes had spent much of his time in Paris and in 1852 married Josephine Coffin-Chevalier, an actress and painter. It is not precisely known who managed his horses at Streatlam at this period, although in 1853 it is reported that a Mr Markwell was leading in his winners. This may be him standing by Daniel O'Rourke. The horse was not successful after the Derby. It was said that Frank Butler took a very large bet the previous winter that he would win the Derby and Oaks. With the first part of his double safely in hand he was fortunate to be mounted on the best filly in the second race. This was John Scott's Songstress who appropriately beat Bird on the Wing! This win also gave Butler his fourth successive Oaks victory.

By the time of the St Leger on 15 September, Stockwell was again fully fit. The race was overshadowed by the death of the Duke of Wellington the previous afternoon but there was a good crowd to see Stockwell win convincingly with Daniel O'Rourke third. Stockwell was later put to stud where he was outstandingly successful siring three Derby winners and fathering the first three horses in the 1866 race. He was the leading sire on seven occasions and was rightly known as the Emperor of Stallions, being the father of seventeen Classic winners. Lord Exeter continued racing until 1855 but without any further Classic successes. Stockwell was sold for 3,100 Guineas in that year to Lord Londesborough and the rest of the stables to Henry Padwick, due to Lord Exeter having to find a large sum of money to cover losses on railway construction.

At the end of 1852 the veteran jockey Jem Robinson was riding a horse belonging to Lord Clifden in a match when it swerved, a stirrup leather snapped and Robinson fell, breaking his thigh. Despite the attention of a host of skilled doctors his damaged leg set almost four inches shorter than the other. Robinson had to give up riding. This was a sad end to a long and brilliant career in which his honesty, courage and generosity were an example to all in the racing world. In the words of The Quarterly: 'He was perfect.' He died in 1865.

— 1853 —

John Bowes was a heavy better if the opportunity arose. When John Scott reported to him in August 1852 that West Australian had gone particularly well in a morning trial in Yorkshire, Bowes went to William Davis in London the same evening and obtained 30,000 to 1,000 against the colt winning the Derby the following year. He made other wagers at long odds until the 'intelligence' was out that Bowes and Scott had another good one when the world followed suit. 'The West', as the colt was known, was favourite for the 1853 2,000 Guineas and won convincingly half a

length ahead of the Duke of Bedford's Sittingbourne. Frank Butler rode West Australian. At Epsom it was the first year that the electric telegraph was extended from Croydon to the stand, allowing last minute instructions to be sent and received, and for the results of races to be 'flashed' to London and Paris where Bowes resided. The West was again the favourite and after an excellent start he and Sittingbourne sorted themselves out from the field of twenty-eight and went into the lead. Sam Rogers on Sittingbourne gave West Australian a more testing race than in the 2,000 Guineas. It was only after a desperate struggle that Butler was home by a neck with Rogers at his shoulder. Cineas, trained at Danebury, was third by a head, and Rataplan, brother of Stockwell was close behind in fourth place. Mentmore Lass gave Baron Meyer de Rothschild his first Classic victory in the 1,000 Guineas in 1853, ridden by the then little known jockey John Charlton. The Baron had to wait a further ten years before his large stud and great wealth began to make itself felt on the turf. The Oaks was won in a canter by Mr Wauchope's Catherine Hayes with Charles Marlow up.

In the eyes of John Scott, West Australian was the best horse he had ever trained and must be the favourite for the St Leger. However, he was worried that other entries were apparently better thought of by the bookmakers. West Australian was guarded night and day for fear of being 'got at' and Frank Butler was accorded much the same treatment. There were some (including Lord Derby and General Anson) who thought that for the right price Butler would do anything for anybody, but on this occasion 'the idea of accomplishing that which no other man ever did' — win the Triple Crown of the 2,000 Guineas, Derby and St Leger — 'was enough for me'. In the race, Sittingbourne set off at a telling pace and Rataplan was well up. The Reiver then overtook Sittingbourne, who faded quickly, and The West was soon at The Reiver's side before taking a clear lead at the stand to the cheers of the crowd. West Australian won by at least three lengths with Butler riding past the post with 'hands down'. The West was successful as a four-year-old before being sold to Lord Londesborough for £4,600 and retiring to stud. Later, he was sold for 4,000 guineas to the Duc de Mornay and exported to France. He was not a success as a sire in either country. Hall painted West Australian on many occasions (Plate 53), sometimes with his great rival Sittingbourne shown in the background. In any other year, Sittingbourne might well have won two of the Classic races for the seventh Duke of Bedford, whose horses were managed by Admiral Rous.

53 *Mr J. Bowes's West Australian, Frank Butler up, with trainer John Scott and manager James Perrin (Triple Crown, 1853)* Strathmore Estates (Holding) Ltd.

As well as the usual portraits of racehorse winners which were engraved and published in *The Sporting Magazine*, Harry Hall painted two more panels, portraits of jockeys (the first of James Chapple appeared in the *Magazine* the year before). James Robinson and Nat Flatman were portrayed in 1853 and later sixteen of these small paintings were acquired by the Jockey Club. They were framed in fours, with the jockeys' names and exploits inscribed below each portrait. At some date the individual panels must have been removed from their frames for some reason, possibly cleaning, and wrongly replaced. The illustrations at Plates 11, 12, 41 and 42 have the correct captions for each jockey. Between April and September 1853, Harry Hall drew eighteen sketches of racehorses and incidents at training which were reproduced in *The Field*. These are crude wood-engravings which do nothing to enhance Hall's reputation as an artist. The association between the *The Field* and Hall came to an abrupt end the following June.

— 1854 —

John Gully was no longer the Member for Pontefract and partly as a result of his fracas with the Days over Old England, he decided to live close to Danebury at Marwell Hall, Winchester from where he could exercise tighter control over the management and training of his horses. He was still very much a part of the Danebury Confederacy, but perhaps trying to disengage himself from the more nefarious activities of some of its members. Sam Day Snr had retired and Alfred Day rode Gully's and Henry Hill's The Hermit to win the 2,000 Guineas. Two days later, Virago, an outstanding daughter of Pyrrhus the First won the 1,000 Guineas for a 'Mr. Howard', one of the racing names used by the Sussex lawyer and money-lender, Henry Padwick. John Day Snr bought Virago for Padwick for £300 from Mr Stephenson and she was trained at Michel Grove near Winchester. Winning the Newmarket Classics with horses trained by John Day Jnr and Snr respectively must have seemed a

9 *Mr William Ridsdale's Bloomsbury, Sim Templeman up, with the owner on his hack (Derby, 1839)* R. Green

10 *Lord George Bentinck's Crucifix, J.B. Day up with John Day Jnr (2,000 Guineas, 1,000 Guineas and Oaks, 1841)* Private collection

11 *Jockeys: (top, left to right) James Robinson, John Charlton; (bottom, left to right) Frank Butler, Ralph Bullock*
Courtesy of the Stewards of the Jockey Club

12 *Jockeys: (top, left to right) J. Bartholemew, John Wells; (bottom, left to right) Thomas Challoner, Alfred Day*
Courtesy of the Stewards of the Jockey Club

13 *Colonel Anson's Attila, Bill Scott up (Derby, 1842)*   Sotheby's

14 *Mr J. Bowes's Cotherstone (2,000 Guineas and Derby, 1843)*   Richard Green

15 *Mr S. Wrather's Nutwith, Job Marson up (St Leger, 1843)*   Sotheby's

16 *Mr W. Gratwicke's The Merry Monarch, F. Bell up (Derby, 1845)*   Anthony Mould Ltd.

17 *Mr W.H. Gregory's Clermont, Trenn Jnr up*   Richard Green

18 *Mr John Day's The Hero, Alfred Day up (Ascot Cup, 1847 and 1848, Goodwood Cup, 1847)*   R. Green

19 *Lord Clifden's Surplice, held by his trainer John Kent Jnr, Sim Templeman on his hack (Derby and St Leger, 1848)*
Private collection

20 *'The Merry Beaglers', Mr Charles Phelips, the Revd, Philip Honywood, and huntsman Tom Pitts 1848*   Private collection

21 *Lord Eglinton's The Flying Dutchman, Charles Marlow up (Derby and St Leger, 1849)*   Frost & Reed Ltd.

22 *The Set To between Voltigeur and The Flying Dutchman in the Doncaster Cup, 1850*
Collection of the Hon, True Davis, Washington DC

23 *'The Great Match' between The Flying Dutchman and Voltigeur at York, 13 May 1851* Private collection

24 *Mr J. Bowes's Daniel O'Rourke, Frank Butler up, with Mr Markwell (Derby, 1852)* Richard Green

54 *Mr J. Gully's Andover, Alfred Day up (Derby, 1854)* Arthur Ackermann & Son Ltd.

promising start to the 1854 season, quite apart from the undoubtedly handsome return on the family's betting ventures.

The favourite for the Blue Riband was Lord Derby's Dervish. King Tom, belonging to Baron de Rothschild, and a half-brother of Stockwell, was also well thought of, as was John Gully's Andover. Andover was tried before the race with The Hermit and showed he was the superior horse. Gully therefore favoured Andover, putting Alfred Day on his back and using The Hermit with John Wells as pacemaker. The start of the twenty-seven runners was excellent. When the field entered the straight The Hermit was in the lead followed hotly by Dervish with Andover and King Tom in close pursuit. Andover went to the front at the half-distance followed by King Tom, at which moment Dervish faded badly having nothing in reserve for Sim Templeman to call upon. Charlton on King Tom tried valiantly to reach Andover but the latter was a strong horse and won easily by a length (Plate

55). The Hermit was third. Again the Days and John Gully won 'a great pot'. In the *Illustrated London News* of 9 September 1854 the Racing Intelligence correspondent reports:

> Mr Hall has just brought out a very capital Derby portrait of Andover with Alfred Day on him. Six or seven of the leading horses are introduced in the background descending from the paddock to the start, the most characteristic of them being the little chestnut, Hospodar [belonging to Lord Zetland]. Alfred Day's likeness has been capitally hit off; but he would have looked all the better if he had worn Mr Gully's time-honoured white cap instead of a red one, in the fray.

Gully's registered colours were 'violet with white cap' and, as was common practice, if an owner had more than one horse running in the same race, the 'second' jockey wore a different cap to avoid confusion among the spectators, stewards and judges. Andover

55 *Baron Meyer de Rothschild's Hungerford, John Charlton up, with trainer William King (Doncaster Cup, 1853)*
Arthur Ackermann & Son Ltd.

won a number of races as a three-year-old and Gully sold him to Sir Tatton Sykes at the end of the season. Sir Tatton put him to stud in Yorkshire but with little success and he was later exported to Russia.

Mr William Cookson's Mincemeat, a daughter of Sweetmeat, won the 1854 Oaks with Charlton up. Sam Chifney Jnr, who won this race on five occasions and looked upon it as a relaxation after the Derby, died at Brighton on 29 August in very reduced circumstances.

Mr J. B. Morris, known as 'Jolly' Morris, was a convivial man as his nickname implied. He was also an astute Irishman who came to England early in life to 'join his brethren of the book-and-pencil'. He was as straight as any bookmaker could be and soon became a trusted commissioner for Colonel Anson before he went to India, and for the young Sir Joseph Hawley whose prodigious bets have already been mentioned. It was not long before he owned racehorses. The first was Hungerford, whom he bought cheaply from George Osbaldeston and ran him unplaced in

the 1851 Derby. Morris sold Hungerford for a good price to Baron de Rothschild for whom he won the Doncaster Cup and other races. He also bought Vatican from Hawley a quarter of an hour before the start of the 1851 Doncaster Cup, which led to Sir Joseph quitting the turf when accused of artifice in the way the sale was negotiated before winning the race with The Ban. Jolly's next success was with Kingston, who won the Goodwood Cup in 1852 and went on to beat Teddington and Stockwell for the Whip at Newmarket. Morris's single Classic victory was in the St Leger with the hot-tempered little colt Knight of St George, (who was among the also ran in the preceding Derby). By 1854 the racing at Doncaster had taken a turn for the better after Admiral Rous had explained with some vigour how the meeting could best be put right. There was a good crowd on the Town Moor on Wednesday 13 September. It might have been larger but for the absence of those turfites among Lord Raglan's and Marshal St Arnaud's troops who were then disembarking thirty miles north of Sebastopol in

56 *Mr. J.B. Morris's Knight of St George, Bob Basham up, being led in by his owner* *(St. Leger, 1854)* Lane Fine Art Ltd.

the distant Crimea. The going was hard after a drought, and Bob Basham on Knight of St George won an exciting race by a head from Ivan. This was a popular win and Jolly Morris was mobbed by the crowd as he led his horse in, although this is not apparent from Hall's painting of the scene, (Plate 56). After the St Leger Morris's racing luck evaporated but he remained a successful bookmaker for many years. In 1865 he was instrumental in raising a subscription to recognise Admiral Rous as 'The Head of the Racing World' (a title given to him in a speech by the Duke of Beaufort). This took the form of a portrait of the Admiral by Weigall, and a candelabra.

During this period Harry Hall also painted genre scenes of country life and a number of these were exhibited at the Royal Academy, Royal Society of British Artists and the British Institute. They were unconnected with racing having titles such as: 'Shooting Companions'; 'To him lads! Another blank'; 'Rabbit Ferreting. Look out Sir! They're Running';

'The First of September — a Welcome Arrival'. In 1854 'Marking the Covey' was shown at the British Institute. It was the practice of the editor of the *Illustrated London News* to select two or three pictures from these annual exhibitions and have them finely engraved and reproduced. 'Marking the Covey' (Plate 6) was dealt with in this manner on 18 March 1854. The over-romanticised description of the picture and the very complimentary remarks about Hall's skill are given in full on page 126. It is unlikely that any of these pictures were commissioned since most of those exhibited were for sale. Perhaps Hall painted them for relaxation as a respite from the stream of racehorse portraits. They may also represent some of the pursuits which he enjoyed, particularly that of shooting with a few friends. As I have already mentioned, the poor quality sketches in *The Field* stopped in mid-1854, but not before one of Coursing Cracks (two greyhounds) was published showing another aspect of Harry Hall's ability to portray animals.

Mr James Merry was the son of a wealthy, self-made Glasgow merchant. Despite a limited education and perhaps not too much intelligence, Merry had shrewd common sense and a determination which served him well both as a successful Scottish ironmaster and owner of racehorses. At the outset of his turf career, Merry's horses were trained by George Dawson at Gullane. The first really successful animal which he owned was a Roman-nosed grey, Chanticleer, who won ten races in 1848, including the Doncaster Cup trouncing Lord Eglinton's Van Tromp (St Leger 1847). Earlier that season the first of what were to become a number of attempts to 'fix' James Merry's horses occurred. In this case Frederick Swindell, Merry's betting commissioner who was a respected and unusually honest man for one of his calling, discovered the reason for the continued long odds laid against Chanticleer. Having first taken advantage of the good price available about the colt, he advised Merry to change his jockey at the last moment. The horse quickly became third favourite for the Goodwood Stakes and a great many bookmakers were then unable to cover themselves in the short time before Chanticleer won the race. Fred Swindell remained Mr Merry's adviser, commissioner and companion securing many betting coups for his patron, who was never slow to lay out money on his own horses. For some reason, whether jealousy, mere snobbery or a dislike of his character, for James Merry could be suspicious and difficult, he had few friends. He became a leading owner and won seven Classic races, but there was never a suggestion that he should be made a member of the Jockey Club. He was very fond of cock-fighting, as were Lord Derby and Admiral Rous, but this mutual interest did not bridge the apparent gap between the ironmaster and the aristocracy of the turf.

— 1855 —

Merry had moved his horses to William Day at Woodyates in 1852 to be nearer the southern circuit and the main races for two and three-year-olds. William Day bought Lord of the Isles as a yearling for £350 for Merry in 1853 and entered the colt for the 2,000 Guineas and Derby in 1855. In the first Classic of the season Aldcroft rode Lord of the Isles to victory a neck in front of Henry Padwick's St Hubert. Henry Hill's Kingstown was third.

The field for the Derby which followed was only twelve strong, the smallest for many years. The crowd was not large either, lacking the presence of the usual division of military supporters who were away in the Crimea. Wild Dayrell, bred by Mr Francis Popham of Littlecote, Berkshire, was an awkward foal. As a result Popham, who only raced a few horses, disposed of the colt but subsequently bought him back again a year later when the Duke of Richmond's stud was put up for sale at Tattersalls in 1853. Lord Craven had a share in the horse who was trained privately by Mr Rickaby at Ashdown Park. Wild Dayrell improved enormously but ran only once as a two-year-old winning a sweepstake at Newmarket in the autumn of 1854. He did not race again before the Derby but outpaced all the opposition matched against him in a number of trials during the spring of 1855. His form became known publicly but, as too often occurred, the price against his winning the Blue Riband remained long. Francis Popham was offered £5,000 to scratch the horse, which naturally he refused to do. It was then suspected that the van which would take Wild Dayrell to Epsom might be sabotaged, so a bullock was loaded into it as a test. The vehicle had hardly moved ten yards before the axles gave way and its unfortunate occupant broke a leg in the crash. The bookmakers' favourite was Kingstown and there is little doubt that his owner, Henry Hill, passively, if not actively, helped the blackguards who were determined that Wild Dayrell should not run. To the embarrassment of Kingstown's supporters, Wild Dayrell reached Epsom safely under heavy guard and before the start the odds shortened dramatically making him favourite. He was in wonderful condition when saddled and the writing was clearly on the wall for those who had backed any other horse in the race. Lord of the Isles made the pace until being overhauled by Kingstown at Tattenham Corner. At the distance Wild Dayrell, ridden by Robert Sherwood, passed them both to win very easily by two lengths. Kingstown was second, a head in front of Lord of the Isles. Francis Popham was disgusted by the dishonesty which surrounded his venture into Classic racing and virtually retired from the turf having only started the year before. Wild Dayrell won one more race before breaking down in the Doncaster Cup. He was sent to stud not far from Littlecote but was not a success as a sire.

Some years before this Derby, Francis Popham commissioned Harry Hall to paint his hunters at grass at Littlecote — a picture which was exhibited at the Royal Academy in 1851. After the Derby, Hall painted a very large portrait of Wild Dayrell with Sherwood and Rickaby. He also painted a smaller canvas for Baily's series of Derby winners and a panel of the colt in a loosebox which appeared, engraved, in *The Sporting Magazine* of July 1855.

The poor performance of James Merry's Lord of the Isles in the Derby came in for some criticism. It was thought that his jockey, Aldcroft, may have been

57 *Mr F.L. Topham's Wild Dayrell, Robert Sherwood up (Derby, 1855). Engraving by John Harris & Charles Quentery*
Julian Armytage

persuaded to hang back to give Henry Hill's Kingstown (Alfred Day up) a chance to win. The outcome was that the suspicious Merry thought using a public trainer such as William Day, under pressure of pleasing a number of owners, let alone relatives or members of the Danebury Confederacy, was too risky for his liking. At the end of the season he moved his horses to Russley, where they were privately trained by John Prince and later by Mathew Dawson.

In 1855 the 1,000 Guineas was won by the Duke of Bedford's Habena with Sam Rogers up, and the Oaks by Marchioness (Sim Templeman) owned by Mr Rudston Read of Frickley Hall, Doncaster, a well-known northern racegoer and naturalist. In the second of these races the favourite, Nettle, was ridden by Charles Marlow, for once not in Lord Eglinton's jacket. Soon after the start Nettle bolted, fell over the chains and Marlow was badly thrown, breaking a leg which put him out of racing for two years.

Thomas Parr started life as an itinerant tea-seller in the West Country. It is difficult to discover his first association with horses, except that he progressed from peddling his wares on foot to owning a pony and trap, but in quite quick succession he became first a jockey and then a trainer-owner. He had an uncanny knack of recognising a good thing in a young horse whom others could not dispose of too quickly. In this last respect Admiral Rous became the butt of some good-natured chafing about the performance of a colt named Weathergage whom he sold on behalf of the Duke of Bedford for £40 before falling into Parr's hands for only £10 more. Weathergage immediately started winning races when trained by Parr, including the Goodwood Stakes and Cesarewitch in 1852. In both races the jockey was 'Tiny' Wells. Possibly the strangest part of Parr's philosophy of racing was constantly to run his horses at little meetings for small stakes all over the country. This practice of winning a £15 stake on one day and another a hundred miles away a week later must have given Parr some satisfaction, but it did not result in his ever having much money in his pocket. He is said to have spent a great deal of his time hiding in a hayloft at his stables near Wantage, while his ancient factotum, George Hall, lied through his few remaining teeth to a queue of anxious creditors that his master was away racing in some distant part of the country.

Thomas Parr bought Saucebox from Henry Hill and Rataplan from Henry Padwick in 1854. A year later Saucebox won the St Leger in fine style. The colt started as an outsider at 40 to 1 and Wells only had to sit still for him to beat Rifleman by three-quarters of a length. Rataplan (in Mr Thelluson's jacket) took the Doncaster Cup. As usual Parr was short of funds and won next to nothing except the stakes for each race. With more prudence and fore-thought he might have been a rich man, but this was not his nature and perhaps he would have lost some of his wayward charm had he been more careful.

At the end of October 1855 Charles Greville wrote in his diary:

> All last week at Newmarket, and probably very nearly the last time as an owner of racehorses, for I have now got rid of them all, and am almost off the turf, after being on it more or less for about forty years. I am sorry that I have not kept any memoranda of my turf life, which might have been curious and amusing; for I have known many odd characters, and have lived with men of whom it would have been interesting to preserve some re-cord. Perhaps I may one day rake together my old recollections and trace the changes that have taken place in this racing life since I first knew it, but I cannot do so now.

Sadly, Greville never wrote about his racing ex-periences in any detail. If he had, and despite being rather a fuss-pot, he would have given a valuable contemporary account written with a sympathy and fairness which are not found among many other writers. Naming the crooks, he would also have men-tioned any redeeming features of their characters; and he would not have shirked criticising his friends if he thought it right to do so. A story of forty years of racing stretching from Whisker by Waxy to Saucebox by St Lawrence, and from the activities of the Duke of Grafton to those of Tom Parr, would be invaluable to the turf historian today.

Harry Hall was now thirty years old with five sons; the eldest at Merchant Taylors' School and the youngest aged four. The first three boys, Sidney, Arthur and Frank, have been mentioned already. Frederick Hall was born in May 1849 but died of pneumonia at the age of 12. Ernest Hall, seen at a later date in the photograph with his father (frontis-piece) was born in April 1851, educated at Felsted School where he showed promise as a cricketer, and then studied to be a surveyor before entering an estate agent's office on the south coast. Hall's position as the principal portrayer of racehorses of the period was now secure and while part of his time was spent in his stable studio at Newmarket, he was also fulfilling commissions on site, to which he travelled on the ever-improving railway network. Although this ac-count is in part about Classic-winning horses, Hall also painted steeplechasers and hunters, often belong-ing to the same owners of the winners on the flat. He was therefore engaged throughout the year, perhaps allowing him to spend less time than he liked with his wife Ellen and their growing family.

1856—1861

As on the struggling coursers press,
So deep the eager silentness,
That underneath their feet the turf
Seems shaken, like the eddying surf.

LORD DERBY'S FAZZOLETTO was bred at Knowsley. As a two-year-old he was a large and ungainly brown colt, whom some thought had a physique only fit for a coach horse — which was surprising for the progeny of Orlando (Derby, 1844) and Canezou (1,000 Guineas, 1848). Fazzoletto did not race before the 2,000 Guineas in 1856 but won easily by half a length with Nat Flatman on his back. Henry Padwick who owned the second horse, Yellow Jack, put in an objection for crossing, but this was overruled. The race was Lord Derby's only 2,000 Guineas win. On 1 May, Manganese beat Henry Hill's Mincepie in the 1,000 Guineas in what was described as a dull meeting at Newmarket. Manganese was raced in the name of Mr W. H. Brook although at the time of the 1,000 Guineas the filly belonged jointly to the Reverend J. W. King of Ashby-de-la-Launde in Lincolnshire and John Osborne Snr, who trained her at Ashgill, near Middleham in Yorkshire. Shortly after the race, Mr King bought Osborne's share. Manganese was ridden by John Osborne Jnr, the younger brother of William and Robert Osborne who became trainers when they could not keep to a jockey's weight. John Jnr (Plate 42) started riding in 1846, when he was thirteen years old, and this 1,000 Guineas was his first of many subsequent Classic victories. His career was one of steady if unspectacular progress. His forte was an ability to judge pace so well that even when he appeared to be almost out of touch with the front runners, he would steadily bring his horse through, finally to win by half a length or less. George Fordham, Jim Snowdon and Osborne were successful exponents of the art of waiting, which the Chifneys would have greatly admired.

Ellington, belonging to Admiral Harcourt, was one of the first foals by The Flying Dutchman. He was trained by Thomas Dawson at Brecongill, also near Middleham, from where he ran in a few races as a two-year-old and again during the spring of 1856, before travelling down to Epsom for the Derby. Two weeks before the race a newspaper correspondent wrote: 'Ellington's chance must be quite out, as he has not grown, but mainly "run to hoof", a point on which he is really enormous.' Despite looking supremely fit on the day, and the heavy going of that year suiting a large-footed horse, the odds against Ellington winning were 20 to 1. Fazzoletto was the favourite at 5 to 2. The Admiral's horse was ridden by Tom Aldcroft who had taken over from Tommy Lye as Dawson's stable jockey when Lye so severely handled Blue Bonnet in the 1842 St Leger. Aldcroft was a rising star among a new group of young jockeys coming into prominence in the wake of Bill Scott, Jem Robinson and Frank Butler. Prince Albert was present in the grandstand with the Prince of Prussia to watch an exciting finish between Yellow Jack and Ellington (Fazzoletto faded early). With a few yards to run, Aldcroft only had to show Ellington the whip once for the little horse with large feet to jump into the lead and win by a length. Ellington was favourite for the St Leger but could not repeat his Derby form and came nowhere. He did not win another race and was not a success as a sire. Henry Hill's Mincepie, with Alfred Day up, won an unspectacular Oaks.

The organisation of racing on the Town Moor was now much improved but while thousands were expected to make the special ten shillings railway journey north from London for the Doncaster St Leger, only 370 turned up at King's Cross Station. The many scratchings of entered horses may have partly accounted for the dearth of southern racegoers, but it is more likely that there were no 'big' names among the remaining runners which led to a suspicion that the result would be a half-guinea wasted. In the event the

58 *Admiral Harcourt's Ellington, Tom Aldcroft up (Derby, 1856)*   Sotheby's

would-be spectators were probably right since Warlock, a roan belonging to Mr Anthony Nichol and trained by John Scott, won easily by two lengths giving both the owner and Nat Flatman their second St Leger successes.

The racegoing crowds were also still depleted by those serving in the Crimea. Although Sebastopol fell in September 1855 and fighting stopped, the peace terms sent to St Petersburg in December were not signed (in Paris) until the end of March 1856. The evacuation of British troops took place during the following July. No sooner had the military element of the turf returned to normal than seven companies of Bengal Native Infantry mutinied at Barrackpore in March 1857, joined by the Sepoys at Meerut on 10 May. However, the Indian Mutiny involved only a few soldiers from England, but 'intelligence from the front' dominated the newspaper columns which would otherwise have been full of the latest prices for the 1857 2,000 Guineas and Derby.

— 1857 —

Lord Zetland's trainer at Aske in 1857 was George Abdale who was married to a sister of John Osborne Jnr. Lord Zetland relied heavily for advice on Abdale and more particularly Mr Williamson, his brother-in-law. It was the latter who persuaded Zetland to buy the ugly Voltigeur whom his old trainer Robert Hill had first admired. Sadly his Lordship fell out with Hill shortly after The Great Match. Hill had been over-optimistic over the prospects of a horse which turned out to be almost useless. It was again Mr Williamson who persuaded Lord Zetland to buy Voltigeur's ungainly son, Vedette. Job Marson rode Vedette in a trial and thought him a worthy successor to 'Volti', if not better than the Derby and St Leger winner. Vedette therefore came to the 2,000 Guineas as the 5 to 2 favourite, ridden by John Osborne Jnr, now in

59 Mr G. Hodgman's Emigrant, Charles Boyce up (Grand National, 1857)   Christie's

the Zetland fold. He won clearly by three-quarters of a length from Anton, a Danebury entry ridden by Alfred Day. After the race Vedette was hobbling and often suffered from rheumatism. He was not entered for the Derby but, if he had been, it seems unlikely that he could have run since he was still lame from Newmarket. However, Vedette later won a number of races, including the Doncaster Cup, and was the sire of the highly successful Galopin.

John Scott of Malton, the 'Wizard of the North' whose prowess as a trainer was without equal during this period, occasionally ran horses in his own name as we have seen. This was the case of the filly Imperieuse which, it was believed, 'fell into his hands' when her noble owner found it necessary to go abroad quickly to avoid his creditors. She was by Orlando, as smart and neat a filly as one could find, but not fancied for the 1,000 Guineas. Mr William I'Anson, a Scotsman, was among that small covey of trainers based around Malton, who also owned a few horses; one in which he had great faith was Blink Bonny. She was by Melbourne out of the despised Queen Mary,

whom I'Anson sought out to breed from, paying £30 for the mare. Blink Bonny won a number of races as a two-year-old but was ill during the winter of 1856/57. Because of her earlier successes she remained favourite for the Derby in the spring of 1857 and I'Anson thought she was fit enough to win the 1,000 Guineas. In this he was mistaken. She ran fifth in an eight-horse race won comfortably by Scott's Imperieuse ridden by Nat Flatman. With this result Blink Bonny's price dropped back to 20 to 1 for the Derby and a Mr Douglas's Tournament became favourite at 4 to 1. Derby Day at Epsom was extremely hot and both Tournament and Blink Bonny were in a lather of sweat before they left the paddock. There were eight false starts which must have affected all the runners and particularly those with difficult temperaments, certainly Tournament. Four jockeys were later fined for unruly behaviour and disobeying the starter — oh for the firm hand and commanding presence of Bentinck! The race, once off, was run at a very fast pace and there were seven horses together in the final furlong. William I'Anson's filly, with three other

60 Count Frederic de Lagrange's Mademoiselle de Chantilly, Spreoty up (City and Suburban Handicap, 1858). Engraving by John Harris   Julian Armytage

horses, passed the judge's post in line abreast, although laterally far apart. Blink Bonny ridden by John Charlton was declared the winner with Tournament well back in the field. On 29 May, Charlton rode her to victory again in the Oaks beating Imperieuse by sixteen lengths. Blink Bonny was only the second horse to win both the Epsom Classics since the races started; the first was Eleanor in 1801.

In this fillies' year both Imperieuse and Blink Bonny were well thought of for the St Leger on their 'home ground'. Blink Bonny was the favourite at 5 to 4 against but a great deal of money was placed on Imperieuse at 100 to 6. The *Illustrated London News* thought:

> The fancy for Scott's mare forms such an era in its history that Harry Hall ought to be commissioned forthwith to paint a life-size portrait of her, to hang as a Turf trophy aloft in the Stock Exchange.

With these two northern horses leading the betting it was natural that there should be a very good crowd at Doncaster on the fine and balmy day of the race. Some time before the meeting William I'Anson was warned that his jockey, John Charlton, might have been 'got at' by a dangerous bookmaker named Jackson who had placed a great deal of money on Imperieuse. I'Anson stayed true to Charlton which probably cost him the race. Blink Bonny was plainly pulled and came fourth to Imperieuse ridden by the invariably 'straight' Nat Flatman; Commotion was second, and Tournament third. After the Derby and Oaks, Harry Hall painted a number of portraits of Blink Bonny, most of them also show I'Anson and a groom, and some have Charlton up (Plate 25). Little is known of John Charlton apart from his successes on Mentmore Lass (1,000 Guineas, 1853) and Mincemeat (Oaks, 1854) which may indicate overall that he was most happy mounted on fillies. He is also portrayed in the Jockey Club collection (Plate 11) but, perhaps significantly, this picture was not engraved and reproduced with an account of his life in the *Sporting Magazine*, as were the majority of the others. His somewhat weak face suggests that it might have taken very little to bend his loyalty to the highest bidder, which was the case in the 1857 St Leger.

At the end of this flat season William Davis retired from his position as the leviathan of turf bookmakers. He was a large man and a few years earlier had fallen through the stand at Rochester. He immediately took it into his head to run twice round the course to overcome the shock of his tumble, which may have hurt his senses more than his physique. However, either the fall or the running signalled the end of his enthusiasm for racing and betting, which had first been aroused when he was sent as a joiner to repair some wainscoting in the Subscription Rooms at Newmarket thirty years before.

— 1858 —

Sir Joseph Hawley's absence from the turf lasted barely a year and he soon had a few horses in training at Danebury. They were largely unsuccessful and he again thought of giving up but received no reasonable offer for his string. It is surprising that Hawley ever used a public trainer since his method was to maintain a very close control of his stud giving little away about his intentions for each animal to either his trainer or jockeys. They were told to have a certain horse and themselves ready for a certain meeting, nothing much else. Equally, after his partnership with J. Massey Stanley, he rarely shared the ownership of a horse with others and he kept their form very much within the small circle of his stables. At the end of 1857 he bought an establishment at Cannon Heath near Basingstoke in Hampshire where he installed young George Manning as his private trainer and 'Tiny' Wells, (Plate 12) on a small retainer, as his first jockey. As before, once master of his own affairs, Sir Josephs's luck returned. He bought Fitz-Roland as a yearling and the chestnut colt looked as fine as the weather on the morning of the 2,000 Guineas on 20 April. Although he started slowly, Wells soon woke Fitz-Roland up and pushed him through the field of fourteen starters with characteristic energy catching the leader, Lord Ribblesdale's The Happy Land, ridden by George Fordham, on the hill. Two days later the 1,000 Guineas was won by Mr Gratwicke's Governess with T. J. Ashmall up; a performance repeated in the Oaks after a dead heat with Gildermere.

It will be recalled that Sir Joseph Hawley had bought Mendicant from John Gully. One of the first foals was Beadsman by Weatherbit. Beadsman was an upright, short-backed (in proportion) and almost black horse. While not outstanding as a two-year-old, Beadsman came on fast in the early spring of 1858 and when tried with Fitz-Roland (for a time the Derby favourite) was found to be the superior horse by a long way. As Hawley's first jockey, Wells was put up on Beadsman and Sim Templeman engaged to ride Fitz-Roland.

By this time 'Tiny' Wells was not as small as when he started his riding career as a featherweight of twelve years. John Wells was tall for his profession but determinedly managed to keep his weight down to around eight stone for many years. He is described as being anything but an elegant rider, but out of the saddle he was evidently a cheerful dandy as well as

61 *Sir Joseph Hawley's Beadsman, John Wells up (Derby, 1858)*   Arthur Ackermann & Son Ltd.

being scrupulously honest and also careful with his money. Harry Hall's paintings of Wells on Beadsman (Plates 26 and 61) give the impression of a cocky young man on an equally alert and proud horse. The photograph of Beadsman at stud in later years (Plate 62) illustrates the accuracy of Hall's portraiture. Well's sleek and foxy appearance may account for his other nickname, 'Brusher', by which he was known in later years. For some reason he and Rous never saw eye to eye, which may have been an extension of the coolness which always existed between the Admiral and Hawley. In a surprisingly eccentric fashion Rous occasionally wore a tartan suit, pushed a feather into his cap and carried a swagger stick. One day Brusher Wells arranged with his fellow jockeys that they scratch from a small race where the Admiral was in charge. Dressing himself in tartan, cap and carrying a cane, Wells then 'walked over' the course as he was required to do, to the immense amusement of the racegoers. One can understand why actions such as this did not endear him to the Admiral.

To return to the 1858 Derby (19 May), the 100 to 30 favourite was Toxophilite, belonging to Lord Derby (now Prime Minister) and trained by John Scott. Beadsman was fourth favourite at 10 to 1 narrowly ahead of Fitz-Roland at 12 to 1. In the race, Fitz-Roland made much of the running until the last furlong when Toxophilite was going well. The twenty-five year old Wells drove Beadsman through with great skill, if not much refinement, to win by a length. The day was excessively hot and when the leading jockeys came to the scales after the race some of them had difficulty in making the weight they started out with. Wells was among these and Beadsman's bridle had to be added to tip the scales. Sir Joseph Hawley made a great deal of money on the race, and, as was his habit, he rewarded his trainer and jockey handsomely. Despite his taciturn way and occasional moodiness, Hawley was an excellent master to work for as all his employees affirmed.

James Merry's string were now trained by John Prince at Russley and their number was added to in 1857 by the purchase of Sir John Scott's small stud of six horses for £6,000. They were bought on the advice

62 *A photograph of Beadsman with his trainer George Manning*

of Mathew Dawson. Among them, Sunbeam was a very fine light bay filly who came into form at the time of the Doncaster meeting after a previously undistinguished short career. Merry recognised her fitness at Russley and plunged heavily on her winning the St Leger. Luke Snowden, a young and modest jockey, rode Sunbeam. While Snowden was self-effacing in character his riding showed a dash and determination expected only from a jockey of far greater experience. Born in 1840 he progressed steadily from winning five races as a fourteen-year-old to sixty-four in 1861 when he was third in the table of leading jockeys. In the St Leger he won neatly by what was described by some as a short half-length. The Hadji (third in the Derby) was second and Toxophilite (the Derby runner-up) was fourth. James Merry's betting coup in the St Leger was almost as large as Sir Joseph Hawley's in the Derby.

Harry Hall was as busy as ever providing sketches for wood engravings in the *Illustrated London News*, small panels for *The Sporting Magazine* and painting genre scenes which were exhibited at the British Institute and Royal Society of British Artists exhibitions. He was also painting a great many racehorse portraits of which some were published by Bailey. This is made clear from *The Sporting Magazine* report of December 1858:

> Harry Hall's Beadsman print has come out; and we hear this eminent artist has just completed a very beautiful picture of Longbow and his groom Forshaw for the Premier. The picture had gone home, but the simple study of the horse, which was painted in the open air, for the sake of the lights, which were especially brilliant, was the leading feature of the studio during the Houghton Meeting [at Newmarket]. There were also several French horses — Monarque, Madame de Chantilly, and Ventre St Gris — whom he crossed the channel specially to paint.

Also in 1858, during Derby week, the paintings owned by Messrs Fuller, from which their fine series of aquatints of Derby and St Leger winners were engraved and published, came up for sale. From *The Times*, 19 May 1858:

> Now on View — The Turf — Messrs Fuller's beautiful Collection of Portraits of the celebrated winners

of the Derby and St Leger painted by Mr Herring Sen. Messrs Foster are directed by Messrs Fuller to sell by auction at the Gallery, 54 Pall Mall, Tomorrow, May 20, about 80 portraits of celebrated RACERS and SIRES of the present winning stock, painted from life, principally by Mr Herring Sen., expressly for Messrs Fuller, and from which they have published their well-known series of engravings; also, The Start for the Derby (Plenipo year), and the celebrated engraved picture, Three Members of the Temperance Society, both fine works by Mr Herring Sen.; and various sporting subjects by the same talented artist and others. Catalogues at Messrs Tattersall's, Hyde Park Corner; or at Messrs Foster's, 54 Pall Mall.

From an examination of this interesting catalogue, there were seven paintings by Harry Hall in the sale. They are of Cotherstone, Orlando, The Merry Monarch and Pyrrhus the First (Derby winners of 1843, 1844, 1845 and 1846), and Blue Bonnet, Nutwith and The Baron (St Legers, 1842, 1843 and 1845), each of which made between 3 and 5½ guineas. The painting of The Merry Monarch may be Plate 16.

— 1859 —

William Day in his *Reminiscences of the Turf*, published in 1886, provides an interesting account of racing and training during his life-time, but the book must be read with caution. There is little doubt that he did not match up to the doubtful 'honest' soubriquet given to his father, John Barham Day. In his early thirties, William left Danebury and set up his own stables at Woodyates near Winchester. A succession of owners placed their horses with him and, after a year or so, a good many removed them elsewhere seeking a more straightforward trainer! William Day treats those who felt it necessary to move on from Woodyates or Danebury with an unpleasant mixture of scorn and spite. Whether writing about Lord George Bentinck or John Gully, who both found him out, he dismisses their remarkable success either with derision or as if it did not exist. Notwithstanding this aspect of his character, his dishonesty and petulance, he could train racehorses and ride them too. He trained Lord of the Isles, the 2,000 Guineas winner, for Mr James Merry in 1855 and now had a further success in this Classic with his own horse, The Promised Land. He was then the joint owner of the brown colt with a Mr Thomas Robinson of High Wycombe. The horse, ridden by Alfred Day, 'won as he liked', with William Day looking on from the rear of the field on the back of Mr Parker's unplaced Nimrod.

Mr W. Stirling Crawfurd came from Scotland and being a modest man of shy temperament he never made a speech of any sort during his thirty-three years membership of the Jockey Club. This is not to say he had no influence in that body; he did. He exercised it through his great friendship with Admiral Rous and Mr George Payne by applying a quiet word when he thought it appropriate, which was quite often. With his considerable financial resources he was able to throw himself into the life of a turfite with enthusiasm. Born in 1819, Stirling Crawfurd's first major success was with The Cur who won the Cesarewitch in 1848. He waited a further eleven years before his first Classic victory when Mayonaise won the 1,000 Guineas ridden by George Fordham; this was also the jockey's first Classic success.

Fordham was born in Cambridge in 1837 and was apprenticed to the trainer Dick Drewett of Lewes, for whom he won his first race at Brighton in 1851 riding at three stone and twelve pounds. The following year he won the Cambridgeshire on Little David in the face of considerable opposition from experienced jockeys. Although Little David ran away with his rider at the finish and did not pull up until they were in Newmarket High Street, Fordham's performance in the race presaged great things to come. He rarely wasted and did not seem to need exercise to keep fit, but he was a keen pedestrian. He never appeared comfortable in the saddle and had a 'bad seat'. 'His little short legs looked almost pinned to the saddle at the knees' which resulted in his riding more with his body and shoulders than his legs. His style was not graceful but marvellously effective as his sixteen Classic victories bear witness. His ability to come through unexpectedly with a late rush led to his acquiring the nickname of The Demon, so clever was he at appearing from nowhere.

The 'lucky baronet', Sir Joseph Hawley, bought a good looking but little-thought-of son of Newminster (St Leger 1851) from Lord Scarbrough for £200. The brown colt was named Musjid. As was often the practice, there was an additional sum payable if the horse subsequently won the Derby; in Musjid's case, £500. The horse was trained by Manning, running little and not very well as a two-year-old. During the winter of 1858/9, he improved considerably and, when tried against other horses from the Cannon Heath stables, showed immense promise. Sir Joseph confidently backed him wherever he could lay money; the public took note and followed suit making Musjid the favourite for the Blue Riband at 9 to 4. The Promised Land was second favourite at 7 to 2 and Trumpeter, owned by Henry Hill and ridden by Alfred Day, was at 4 to 1. Alfred Day was part owner of another starter, Marionette ridden by Sam Rogers,

63 *Sir Charles Monck's Gamester, with his trainer (St Leger, 1859)*   Richard Green

and was said to have a large bet on her winning. This melange of interests among the Danebury circle promised a rough race for Musjid, and so it proved to be. The start was a poor one but William Day, going at a fast pace, managed to put The Promised Land in front. Trumpeter and Marionette were forward of the rest of the field in which Musjid was struggling to shake off the attentions of at least two jockeys paid by the bookmakers to give the favourite a hard time. John Wells finally extricated his mount in the straight and drove Musjid on with all the determination and energy for which he was so well known. In the meantime The Promised Land began to fade quickly having run too fast too early (possibly as William Day intended), and Alfred Day was said to be holding Trumpeter back to let Rogers on Marionette go by. Musjid won neatly by half a length and on settling day Sir Joseph Hawley collected all but a few pounds of his £75,000 winnings. Musjid did not run again and was retired to stud where he died six years later.

Lord Albert Conyngham was the second son of the first Marquis of Conyngham and Lady Conyngham; the former a courtier of George IV and the latter a strong influence during the life of the King and earlier when he was Prince Regent. Lord Albert was born in 1805. After marrying, he lived in Yorkshire where he was created Baron Londesborough in 1850. So far, Lord Londesborough has been mentioned only as a purchaser of horses for stud: Stockwell and West Australian. He also tried unsuccessfully to buy Blink Bonny as a two-year-old from William I'Anson in 1856. Racing for many years, his only Classic winner was Summerside (by West Australian) who won the Oaks the year before Londesborough died. George Fordham was her jockey.

Sir Charles Monck's interest in racing started when he was a young man but, like Lord Londesborough, it was some time before he achieved a Classic victory. He took Gamester to Doncaster for the St Leger in 1859 but without much confidence in his winning, since he was unplaced in the Derby. Sir Charles was eighty-four and time was running against him. As well as The Promised Land (the favourite), with Alfred Day again in the saddle, the winner of the Oaks was also

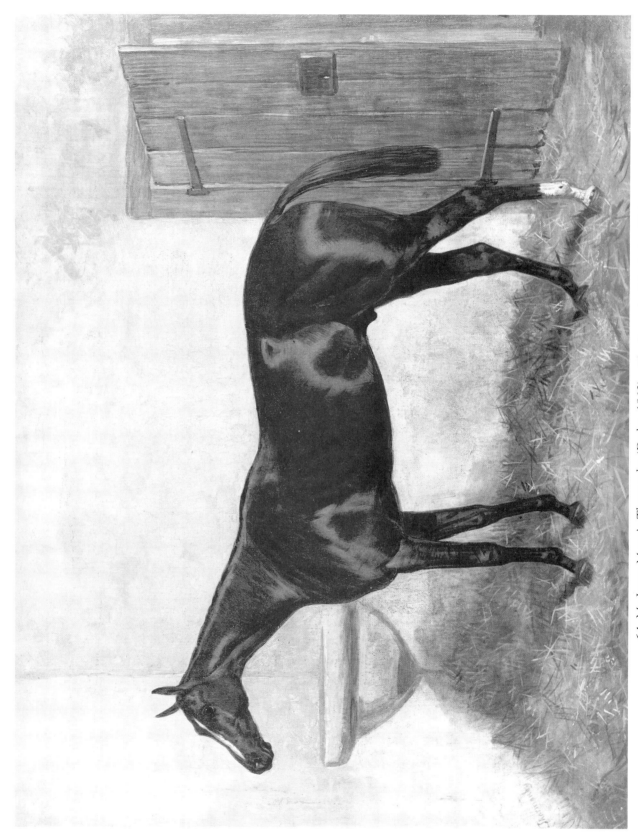

64 Mr James Merry's *Thormanby (Derby, 1860)* The Stewards of the Jockey Club

running. It is fair to say, however, that none of the 1859 batch of three-year-olds was remarkable — they were a moderate lot. The weather on 14 September started well but there was some rain in the morning. Gamester (Plate 63) was a strong horse and well-suited to the slightly tacky going on the Town Moor allowing Tom Aldcroft to bring the colt up in the last few yards to win by half a length. A horse named Defender was second, Magnum third, Summerside fourth and The Promised Land a disappointing fifth. The crowds had backed the favourite strongly and gave Alfred Day an unpleasant time after the race. William Day and Thomas Robinson then sold The Promised Land to Lord William Powlett for £2,500 of which £400 was represented by the acceptance of Lord William's little filly Dulcibella. To Powlett's annoyance The Land never ran well thereafter while Dulcibella won a number of races for Messrs Day and Robinson.

— 1860 —

John Barham Day had been living with his son William at Woodyates for the past five years when he died in March 1860. Born in 1793, he was soon riding as a lightweight at small race meetings in Hampshire and the surrounding counties. Making slow but steady progress as a jockey, his first Classic successes came in 1826 when he won the 2,000 and 1,000 Guineas riding for the Duke of Grafton. He also won the Oaks in 1828 and 1831 for the same patron. In all, he rode the winners of sixteen Classic races, the last being his run of the 2,000, 1,000 Guineas and Oaks on Lord George Bentinck's Crucifix in 1840. By that year he was also a highly successful trainer of racehorses at Danebury near Stockbridge, Hampshire. Both as a jockey and trainer, the soubriquet of 'Honest John' fitted him ill since he was motivated in nearly everything he attempted by greed for a gambling coup. No means was discarded to ensure a favourable result for himself or the Danebury Confederacy. In the late 1840s, J. B. Day became private trainer to Henry Padwick at Michel Grove leaving Danebury in the hands of his son John Day Jnr. By 1855 Padwick had had enough of his skulduggery and dismissed him, now aware, as many others before him had realised, that the Days trained horses entirely for their own gambling convenience. John Day Snr was a familiar figure at race meetings, his ever-ready black gamp tucked under his arm to provide shelter or point to a horse on which his eye fell. It is sad that so much turf history is connected with such a rogue, but at the time this was par for the course.

Mr Anthony Nichol's last Classic success was with his colt The Wizard, by West Australia. The Wizard started well by comfortably winning the 2,000 Guineas; he was then favourite for the Derby, coming second, and later came third in the St Leger, beaten one and a half lengths and a neck. In the first race T. Ashmall was his jockey, in the second A. French and the third, Tom Aldcroft. This appears to be a surprising succession of riders, but arose simply from the 'first claims' on jockeys made by owners able to pay a retaining fee rather more easily than Mr Nichol who raced in a small way, but successfully.

Lord Derby was Prime Minister from February to December 1852 and again between February 1858 and June 1859. At the end of this second term he could again devote more time to racing although, like Nichol, the fourteenth Earl's last Classic success was in 1860. His filly Sagitta won the 1,000 Guineas with Tom Aldcroft up.

Mr Merry has been dealt with harshly by a number of writers, and possibly rightly so, since there is no doubt that he enjoyed winning money in rather too obvious a fashion. As Charles Greville wrote about Bentinck counting his betting coups as a general might count the enemy dead or captured, so Mr Merry counted his winnings pound by pound and cheque by cheque, sometimes publicly. A redeeming feature was that he ran his horses in a straightforward manner with little of the deviousness employed by one or two of his aristocratic contemporaries. John Prince was Merry's private trainer at Russley in Wiltshire until 1858, when there was a disagreement between them about the performance of Sunbeam subsequent to his winning the St Leger. Mathew Dawson was helping with the management of the Russley stables and now succeeded Prince, remaining James Merry's private trainer for the next ten years.

In reading accounts of Classic-winning horses, hindsight often helps to portray the position that they attracted little attention as foals or failed to sell as yearlings. Time and again an owner was persuaded by his trainer, or some other adviser, of the potential merit of an awkward and ugly young animal languishing on the books of a despondent breeder. So it was with Thormanby. Mr Benjamin Plummer failed to find anybody in the least interested in his light-fleshed yearling until Mat Dawson was asked to look at him. Dawson saw something in the colt whom he bought for £350 for Mr Merry. He may have regretted his purchase initially since it is alleged that James Merry was so unimpressed with the horse that Dawson had to stable him at his own expense. As a two-year-old Thormanby was turned out for fourteen races, winning nine. He was a tough little animal and the following year Dawson knew he was training a sure thing for the

Derby. By this time Merry was also convinced of the colt's form and backed him accordingly.

The exodus from London to Epsom started early in the morning and by ten o'clock the road between the two was so thick with horses, vehicles and dust that there was as much chance of crossing it safely as there is of interrupting an Orange Order parade in Belfast.

On it [the road] might be seen everything that would go upon wheels, and not a few which, as it eventually turned out, would not go at all. There was everything in the way of vehicular contrivance — grand, moderate, seedy, and used up — from the very fast drag down to the humble costermonger's cart, or the not much better post-chaise which had been a pigeon roost any time these months past in the worst inn's worst yard. The quadrupeds, as a matter of course, were as numerous and not less varied, comprising a liberal percentage of those that wouldn't go and those that couldn't, and never should have been tried at all. All through Clapham and Cheam the road was lively, and the turnpikes as annoying and obstructive as ever.

As *The Times* goes on to describe, it seems the most ambitious carriages were the ones to fall by the wayside while 'the costermonger, with his family of nine inside and a select circle of immediate relatives on the shafts, manages to job on well enough. The hill up to the course is, however, the great touchstone of equine merit.' Once on the course, and joined by those who travelled by rail, the dense crowd pressed round the exhibitions of pugilists, acrobats, conjurers, clowns, organ-grinders, gipsies telling fortunes, German bands, Punch and Judy shows and those, for a halfpenny, providing the exhilaration of experiencing electric shocks from a 'voltaic battery'.

This was the scene confronting young Harry Custance whose first ride it was in the Derby, up on Thormanby, the second favourite to The Wizard. Umpire, belonging to an American Mr Ten Broeck was third favourite and a Mr Wyatt's Nutbourne was fourth in the betting at 7 to 1.

After one abortive attempt to start they were off with Lord Stamford's Bentinck taking the lead. Three furlongs from the finish Nutbourne, Umpire, The Wizard and Thormanby were all together with Dangu and Horror. Nutbourne broke down and was pulled up while Umpire faded. The Wizard then temporarily took the lead followed by Dangu, Horror and Thormanby, the last quickly forging through to win by a length and a half in fine style. Custance rode a clever and sensible race well beyond the expectation of his limited experience. The Wizard was second, Horror third and Dangu, owned by Count Frederic de Lagrange was fourth. The value of the winning stakes was over £6,000 and James Merry won £70,000 in bets. He gave Dawson £1,000 and Custance £100 which were somewhat meagre rewards compared with his overall gain, but Merry threw a party for all the villagers at Russley which showed there was some generosity in the heart of this strange man.

The Oaks was won by Mr R. Eastwood's Butterfly with James (Jim) Snowden up. Jim was the younger brother of Luke Snowden but although successful was neither half the gentleman nor a quarter the jockey of Luke. He had not reached his majority when he rode Butterfly but was already gaining a reputation for being a little too fond of both the ladies and the bottle.

As at Epsom for the Derby, the annual invasion of Doncaster for the St Leger made it more of an opportunity for the hoi polloi to escape from the industrial grime of the northern towns than, for them, a serious racing occasion. The weather on Wednesday 12 September 1860 was particularly kind resulting in the stands being full, although the overall crowd on the Town Moor was thought to be smaller than for some years.

The scene presented just prior to the start for the St Leger was one of the most animated and picturesque descriptions. The entire straight 'run in' was lined on each side with double and treble rows of spectators; opposite the stand were carriages filled by ladies; down the smooth green course between the dark thick line of people centered the competitors, the colours of their riders glistening in the sun; streamers and gay colours were waving from drinking booths and stands, bands of music filled the air with their strains, and above the roar and excitement were heard the vociferation in the betting-ring offering to lay against the favourites and outsiders.

The Derby winner, Thormanby, again with Custance up, was the favourite and the 2,000 Guineas winner The Wizard was well thought of. Despite his poor performance in the Derby, the American horse Umpire was also well liked. Luke Snowden was riding Lord Ailesbury's St Albans, a son of Stockwell (2,000 Guineas and St Leger, 1852). The fifteen runners were saddled promptly and their punctual canter to the start prompted a buzz of excitement and some last minute adjustments in the betting. Once at the start orderliness disappeared. The Wizard took off and ran a short distance before Tom Aldcroft could stop him. At a second attempt two other horses, and again The Wizard, broke ranks, and the unfortunately named Stampedo would not come into line at all before a whip was produced. Umpire then proved awkward. Lord Coventry, a steward, went down the course to

65 *Lord Stamford's Diophantus, Arthur Edwards up (2,000 Guineas, 1861)*   Christie's

give Mr Marshall, the starter, some advice which the latter could perhaps have done well without. Finally they were away with Lord Zetland's Sabreur (by Voltigeur) taking an early lead. Luke Snowden rode a clever race holding St Albans in fifth place for much of the way before coming in an easy winner by a length and a half. The Wizard was third; Thomanby fifth and Umpire who again showed he was a better sprinter than stayer finished sixth. Harry Hall painted Luke Snowden (Plate 41) in Lord Ailesbury's red and yellow jacket.

— 1861 —

In the early years of the century the turf was as full of members of the Edwards family as it later became of the Days. In the 1820s Lord Jersey's trainer was James or 'Tiny' Edwards and his one-eyed brother Harry rode for his Lordship. Harry was a fine jockey but none too

honest while Tiny was a conscientious and thoughtful trainer at Mickleham in Surrey. By 1860 the number of Edwards was depleted and could be counted on one hand. Arthur Edwards, the son of the late Edward Edwards (a jockey) and grandson of Tiny, was the first jockey to Lord Stamford. George Harry Grey, the seventh Earl of Stamford succeeded his grandfather in 1845 and lived at Dunham Massey in Cheshire. He kept a large stud and was a conspicuous patron of the turf for much of his life. In 1861 he entered his three-year-olds Diophantus, Imaus and Lara in four out of the five Classic races, usually ridden by Arthur Edwards.

Starting at 25 to 1 against, Diophantus (Plate 65) won the 2,000 Guineas with surprising ease from Kettledrum and Klarikoff. Kettledrum belonged to Stamford's fellow northcountryman, Colonel Towneley, and Klarikoff was owned by John Scott. Shortly before the Derby, Lord St Vincent bought a half-share in Klarikoff from Scott for 5,000 Guineas.

66 *Mr Saxon's Brown Duchess (Oaks, 1861) (with Miss Livingstone)* Arthur Ackermann & Son Ltd.

67 *Colonel Towneley's Kettledrum, Ralph Bullock up, with his owner, John and Richard Towneley, William Oates and Richard Eastwood (Derby, 1861)* Arthur Ackermann & Son Ltd.

The favourite for the Derby at the end of May was Mr James Merry's Dundee, a son of Lord of the Isles, Merry's 2,000 Guineas winner in 1855. In his owner's view Dundee was a better horse than Thormanby giving the ironmaster the hope of winning the Blue Riband of the turf in consecutive years, emulating Sir Joseph Hawley's feat. There was a problem with Dundee's forelegs, but the betting public remained confident of his ability and could only obtain odds of 3 to 1 against him from the bookmakers. Diophantus was at 4 to 1.

Everyone is waiting for the favourites, and at last they enter from opposite sides of the paddock, Diophantus an exquisite chestnut colt, and Dundee, if possible, a still more beautiful black [in fact bay].

Kettledrum walked round in a corner quite unnoticed. The start conducted by Mr McGeorge was on time, but four horses, including Klarikoff the third favourite, were well out of line and had a great deal to make up to be in contact with the body of the field. George Fordham on Klarikoff succeeded in reaching the leaders a little too quickly; the effort probably cost him the race. Just before the distance one of Dundee's foreglegs 'went' but he very gamely struggled on to be up with Klarikoff, Aurelian, Diophantus and Kettledrum at the Stand. The young Ralph Bullock on Kettledrum (Plate 67) then made his move followed courageously by Dundee with Custance up. The former won by a length from the now three-legged Dundee who was a head in front of Diophantus. Aurelian was fourth and Klarikoff a bad fifth. Lord Stamford's other horse in the race, Imaus, ridden by Tom French was in seventh place. James Merry was naturally disappointed but the gameness of Dundee won the admiration of the spectators and sympathy for his owner. The riding of the winner by Ralph Bullock was also much admired. 'Geordie' Bullock (Plate 11) was born in 1841 and was apprenticed to the trainer Thomas Dawson at Tupgill. He was registered as a jockey at the age of thirteen when he weighed four stone three pounds. Making steady progress, his first ride in the Derby was in 1859 and he was second in the St Leger the following year behind Luke Snowden on St Albans. A cheerful yet quiet man with abstemious habits, he was regarded as an up-and-coming, stylish and elegant jockey. Bullock was much in demand for the few years that he was able to follow his profession.

The 1,000 Guineas was won by Mr Fleming's Nemesis from Mr Cartwright's Fairwater. These two horses were joint favourites for the Oaks on Friday 31 May. Mr McGeorge was sharply criticised for the bad start of the Derby, not least by the followers of Klarikoff, and he was in difficulties again with the seventeen Oaks' fillies who, 'with characteristic impatience of their sex', broke away on a number of occasions. They were finally off thirty minutes behind schedule. William I'Anson's Caller Ou made the pace for much of the course but in a close and exciting finish Mr Saxon's Brown Duchess (Plate 66), ridden brilliantly by Luke Snowden, won by a neck from Lady Ripon, with Geordie Bullock maintaining his Epsom form.

The news that the Corporation of Doncaster would no longer pay the bell-ringers of the town to add to the cacophony of noise of St Leger Day was greeted with delight. For years the constant and bewildering din of the bells had rung out raising the hubbub of the meeting to an unbearable level and drowning the efforts of Pritchard's Band which was far more musical. On a warm September afternoon, the 17th, a very large crowd assembled on the Town Moor. Kettledrum was the favourite at 6 to 4 against. Hopefully Tom Parr the owner of the second favourite, Kildonan, was able to be present and not in hiding at Wantage avoiding his creditors. The start was delayed due to a number of horses, including Kildonan, perpetually breaking away from the line just as it was about to become straight. At the sixth attempt they were off and the fastest race so far recorded ensued. At the distance Kildonan, Janus (belonging to Baron de Rothschild) and Kettledrum were joined by I'Anson's Caller Ou ridden by Challoner. The last two named then set to and a tremendous struggle followed with Caller Ou beating Kettledrum by a head at the finishing post. Kildonan was a bad third, a head in front of Janus. Caller Ou (Plate 28), by the emperor of stallions, Stockwell, was a rank outsider at 66 to 1. William I'Anson had not placed a bet on her since he thought she had no chance and Harry Grimshaw had excused himself from riding for the same reason. In the Oaks Caller Ou had led for a time but then faded quickly; by the St Leger, Challoner understood her better and made good use of her ability to come through strongly when not hurried too early. Tom Challoner (Plate 12) was 'trained' at John Osborne Snr's stables at Ashgill and was riding with increasing success. This was his first of many Classic victories.

Two days after the St Leger Kettledrum was turned out for the Doncaster Cup in which he ran a dead heat with Brown Duchess. The Oaks winner carried ten pounds less than Kettledrum as was appropriate between a colt and a filly of their respective ages and merits. This was almost Luke Snowden's last race (Brown Duchess) for he died the following January of typhus. 'Never, we believe, was so young a man so much regretted by those who had knowledge of him.'

CHAPTER 6

1862−1868

Still ahead of the glitt'ring throng
Dashes the eager mare along,
And round the turn, and past the hill,
Slides up the Derby winner still.

HARRY HALL COULD NOW be described as being at the height of his profession as a portrayer of racehorses; however, without belittling his ability, the number practising this specialisation of sporting painting was not many. Abraham Cooper was seventy-five and had stopped painting racehorses many years before; he died on Christmas Eve 1868. As has already been mentioned, J. F. Herring Snr was immersed in rural and farmyard scenes although his health was failing. He was plagued with asthma throughout his life and was now losing the use of his legs, becoming dependent on a wheelchair to move about the garden of his house, Meopham, in Kent. Within three years he was dead. J. F. Herring's son, Ben Herring, was painting in his father's style but without his ability, in much the same way that Henry Gordon Alken traded on his father's (Henry Alken's) genius. Charles Hancock turned from the role of artist to that of inventor in 1846. Among his many ideas the most successful was the discovery of a substance useful in the coating of underwater cables. However, he ran into patenting problems and was often in some financial difficulty. He painted occasionally for friends and at the end of his life, after a long absence, exhibited at the Royal Academy in 1873 and 1874. Hall was therefore much in demand and there is evidence to support the proposition that his work was both decorative and accurate.

Photography was still in an early stage of development in the 1860s. Comparing early plates of owners and trainers with Hall's paintings of the same individuals shows him to be a master of human portraiture. It seems that only in France the photographic medium was considered to be a useful way of recording horses at this period, among them English stallions at stud. Those portrayed at Le Haras du Pin, with their uniformed grooms, are shown standing rather nervously in front of a large stage back-cloth depicting a classical garden. To compare these photographs with Hall's equine portraits is instructive. Making allowances for the artificially small head and slender neck of the three-year-old in a painting and the 'thickening' of the body of the photographed stallion, the similarity of the two is remarkable. The stance and the character of the animal in paint is exactly right. Being able to make these comparisons gives one confidence that contemporary accounts of how well Hall caught the likeness of a horse are not exaggerated.

Another reason for Harry Hall being much in demand was the growth of Newmarket itself. Newmarket Heath is recognised as the birthplace of English racing but at the end of the eighteenth and beginning of the nineteenth centuries the poor communications between the north and the south of the country resulted in two distinct racing circuits and fraternities. As roads and the means of travel improved, horses from the north raced in the south and southern-trained horses took part in the Doncaster and York meetings with greater regularity. Regional loyalties to horses, owners and trainers remained among the two groups of racing public. Despite these ties, the authority of the Jockey Club was increasingly recognised and for this reason Newmarket was regarded as the centre of nearly all turf activities. While there had been stables at the edges of the town for many years, more were being established in the surrounding countryside by owners who wanted their studs to be close to the home of the turf. A large number of horses from the north of England and from as far away as America, France and later Austria, were kept for long periods at Newmarket during the racing season. For the most part, the winners painted by Harry Hall were walked from their stables to his studio in Church Lane in a matter of minutes.

In early 1862 Harry and Ellen Hall's sons Sidney, Arthur and Frank were away at school, and Frederick aged twelve, Ernest aged ten and their infant daughter Kate Marian lived at home with them in Park Cottage across the High Street from the entrance to Church Lane. After a short illness, Frederick died of Scarlet Fever on the fourth of February. The boy was buried in the cemetery at the top of the High Street among the graves of grooms and jockeys, some of whose portraits his father had painted in recent years. This was a sudden and unexpected blow to Hall who was immensely fond of all his children. It took time for him to recover his old spirits but he was helped by the kindness of a wide circle of Newmarket friends. He turned more than before to the church for comfort and redoubled his efforts to ensure his sons were as well-educated as possible to make their own marks in life. He was rewarded by the successful careers of Sidney and Ernest; but the lives of Frank and a further son Roland, born in 1864, ended in tragedy, fortunately some years after their father's death.

The field for the 2,000 Guineas in 1862 was the largest so far: seventeen runners, which did not include Old Calabar who was scratched at the last moment by his owner Sir Richard Buckley. There was heavy betting against Calabar despite his obviously excellent preparation and good form — he was found, or made, lame the day before the race. This left a somewhat moderate lot with Mr Richard Sutton's Nottingham and Mr S. Hawke's The Marquis among the four joint favourites at 5 to 1 against. It was hot and oppressive at Newmarket and there was a large crowd at the meeting. Mr McGeorge's appointment as the Jockey Club Starter had been confirmed at the beginning of the season despite his ineptness the previous year. At the start of the 2,000 Guineas he was again in difficulties but through no fault of his own. A number of horses were fractious, possibly because of the heat. The Marquis, wearing blinkers, was expected to be hot tempered but in fact remained calm with Tom Ashmall on his back. They were off at the fifth attempt. At the end of a rather slow race The Marquis, trained by John Scott, beat Mr Richard Naylor's Caterer by half a length. Three of the first four horses were by Stockwell whose prowess as a sire was quickly becoming evident.

Two days later, on Thursday 8 May, Ashmall was again riding the winner of the 1,000 Guineas: Lord Falmouth's Hurricane. The filly was also trained by John Scott and signalled the start of Lord Falmouth's long run of Classic victories and near domination of the turf during the next twenty-two years.

Mr C. Snewing has been variously described as a veterinary surgeon from Rugby or a publican from the Tottenham Court Road, London. He was certainly a bookmaker and described in *The Sporting Magazine* as 'one of the very few commission agents . . . who may be trusted with the money of the British public'. The odds offered on his lists were never generous but those who were successful were promptly paid. As an owner he was said to have won his first race, a steeplechase, at Rugby in 1840. Mr Snewing's few horses were trained for some time by William Day but later at Harpenden in Hertfordshire by a Robert Smith, who had learnt his trade with the Days. Caractacus, belonging to Snewing, ran moderately well as a two-year-old and was well prepared for the Derby in 1862. At Epsom, the brown colt was quietly saddled by Snewing and Bob Smith in the shade of the ash and thorn trees which were then in the centre of the paddock. Caractacus looked in marvellous condition and was known to be fit, but the ring marked him as a 40 to 1 outsider. The reason for this may have been that Snewing held an interest in William Goater's Spite. William's son James was retained by Snewing as his first jockey and when given the choice of riding Caractacus or Spite chose the latter despite the horse being at 50 to 1. Caractacus was ridden by his lad, J. Parsons. The public naturally assumed that Spite must be the better horse, but they were disappointed. The Marquis was the Derby favourite and Mr James Merry's Buckstone was well thought of. The start was again badly handled and Mr McGeorge was told that any more failures would result in the sack. At the half-distance the leaders were The Marquis, Buckstone, Neptunus (who suddenly faded) and Nottingham with Caractacus, skilfully ridden by his lad, making ground quickly.

> the struggle was so keen that the Japanese Ambassadors, who occupied special seats in the Stewards' box, warmed up into something like the interest of ordinary mortals, and leant forward to discover the winner,

which was Caractacus by a neck in front of The Marquis; Buckstone was third. Spite ran well until approaching the distance then he broke down; James Goater dismounted to avoid a fall.

This was the first occasion at Epsom that 'Mr Bennett's new chronograph dial clock', which allowed the recording of tenths of a second, was used. The race was run in '2 minutes and 45 and 5 tenths seconds', (a half is easier to comprehend!) which was the third fastest Derby since timing was introduced in 1846.

Hurricane was favourite for the Oaks but was easily beaten into third place by Mr Naylor's Feu de Joie, with Tom Challoner up, who was two lengths in front of Colonel Towneley's Imperatrice ridden by Jim

Snowden. By the date of the St Leger, 17 September, Caractacus had sadly broken down but Old Calabar was sound but by no means fit. Mr Merry's Buckstone was favourite with The Marquis not far behind. While it took some time to clear the course of spectators, which caused a delay, the start was admirable. Buckstone and The Marquis were soon well clear of the rest of the field and in the end Mr Hawke's colt defeated Buckstone by a head. Lord Glasgow's chestnut colt Clarissimus was third. Both the first and second horses were sons of St Leger winners, and Stockwell was now the sire of the winner for the past three years.

— 1863 —

On 24 January 1863 followers of the turf were surprised and distressed to read in *Bell's Life* that the young jockey Ralph Bullock had died the day before from an infection in the throat. Since 1856 he had been winning between twenty and forty races each season although only one was a Classic (Kettledrum in the 1861 Derby, owned by Colonel Towneley). The future seemed immensely promising. One of his last races was for the same owner as Kettledrum, for whom he rode Imperatrice in the recent St Leger. In a period of twelve months Luke Snowden, John Charlton, a jockey named Creswell and now Ralph Bullock had died, of whom Bullock was the best both in riding and character.

Echoes of the past were stirred early in 1863 by the announcement that John Gully had died on 9 March. When he gave up racing he left Winchester, buying Cocken Hall near Durham to be close to his coal-mining interests; towards the end of his life he moved into a town house in that city. He was buried with great ceremony in consecrated ground at his old home, Ackworth Park near Pontefract. By his strong character he transformed his life from a situation of almost certain poverty to a position of affluence and some power. This inevitably incurred the jealousy of many less successful than himself. Among such people was William Day who describes Gully as 'of tyrannical and overbearing disposition, extremely avaricious and, like men of his class, not over-scrupulously nice in the acquiring of wealth'. No doubt he had faults, but I prefer another writer's comment that he was: 'A true sportsman and sterling Englishman'.

Mr R. C. Naylor, a Liverpool chemist, founded a stud at Hooton Park near Chester in 1858. He was enabled to do this when he inherited a fortune from an uncle and could give up his profession and devote all his energy to racing. In a short time he owned

Classic winners. In 1861 he made a particularly fortunate purchase of yearlings from Eaton Hall, the seat of the Marquis of Westminster. The six horses had been ill and were sold en bloc by the Marquis to his neighbour for £700. Among this draft was Macaroni who ran moderately well as a two-year-old in the autumn of 1862. His new owner recognised his potential and backed Macaroni heavily for the Derby the following year. This must have been kept a good secret at the Newmarket First Spring Meeting since the public thought Macaroni had little chance in the 2,000 Guineas because, at that time, Naylor was not backing him. A French syndicate headed by Count Frederic de Lagrange, whose horses were trained by Tom Jennings at Newmarket, owned Hospodar, the firm favourite for the first Classic of the year, with Lord Strathmore's Saccharometer at the next shortest odds. Macaroni was 10 to 1 against. A strong wind kept off the rain but stirred up the dust to the discomfort of the large crowd on Newmarket Heath. The going was hard, and the start was successful at the first attempt. As the leaders entered the rails (in fact cords) approaching the finish, Macaroni, ridden by Tom Challoner, drew ahead of Saccharometer to win by just under a length. Baron de Rothschild's King of the Vale was third and the favourite a poor fourth.

Lord Stamford saw his two horses, Lady Augusta and Flying Fish, take first and second place in the 1,000 Guineas by coming out of the ruck half a mile from home and enjoying a gentle duel to the finish, with Arthur Edwards on Lady Augusta taking first place. This Newmarket meeting was reported as uninteresting so far as the racing was concerned but allowed one correspondent to:

> escape early from the Heath to that pleasant little studio of Harry Hall's where the showy Fantastic with Custance up, Tim in his box, an excellent portrait of the very good looking Brick, with Jennings and Grimshaw, etc, and a spirited sketch of the 'Set-To' between Stradella and The Marquis ...

were on show.

Derby Day in 1863 was extremely wet. Allegedly the Prince of Wales made his first appearance at Epsom, (although this is not reported in *The Times*). He was well received, but those spectators able to cast their minds back to the last rain-sodden Derby in 1856 when the Prince Consort was present might be forgiven for associating the rare foul conditions with the equally infrequent Royal visits up to that time.

The weather did not help Mr McGeorge in his task of starting his thirty-one entries. After his previous warnings he was particularly careful, perhaps too much so, for it took an hour, and more false starts than there were runners, before the field was finally away in a steaming mass. Lord St Vincent's Lord Clifden was the favourite and made much of the running. At the final bend the race was between this bay colt with George Fordham up and Macaroni, again skilfully ridden by Tom Challoner. The crowd had to wait for the numbers to be telegraphed to discover the winner: Macaroni by a head. Lord St Vincent had plunged heavily on his horse and lost almost as much as Mr Naylor was reported to have won with Macaroni — at least £70,000. He gave Godding, his Newmarket trainer, £3,000 and Challoner £1,000. Undoubtedly Tom Challoner rode the best race and there was some criticism of Fordham, which he bitterly resented.

Evelyn Boscawen was born in March 1819, the eldest son of Canon John Boscawen, and related to Admiral Boscawen of Lagos Bay fame. Evelyn was educated at Eton and Oxford before being called to the Bar in 1841. When twenty-three years old this intelligent and unassuming man unexpectedly succeeded to the title of Viscount Falmouth and inherited a large estate at Tregothnan in Cornwall. He immediately adopted the role of the country landowner and, like so many others of the period, turned to improving strains of sheep and cattle by breeding. It was not long before he progressed with equal enthusiasm to the breeding of thoroughbred horses followed by a passion for testing them on the turf. In 1845, the sixth Viscount Falmouth married Baroness Le Despenser, the owner of Mereworth Castle in Kent, adding a further estate on which he could practise farming and horse breeding. The Castle, or more properly house, was erected in the early eighteenth century for the Earl of Westmorland. It was built as a replica of a sixteenth century Palladian villa near Vicenze. The transposition of an Italianate villa into the Kentish landscape made it a curiosity, if not quite a folly. However, with a base for operations in both the south-east and south-west of England, Lord Falmouth was well able to proceed in his quietly determined way to become a leading owner on the turf. He started racing in 1857 and, after a short period of training at Newmarket, he sent his horses to the north to be trained by John Scott of Whitewall, from whence Hurricane came south again to win the 1,000 Guineas in 1862. Queen Bertha was trained by Scott at Malton as well. She was entered for the 1863 Oaks in the name of 'Mr T. Valentine', a *nom de guerre* which Lord Falmouth soon dropped. Queen Bertha neither performed well in trials nor in a race early in the year; however, Scott was confident she could run if she put her mind to it. The bookmakers were not impressed and she started at 40 to 1 against. Nearing the finishing post a Mr Hargreaves' Marigold was leading but within half-a-dozen strides of the judge Tom Aldcroft came up with Queen Bertha to snatch victory by a short head. Count Lagrange's Vivid was third and the 1,000 Guineas winner, Lord Stamford's Lady Augusta, could only make seventh place in a field of twenty.

Lord Falmouth and Mr R. C. Naylor were friends, jointly renting a house at Newmarket for the season. The landlord had the weathercock over the establishment painted in the colours of the owners of Queen Bertha and Macaroni to make quite certain everyone knew who were his tenants.

Lord Clifden was nicknamed the 'Shuttlecock' since his performance bobbed about in a similar manner. Two days after the Derby he beat a very moderate French horse with difficulty in the Surrey Foal Stakes and just over a week later was fifth in the inaugural Grand Prix de Paris, (won by Mr Savile's The Ranger). He was thought to be ill-prepared for the St Leger but the bookmakers were probably unaware that he had been trained at night to avoid the attentions of 'the men of observation'. Lord Clifden's changes in the betting before the St Leger were as erratic as his nickname implied until, shortly before the race, the 'Shuttlecock' settled at 100 to 30 against. Lord Clifden was left at the post after a bad start but John Osborne kept his head and moved the colt up steadily before cutting through the rest of the field at the distance. Queen Bertha, ridden on this occasion by Wells, was second and Mr William I'Anson's filly Borealis (the Oaks favourite who came nowhere in that race) was third. Lord St Vincent recouped some of his Derby losses at Doncaster but soon afterwards had to turn to the moneylender Henry Padwick for help. The following year 'a very highly finished and faithful study' of Lord Clifden by Harry Hall was shown at the Suffolk Street exhibition of the Royal Society of British Artists. In the series of portraits of jockeys painted by Hall, Osborne is shown in the chocolate colours of Lord St Vincent, a jacket which was soon to disappear from the turf.

— 1864 —

On 26 April 1864, the day of the 2,000 Guineas Stakes, the Prince of Wales made his first appearance on Newmarket Heath since becoming a member of the Jockey Club. The large crowd gave him a warm welcome. The presence of Royalty on the turf had at best been spasmodic in recent years. At the death of William IV the Hampton Court Stud was sold to Prussia. After her visit to the Derby in 1840 Queen Victoria only went to Ascot, and then from social duty rather than out of interest or enjoyment of racing. Prince Albert had tried to resuscitate the Hampton Court establishment in 1851, which was kept going on a small scale but with little success until the mid-1870s. After the death of the Prince Consort in 1861 Her Majesty never went racing again. The interest of the Prince of Wales was therefore welcome and he soon became a prominent turfite.

Lord Glasgow's eccentricity in what he wore, in the strange management of his horses and his passion for the turf were undiminished as the years went by, despite his not winning a Classic race until he was seventy-two. Neuralgia in the back of his neck plagued him constantly resulting in a short temper; a feared characteristic in a man otherwise recognised as generous, open-hearted and well meaning to man and beast alike. His trainers and jockeys continued to be hired, fired and re-hired when a storm had passed. If one of their number fell on hard times, he invariably received some unsolicited pecuniary help from his Lordship. He bred nearly all the horses he raced while naming few of them. An exception was a fine bay colt called General Peel after Glasgow's lifelong friend and fellow turfite. Fille de L'Air, an outstanding filly belonging to Count Frederick de Lagrange and trained by Tom Jennings was the favourite for the 2,000 Guineas. General Peel, ridden by Tom Aldcroft was second in the market at 7 to 2 against and, encouraged by the tremendous cheering of the crowd, won the race by a length from Paris owned by the American Mr Ten Broeck. This was an immensely popular win for Lord Glasgow – the only Classic success of his lifetime. Fille de L'Air was nowhere and Tom Jennings was suspicious that her jockey Arthur Edwards had pulled her having been persuaded by certain bookmakers to do so. Edwards claimed: 'She was out of the race the instant the flag fell', but many thought this explanation would have been just as true if it had been made some weeks before! Fille de L'Air's failure added insult to injury to those who backed her, for the running (and obviously the success) of French horses in England was generally unpopular.

Baron Meyer de Rothschild was the owner of the 1,000 Guineas winner in 1853 and now, eleven years later, repeated his success with Tomato ridden by Wells. He also owned the second horse, Breeze, and in this year was elected a member of the Jockey Club.

Mr William I'Anson's remarkable faith in the mare Queen Mary was more than rewarded by the performance of her daughter Blink Bonny in 1857. The latter's son, Blair Athol by Stockwell, showed I'Anson's vision to be more prescient than even he may have expected. Blair Athol was bred at Malton but did not race as a two-year-old. However his star quality was recognised by I'Anson as it was by the unscrupulous bookmaker John Jackson who offered to buy him for 7,000 guineas during the autumn of 1863. I'Anson turned down the offer and Jackson rightly concluded the colt's potential was considerable and backed him heavily for the Derby the following year. Like his mother, Blair Athol was not very fit as a young three-year-old and in addition was apparently prone to lameness. The cause of this could not be detected until it was found by chance that Blair Athol's lad, who harboured a grudge against I'Anson, was kicking the horse in the genitals from time to time. Once this outrage was discovered the colt's performance in trials showed him to be exceptional.

Mr James Merry's Scottish Chief, trained by Mathew Dawson at Russley, and Lord Glasgow's General Peel were joint favourites for the Derby. Blair Athol was 14 to 1 against and this position reflected the wishes of a number of bookmakers other than Jackson to see General Peel win. With some difficulty, Jackson persuaded his 'friends' not to get at Blair Athol by whom he hoped to win a small fortune. It could be said, therefore, that the horses ran on their own unnobbled merits. The day of 25 May was fine and calm, and the road to Epsom, the Downs and the course were less dusty than usual allowing the Prince of Wales and practically every member of Parliament to enjoy their day in the country. For a fine of £5 Blair Athol was saddled outside the paddock but his fitness and perfect action were immediately apparent as he cantered to the start. Despite the eight false starts Blair Athol remained quiet in the hands of Jim Snowden, the late Luke's brother. However, while Mr McGeorge's ninth attempt was successful Blair Athol did not jump off well. At the distance it appeared that General Peel would win easily but Snowden, riding vigorously and spurring on Blair Athol, (Plate 29) quickly brought him through to win by two lengths. Scottish Chief was three lengths behind General Peel in third place.

A small confederacy led by Count Frederic de Lagrange bought the stud of the successful but ailing M. Alexander Aumont in 1856. The Count was the son of one of France's better generals of the Napoleonic Wars. He inherited a large fortune from his father which he augmented by marrying into a European royal house. On the advice of Tom Jennings, Lagrange established a breeding stud near Gisors where he lived. The confederacy was quickly successful in France and they decided to race in England as well. Training establishments were set up at Newmarket and Royaleau near Compiegne. Both were controlled by Tom Jennings who had previously trained for Aumont. It was not long before French horses, often of English thoroughbred parentage, were making their unwelcome presence felt on the English turf, racing in

68 *The Duke of Beaufort's Siberia, George Fordham up (1,000 Guineas, 1865)* Arthur Ackermann & Son Ltd.

Lagrange's name. Fille de L'Air was among that number and despite her unexpectedly poor performance in the 2,000 Guineas she started favourite for the Oaks. Although she had run well in France since the Guineas, her position in the betting was surprising. It may also have been due to the manipulations of John Preston, a Newmarket bookmaker, who cultivated the friendship of jockeys including that of the doubtful Arthur Edwards. Fille de L'Air won the Oaks comfortably in front of Breeze and Tomato, Baron de Rothschild's 1,000 Guineas first and second, (but now in reversed order). This was not a popular victory.

> There was a demonstration, not of a complimentary character, when Fille de L'Air's number was hoisted . . . a very hostile-looking crowd pressed on horse and jockey as they returned to the scales. Jennings, as if anticipating something of the sort, had taken care to provide a few extra policemen . . . The entrance to the weighing-room had to be barricaded to prevent the entrance of the hostile forces. It was altogether a scene suggestive of many reflections, and one we hope never to see again on Epsom Downs.

A similar demonstration, but this time aimed solely at Edwards took place when he rode Fille de L'Air to third place (behind Vermout and Blair Athol) in the Grand Prix de Paris. Having led for some way and apparently with the race in his grasp, Fille de L'Air ran extremely wide at the last bend, aided no doubt by Edwards, and lost so much ground that she was easily overtaken before the final straight. On this occasion Edwards lost his nerve completely and bolted from the course before weighing, which resulted in the stewards disqualifying the filly. Edwards did not ride again for Count Lagrange or Jennings but he continued as Lord Stamford's first jockey, coming third in the following St Leger on Cambuscan. He was a clever but dishonest rider. Towards the end of 1864 Harry Hall painted a number of portraits of Fille de L'Air at Newmarket. One of these, and others of French horses, were engraved in aquatint by John Harris and published by Goupil & Cie in Paris.

William I'Anson's Blair Athol, the fourth son of Stockwell to win the St Leger, was favourite with Lord Glasgow's General Peel close behind him at 3 to 1 against. This was their order at the finish of the race, run in a heavy downpour. The wet weather failed to dampen the excitement of the spectators who cheered their locally trained horse past the post. 'Baldy Face', as Blair Athol was known, was accidentally struck as they pulled up in the gloom resulting in his being unable to race again. Passing through a number of hands, Blair Athol proved a highly successful sire. He died in 1882.

— 1865 —

1865 was Gladiateur's year. The colt struggled in the 2,000 Guineas but then went on to win the Triple Crown in unassailable style to the discomfort of British turfites. He was owned by Lagrange and the marvellous performance of the horse resulted in a good deal of ill-feeling being vented on Tom Jennings, Gladiateur's English trainer. 'The position became so serious', wrote Tom Jennings Jnr, 'that Father found it necessary to employ prize-fighters and other ruffians to guard his horses when going to and from the principal meetings.'

Tom Jennings Snr was the son of a publican and horse-dealer. It was from the latter profession that young Tom developed an early eye for good and bad horse-flesh. He was born in Cambridgeshire in 1823 and after some education at a dame-school he and his elder brother Henry were apprenticed to Thomas Carter who, at the time, was the best known English trainer working in France. Much later, Tom Jennings married Carter's niece, the daughter of Richard Carter, for a time stud manager to Lord Henry Seymour. From early in his apprenticeship Tom rode as jockey to Mr Edwards who was then trainer to Lord Henry and the Duc d'Orleans. This 'Edwards' had been a rider in England but, falling foul of the Jockey Club like so many of his relatives, he crossed the Channel to France. For a short period at the end of his time with Carter, Tom joined forces with his brother but by 1847 the partnership foundered; they avoided each other for the next twenty years. Tom was then recommended to Prince Eugene de Savoie who was keen to start racing in Piedmont. Among a draft of English horses which Jennings took to Italy was Julia. With Tom up, Julia won all her races in Italy. At the same time Richard Carter was introducing racing to Lombardy for the Duc de Litta, and there was fierce competition between the two states. When Julia beat the Lombardy champion, Mainstay, it became necessary to guard Tom Jenning's Julia since it was feared she might be abducted to Lombardy. Tom was also commissioned by Prince Carignan to go to England and buy chargers for the staff officers of the Italian Army. This draft of twenty-two horses travelled overland. Hostility between Austria and Italy forced Tom, with only an English lad to help him, secretly to take the horses, tied head to tail, over the Mount Cenis pass. After a hazardous journey they arrived safely in Turin. Almost immediately Tom Jennings contracted smallpox from which he was very fortunate to make a good recovery. Perhaps the adventurous times he experienced in Italy began to pall and in 1850 he returned to France. He was immediately successful as the private trainer to M. Alexander Aumont. Among the many French Classics which were won by Aumont's horses were the Derby of 1855 and English Goodwood Cup of 1857 with Monarque, who five years later was to be the sire of Gladiateur.

It will be recalled that Aumont gave up racing in 1856 due to illness, and a syndicate, headed by Count Frederic de Lagrange, bought his stud. Tom Jennings transferred his allegiance to Lagrange and a few years later was established at Phantom Cottage, Newmarket, but also responsible for Count Frederick's horses near Compiegne. Tom saw Gladiateur trialled as a yearling and was impressed by his performance. 'Jolly' Morris (J. B. Morris the bookmaker and owner of Knight of St George, St Leger 1854) offered him a total of £55,000 to £2,000 against the colt winning the Derby two years later. Lagrange and his confederacy took on £45,000 to £2,000 of this bet leaving Tom with the possibility of winning £10,000 to nothing. As time passed Tom Jennings accumulated a number of other personal bets on Gladiateur.

The doubtful services of Arthur Edwards having been dispensed with, Lagrange employed Harry Grimshaw in his place. Grimshaw was a first-class jockey with fifth-class eyesight. His shortsightedness cost him a few races during his career, but if he could keep track of the field and did not find himself too far behind, his ability to judge pace made him a formidable opponent. Gladiateur was often lame in his forelegs, due to an accident while a foal, and he was not fully fit for the 2,000 Guineas, added to which the ground on 2 May was very hard. However, starting at 7 to 1 against, Grimshaw rode him cleverly stalling off Tom Aldcroft's rush on Archimedes to win by a neck in the last stride.

By the date of the Derby Gladiateur was sound and started as favourite at 5 to 2 against. Mr Henry Chaplin's Breadalbane, recently bought with Broomielaw from William l'Anson for £11,000, was second favourite at 7 to 2. In fact the field was not a strong one and Harry Grimshaw steered Gladiateur to an easy victory by two lengths. The crowd appreciated a favourite winning and gave the colt a good cheer allowing his 'quarter-guard' of ruffians to relax a little on this occasion. However the Press was unnecessarily vicious towards Lagrange, and Jennings in particular. The loss of the Blue Riband to France cut deep into the previously friendly relations which existed between the two countries' owners and trainers. There were even unofficial discussions among members of the Jockey Club to consider limiting the English Classics to English horses. Nothing came of the matter but Gladiateur was soon nicknamed the 'Avenger of Waterloo'. The crowd at Epsom had been well behaved

but at Goodwood the ill-feeling, which really started with Fille de L'Air, was renewed and Gladiateur and Grimshaw were both given a hard time when they won one race and walked over another.

Gladiateur (Plate 30) won the richest St Leger to date (£5,875) by three lengths in front of Mr J. Graham's Regalia (the winner of the Oaks, running in the colours of Mr W. Graham). Archimedes was third; The Duke, owned by the Marquis of Hastings, fourth; and Breadalbane fifth. Graham, who was once a wrestler and now a successful gin distiller, objected to Gladiateur on the grounds of age, both before and after the St Leger. Since the vet appointed by the Jockey Club had certified the colt's age before the Derby, both these protests were quickly overruled. One cannot help suspecting that Graham's motive was more to achieve personal popularity in the general vilification of the French horse than a real belief that Gladiateur was a four-year-old. A heavily penalised Gladiateur won the subsequent Newmarket Derby but was unplaced in the Cambridgeshire, due partly to Grimshaw losing his way! As a four-year-old he won the Ascot Gold Cup, again beating Regalia, and the Grand Prix de L'Empereur in Paris. He was then retired to stud but was unsuccessful in this capacity.

As will be seen, Tom Jennings continued to be a successful trainer and soon found himself sufficiently well off to pursue some philanthropic ideas. These included helping to establish the Fever Hospital at Newmarket and proposing the construction of the Waterworks to supply pure drinking water to the community for the first time. Undoubtedly both schemes were born of his experiences when he was so ill with smallpox in Italy.

— 1866 —

Colonel Pearson was as much interested in breeding racehorses as in racing them, but he was not a gambling man. His contemporaries considered him to be the best kind of sportsman, one whose interest in the turf was rooted in racing for its own sake. He sold many of the horses which he bred and leased others. Among the latter was Lord Lyon, a Stockwell colt, leased to Mr Richard Sutton, a son of the sportsman Sir Richard Sutton, well known for his lavish expenditure to ensure superlative hunting when he was Master of the Quorn and the Cottesmore. Richard Sutton Jnr served under the then Captain Rous, sharing with the older man the hazardous voyage home across the Atlantic in the Pique. Possibly in the hope of being able to spend more time on the turf young Sutton made the unusual transfer from the Royal Navy to the Life Guards, but only stuck this duty for a short time

69 *The Duke of Newcastle's Julius, Tom Challoner up, with trainer Mathew Dawson*   Arthur Ackermann & Son Ltd.

too. Richard Sutton's racing career started when he was thirty-five years old, but his love of heavy gambling was by then in full swing. Lord Lyon, trained by James Dover, ran well as a two-year-old and came to the 2,000 Guineas of 1866 as 7 to 4 on favourite. Harry Custance was beginning to make his presence felt as a jockey and would normally have ridden Lord Lyon but he broke a collar bone in a fall just before the Guineas, on 17 April. A lad, Thomas, who rode the horse at exercise, was therefore given his chance at Newmarket. He made excellent use of this unforeseen opportunity to win by a clear length defeating Monarch of the Glen and Knight of the Crescent. As *The Times* correspondent remarked, the usual order of precedence was quite muddled up by the result!

Another novice Classic success was the performance of Tom Cannon when he won the 1,000 Guineas on Repulse for the young Marquis of Hastings. Cannon had a marvellous 'seat' and appeared to be part and parcel of whatever horse he rode. In a set to he sat well down in the saddle with the reins in his left hand while driving on his mount with ferocious determination. In his right hand was his whip which he rarely found necessary to use except sometimes in the last two or three strides of a finish, and then not in mid-stride. He rode a very fine race on Repulse. The Marquis's horses were trained by the Days at Danebury where the fortunes of the stable were experiencing a revival after some lean years.

Richard Sutton's Lord Lyon was also favourite for the Derby at 6 to 5 on winning. The weather was fine and clear and the usual immense crowd included four Royal Princes: The Prince of Wales, Prince Alfred, Prince George of Denmark and Prince Teck, who took their places in Mr Heatley's Stand. Custance's collar bone had mended so he was put up on Lord Lyon, who appeared extremely fit justifying his very short odds. In the event, the finish was close with Lord Ailesbury's Bribery colt (later named Savernake) only a head behind the favourite with the Duke of Beaufort's Rustic third. Rustic was also bred by Colonel Pearson, and the first three in the race were all sons of Stockwell. Like his employer's father, Custance was a very fine rider to hounds, sharing a hunting-box in Leicestershire with Fred Archer for several seasons. He was a strong and efficient jockey who rode horses hard and well. He was also very popular due to his unassuming manner and good humour. Having won a great deal of money, Richard Sutton could well afford to reward Custance generously for his Derby performance, which he did. Tormentor won the Oaks. She was an unusual yellow bay in colour, trained by Charles Blanton at Newmarket and ridden by James Mann in the jacket (black body, sky blue sleeves and cap) then registered by a Mr B. E. Dunbar and later by a Mr B. Ellam.

Between the Derby and St Leger Lord Lyon achieved mixed success and was again ridden by Custance in mid-September. As in the Derby, the finish was very close with Lord Lyon and Savernake fighting out the last 200 yards as if engaged in a Match, there being no other horses anywhere near them. Lord Lyon won again by a head to give his owner the Triple Crown. The domination of the French the previous year was temporarily forgotten. Harry Hall painted a number of portraits of Lord Lyon, including one showing him with Elland (Ascot Gold Vase) also owned by Richard Sutton, and their trainer James Dover. Nine years later Hall exhibited a painting of the 'Set To for the St Leger by Lord Lyon and Savernake' at the Royal Society of British Artists; the picture was priced at £210.

Returning to 1866, Hall was continuing to paint oil sketches which were engraved and published in *The Sporting Magazine*, as well as supplying more finished canvasses for the Print Publisher, Baily. His portrait of Lord Lyon in his loose-box (with a cat) was published first on 10 July in the series of Baily's Derby winners. The plate was reissued (still with the July publication date) after the St Leger, with the additional legend of: 'Winner of the Two Thousand Guineas Stakes at Newmarket — The Derby Stakes at Epsom and of the Great St Leger at Doncaster 1866'. The engraver was William Summers, replacing John Harris who had died the previous year. Summers continued with Baily until the end of the decade when E.G. Hester became the publisher's principal engraver. Also in 1866, Harry Hall showed a genre picture titled 'Rough and Ready' at the British Institute; a year later these Exhibitions ceased. Hall was now busier than ever and he found himself attending, and apparently quietly enjoying, the main meetings of the Calendar, as well as travelling the country to undertake commissions.

— 1867 —

The very large bets which owners were prepared to make on their own and others' horses during the 1840s were not continued into the 1850s. Sir Joseph Hawley, who seemed at first to be the natural successor in this way to Lord George Bentinck, was having a lean time with his own stables. By coincidence, a few gentlemen with varying degrees of intellect, sense and foolishness entered the racing scene together in the early 1860s. Their betting was prodigious even compared with that of twenty years before. Disaster often followed great coups making the bookmakers happy, but Admiral Rous and the more sober-minded members of the Jockey Club were horrified, aware that, as sure as night follows day, scandals would ensue and the still fragile reputation of the turf could be damaged again. And so, to an extent, it was.

The eighth Duke of Beaufort was not one of these plungers. He kept a few good racehorses which were trained at Danebury. In 1865 he had won the 1,000 Guineas with Siberia (Plate 68). Siberia, as her name might suggest, was by Muscovite, and Muscovite was the sire of Vauban (Plate 31) with whom the Duke comfortably won the 1867 2,000 Guineas, making the brown colt the favourite for the Derby. Knight of the Garter was second in the Guineas and Mr James Merry's Marksman third. A few days after the race at Newmarket it was reported:

> Vauban has been taking it quietly since his victory, and has been encouraging the arts in the shape of Mr Harry Hall, who has been at Danebury, painting him for his noble owner. He is a low and rather short horse, with a beautiful back and barrel.

Colonel Pearson ran Achievement in his own colours for the 1,000 Guineas. She made short work of the opposition promising to be one of the best fillies of both the season and the turf for a number of years.

Henry Chaplin was born in 1840. He was the son of the Reverend Henry Chaplin, vicar of Ryhill near Stamford. When nineteen years old he inherited from an uncle the fine estate of Blankney in Lincolnshire. Once of age he also received a fortune which had accumulated during his minority allowing him to pursue the many field sports of which he was very fond. Sir Frederick Johnstone was a lifelong friend and may have introduced Chaplin to the turf, although as a member of the fast set of socialites during his time at Oxford, he may not have required much persuasion. Among that set was Lady Florence Paget, the vivacious and beautiful younger daughter of the Marquis of Anglesey. Everyone loved her, but it was Henry Chaplin to whom she became engaged in early 1864. Blankney was prepared and she visited the house one Thursday, shortly before the wedding. On the Friday Henry took Florence to the opera and the following morning she wrote a letter to him, showed her wedding dress to her father and quietly left their London house just before midday. By arrangement she met the young Marquis of Hastings at Marshall and Snelgrove's in Oxford Street, and they were married at St George's,

Hanover Square that afternoon. As neat and cowardly a piece of jilting as can be imagined!

Henry Weysford Charles Plantagenet was the younger son of the second Marquis of Hastings who died in 1844 when Harry Plantagenet was two years old. Harry's older brother died in 1851, so that at the age of ten he inherited not only the title but large estates in England, Ireland and Scotland, and a great deal of money besides. The youthful Lord Hastings went up to Oxford for a short time before flinging himself wholeheartedly into a dissolute and aimless life, relieved by his passion for gambling, racing and being thought of as the perfect Cocker of his time; however, in the matter of betting on horses he was not entirely without intelligence, as some bookmakers discovered. His own horses were trained at Danebury and in 1864 he was hopeful that The Duke would win the Derby the following year. At the same time Henry Chaplin invested what was considered a large amount of money in Breadalbane and Broomielaw, the second a vicious horse. Not to be outdone, Hastings bought a colt named Kangaroo from Henry Padwick for £12,000 — far too great a sum even without the hindsight of his proving quite useless. This was the first of many occasions that Padwick relieved the Marquis of his money and property by helping him with his debts! The Duke did not run in Gladiateur's Derby which meant that Hastings had to find substantial sums to settle the bets he had made on the horse. However, his other horses were already winning him a considerable income in stakes' money: £12,800 in 1866.

After Breadalbane's failure in the Derby, Henry Chaplin removed his horses from William I'Anson and placed them with the brothers Bloss at Newmarket. They were managed by Captain Machell. Machell had recently left the Army and was quickly making a name as an astute, hardworking and sometimes ruthless manager and trainer. He was extremely shrewd and not only looked after Chaplin's horses, but also brought his patron to his senses in his method of betting. He encouraged him only to back his own animals where Machell had some control over the outcome of their performance. Backing other people's horses was an additional, and in Machell's view, unnecessary gamble. In 1865 Machell bought Hermit for Chaplin, a Newminster yearling who proved to be a good two-year-old the following season.

There were other promising horses in 1866 and Sir Joseph Hawley was so confident of The Palmer that he bet Chaplin £50,000 that his colt would beat Hermit in the 1867 Derby. The young Duke of Hamilton, who was the worst of the foolish plungers of the period, took Machell £180,000 to £6,000 that Hermit would not win. Fortunately this bet was called off by Machell but Hamilton succeeded in ruining himself by other gambles in a short space of years. During the winter of 1866/7 the Marquis of Hastings laid money against Hermit wherever he found takers, and there were quite a few bookmakers ready to do so. Lady Florence wrote to a friend: 'Harry is laying against Hermit as though the horse were already dead.' Hermit did not run in the 2,000 Guineas. Chaplin's colt came on well in the hands of Bloss and Machell throughout the late spring of 1867 until breaking a blood vessel during training two weeks before the race. Henry Chaplin decided he must be scratched but was persuaded by Machell to keep him in. By careful nursing and light training Hermit remained tolerably fit, but the bookmakers marked him down at 100 to 1 against winning. After some argument, Custance, who was to have ridden Hermit, was released from this commitment and John Daley took his place. Daley was a useful, unspectacular jockey who conscientiously interpreted the riding instructions of owners and trainers.

The weather at Epsom was atrocious. A biting wind and falling snow made both men and horses look miserable at the saddling. Vauban was the firm favourite at 6 to 4 against; The Palmer, Van Amburgh, The Rake (ridden by Custance) and Marksman (Harry Grimshaw) were at 7, 8, 9 and 10 to 1 respectively. Hermit was at 66 to 1 with two other horses. Thirty ran. The start was delayed by no less than ten attempts but once they were off Vauban, with Fordham up, went to the front. Vauban, Marksman and Van Amburgh were the leaders two furlongs from home but at the distance the last fell back, Vauban seemed unhappy and Marksman looked set to win. John Daley who had been nursing Hermit carefully now started his run. Cruising past Vauban he overtook the astonished Harry Grimshaw whose eyes were myopically focused on what he thought was the main threat, Vauban. Hermit won by a neck. Henry Chaplin's winnings were nearly as much as Harry Hasting's losses: £120,000. Of this sum, Hastings owed Chaplin £20,000 which the victor magnanimously told the Marquis not to pay until convenient — perhaps for the sake of the Marchioness with whom he was still on surprisingly good terms. The following Monday the loser's commissioners paid out £120,000 at Tattersalls and Hastings appeared outwardly untroubled by his staggering loss. It was, however, the start of a downward and accelerating spiral of both his fortunes and health.

Achievement, the 1,000 Guineas winner, was favourite for the Oaks and well backed by the public, including Lord Hastings. Surprisingly the race was won by Baron de Rothschild's little thought of Hippia. She was ridden by John Daley who pulled off the Epsom double in style, never winning another Classic race. Achievement ran a dead heat with Romping Girl for second place and her failure to do better could not be understood.

The St Leger was run on a fine, early autumn afternoon before a large crowd of racegoers eager to see Hermit and Achievement running together. The filly, ridden by Tom Challoner, looked very fit as did Hermit with Custance up. Both horses remained quite composed during the two or three false starts. Challoner rode with great judgement and the filly beat Hermit by a length with the Duke of Newcastle's Julius not far behind. Achievement beat Hermit in the Doncaster Cup a few days later and although Chaplin's horse won one more race, thereafter he could do nothing. Hermit went to stud at Blankney in 1869 and was Champion Sire each year from 1880 to 1886. His progeny, including two Derby and two Oaks' winners, won stakes valued at more than £356,000 between 1873 and 1897.

Lord Hastings, hardly twenty-five years old, recouped some of his Derby losses during the summer with Lecturer and his brilliant two-year-old filly Lady Elizabeth who won twelve of the thirteen races for which she started. One of the last was a Match with the three-year-old Julius (who had just won the Cesarewitch) (Plate 69) whom she just managed to beat. The struggle practically knocked the heart out of her as became evident the following year. The Earl was another successful two-year-old and promising Derby entrant owned by Hastings and in whom he set great store. As well as backing his own horses, often successfully, he was also gambling on others' but usually without much luck. He sold his Scottish estates and other property to placate a string of creditors but at the end of the year was forced to sell his horses to meet his debts to the pressing bookmakers and other predators. He bought in The Earl and Lady Elizabeth and turned to Henry Padwick for help for whom part of the security for a loan was ownership of The Earl.

— 1868 —

It is difficult to discover when the brilliant filly Formosa passed from the ownership of a Mr G. Jones to Mr W. Graham; it was possibly between the Oaks and the St Leger. In the 2,000 Guineas Formosa ran a dead heat with Mr Stirling Crawfurd's Moslem. The two horses led throughout and provided a splendidly exciting finish for the Newmarket crowd. To save Formosa for the 1,000 Guineas two days later the stakes were divided and Moslem walked over. On 30 April 1868, with George Fordham again in the saddle,

Formosa beat Athena to win the 1,000 Guineas with ease.

This spring the Marquis of Hastings found himself a defaulter unable to pay his gambling debts to the tune of about £50,000. He quietly resigned from the Jockey Club before being asked to do so. Lady Elizabeth, his filly who had done so much to ameliorate her owner's losses during 1867, wintered badly and was plainly still suffering from over-racing as a two-year-old, not least in her Match with Julius. The public however were unaware that she had lost her form and she started favourite for the Derby. There is evidence that Danebury and a ring of bookmakers who backed her strongly for the race when she was carrying all before her the previous year, now sought ways of neutralising any possible opposition she might face. Among such horses was The Earl, mortgaged by Hastings to the 'Sussex Lawyer'. The Earl beat Sir Joseph Hawley's Blue Gown in the spring while carrying Padwick's jacket. A little later the colt returned to Hastings' ownership but was unexpectedly scratched from the Derby shortly before the race.

John Porter was a Godson of the jockey Charles Marlow. He came from Rugeley in Staffordshire, a town which had achieved notoriety through the activities of one of its citizens, a Dr Palmer who, before being caught, successfully poisoned a number of men coming between him and success on the racecourse. Porter was apprenticed to John Day Snr who for a time managed Padwick's horses at Michel Grove. Day subsequently quarrelled with Padwick and the latter moved his horses to William Goater at Findon. Porter moved as well, and at the age of seventeen found himself in sole charge of the administration and accountancy of the stables, these two facets of management not being Goater's forte. Porter also 'did' a horse himself. His serious, zealous and conscientious efforts were rewarded in 1863 when Sir Joseph Hawley engaged him to take over as his trainer at Cannon Heath after the untimely death of George Manning. Two years later Porter contracted typhoid following a visit to Doncaster and Sir Joseph's horses were temporarily stabled with James Dover at Ilsley. It was at about this time that Hawley decided to build a new stables at Kingsclere, a short distance from the dilapidated Cannon Heath. They were in part designed by John Porter, and the Baronet's small string moved into the fourteen boxes at Kingsclere during the winter of 1867/8. Among the occupants of the new loose-boxes were Blue Gown, Rosicrucian and Green Sleeve, all the offspring of Beadsman. Each had shown great promise as a two-year-old, although Blue Gown was the least consistent in his performance. Despite Rosicrucian and Green Sleeve catching chills in the still construction-damp stables, Hawley declared

70 *The Marquis of Hastings' The Earl (Grand Prix de Paris, 1867)* Sotheby's

either of them to win the Derby, leaving Blue Gown (whom John Wells chose to ride) to run on his merits. As with Lady Elizabeth, the public felt they knew best and were certainly more aware of Blue Gown's form making him the second favourite at 7 to 2 against.

The weather on 27 May was excellent and the crowd gave a sallow complexioned Marquis of Hastings a cheer as he went with his wife to watch the race from Lord Anglesey's stand. Fordham rode Lady Elizabeth and at the start she 'turned stupid' as was her practice. However, she was away well, but faded quickly as John Day and Henry Padwick must have expected. At the distance the race was between Blue Gown and Baron de Rothschild's outsider King Alfred. Wells landed Blue Gown (Plate 35) a clear winner by half a length and Hawley, who had hardly backed the bay colt, generously gave his jockey the stake: £6,800. Blue Gown won a number of races including the Ascot Gold Cup, but was not a success as a sire.

In the Oaks George Fordham was again riding Formosa. They won easily with Leonie and Athena second and third, but well behind. Lady Elizabeth was seventh. It was reported at the end of this Epsom week that Hastings' gambling was successful showing only a net loss of £2,000! If true, he must have 'covered' himself well since, like the Days and Padwick he had presumably backed Lady Elizabeth the year before and the decision to pull out The Earl was not a cheap one.

The scratching of The Earl (Plate 70) just before the Derby naturally upset those members of the public who had backed him earlier. Their disappointment turned to anger when shortly after the Epsom Meeting the horse won the Grand Prix de Paris on 7 June and three races at Ascot on the 10th and 11th — all in the Marquis's colours. They recalled as well that the colt beat Blue Gown in the spring. To protect the name of the turf, the Jockey Club began to investigate this irregularity, if it was one. They were partly forestalled by the individual initiative of Admiral Rous. One of the Admiral's few failings was a quite irresistible urge to rush into print without first thinking a matter through. He wrote to *The Times* on 15 June 1868. Rous had no love for reckless plungers but his dislike of blackguards was even greater. He accused the Days of concealing from their employer Lady Elizabeth's catastrophic loss of form and wrote that Hastings had nothing to do with the scratching of The Earl, for which Henry Hill and Padwick were responsible for their own gambling ends. The letter ended with a thoroughly libellous shot: 'What can the fly demand from the spider in whose web he is enveloped?.' Hastings and Padwick denied these accusations but their explanation for not running The Earl was thin to say the least and simply not believed. John Day Jnr started proceedings and the Admiral was encouraged by his friends to withdraw his letter — which he refused to do. The whole row dragged on into the autumn since those who might be described as the aggrieved parties were aware that in taking Rous to court malpractices, which clearly existed, could come out into the open and rebound on them.

In the late summer The Earl broke down and was quite properly scratched from the St Leger. Formosa was the joint favourite with Baron de Rothschild's King Alfred. The race was run on a bright, clear day before a good crowd. The filly won convincingly, this time in the hands of Tom Challoner. Mr George Hodgman's Paul Jones with George Fordham up was second and Mercury with Johnnie Osborne third.

The young Marquis of Hastings was ill and his health deteriorated rapidly in the autumn. He died on 10 November 1868 aged twenty-six. Soon after Hastings' death Admiral Rous withdrew his letter and the case with the Days was quickly settled out of court. The Marquis's short life and mercurial racing career provided the turf with renewed, unwanted notoriety and London society a subject of endless speculation and discussion. Since Lady Florence bore him no children the title became extinct, although

his name remained familiar in racing circles and among his contemporaries who survived so much longer than he did. Two years after his death Lady Florence married Sir George Chetwynd, also a racing man whose gambling activities supported a rather longer but in some ways just as notorious turf career.

Henry Chaplin reduced his stud at the end of 1867. In the spring of 1869 he disposed of nearly all his horses but not before Harry Hall painted Broomielaw and Breadalbane, as well as Hermit with Daley up in the owner's distinctive all rose colours (Plate 32). Chaplin maintained his interest in racing, became a Steward of the Jockey Club in 1873 and a successful owner of a few steeplechasers, also managed by Captain 'Jem' Machell. He represented Lincolnshire constituencies in Parliament from 1868 to 1916 when he was created Viscount Chaplin. In 1876 he married (another) Florence, a daughter of the Duke of Sutherland. Epitomising the country squire, although the Blankney estate ran into difficult times, he showed a keen interest in politics which led him to be a member of Commissions of Inquiry into a wide variety of causes and subjects. At his death in 1923, *The Times* wrote in a leader: 'In the annals of the Turf his name is never likely to be forgotten', not forgotten for very different reasons to those for which the Marquis of Hastings is also remembered.

So ended a brief, exciting era of heavy turf gambling with its inevitable partners of scandal and skulduggery. It was exhilarating for the players but debilitating for the game at a time when Victorian rectitude was fast becoming fashionable. This last factor reduced the number of individuals who could otherwise have been expected to enter racing each year to invigorate the turf with fresh enthusiasm, money and ideas. The decline was unexpectedly halted. In 1870 an influx of French and German owners came to England for the opportunity to race which was denied them in their own countries due to the outbreak of the Franco-Prussian War. On this occasion the foreigners were given a warmer welcome to the English turf than in Gladiateur's year!

CHAPTER 7
1869–1875

And head to head, and stride to stride
Newmarket's hope, and Yorkshire's pride,
Like horses harnessed side by side,
Are struggling for the goal.

DESPITE THE LARGE number of horses in training at Newmarket the standard of sport shown on the Heath was low in the late 1860s and early 1870s. Sir George Chetwynd in his reminiscences twenty years later describes how there was only one small stand comprising a luncheon room with a balcony outside, and a room below for sheltering from the rain. The best way to see what racing there was being to spend the whole day in the saddle. In 1869 and 1870, Matches swelled the mediocre card and Sir George recalls attending four walks-over in one day. In an acerbic account of Newmarket in May 1874 the *Illustrated London News* correspondent wrote:

When we complained, last week, of the parsimony and inactivity of the ruling powers at Newmarket, we imagined that such wretched programmes as those of the Tuesday and Wednesday could scarcely be equalled. There was, however, a lower depth, and the Friday's card ought to be preserved as one of the curiosities of racing in 1874. It was made up of the appropriately named Refuse Two-Year-Old Selling Plate, a £50 plate and a selling stakes. Happily we were not there to witness the sport (!), nor have we been able to meet with anyone who was; but we should imagine that the starter and judge, and one or two members of the Jockey Club, had all the fun to themselves. We are not one of those who wish to see the sacred heath disfigured with a monster grandstand, or to have it invaded by the motley throng who annually swarm to Epsom; indeed it is too far from the town to be in danger of such a misfortune; but we do desire to see some radical reforms, which would make the racing at Newmarket more what it should be at a place with a thousand horses in training, and more worthy of such classic ground.

The lack of good racing would not have affected Harry Hall except in so far as he may have shared in the feeling among turfites that the enjoyment of a day out at Newmarket was not what it used to be.

The concentration of training around the town resulted in northern horses being regarded as somewhat second rate. This impression was manifested in the dislike of Pretender who came down from Yorkshire where he was trained by Tom Dawson at Tupgill. John Osborne Snr, the trainer, died in 1865. His own horses were sold, but the Ashgill stables continued to be used by a number of owners who placed their horses in the hands of his sons. John Osborne Jnr was so involved in the new arrangements at Ashgill that for a few years there was little time for him to pursue his career as a jockey until Tom Dawson, a great friend of Johnnie Osborne, put him up on Pretender. Pretender won the Guineas by half a length at the end of an exciting race against Mr James Merry's Belladrum, a much favoured southern horse. After the race Pretender became favourite for the Derby, his merit recognised by the southern turfites and bookmakers at last.

Whatever other criticisms there were of Newmarket, the weather at the end of April was perfect except for a slight east wind which stirred up the dust of a long dry spell. The Duke of Beaufort's Scottish Queen won the 1,000 Guineas very easily with George Fordham in the Duke's jacket.

At Epsom a wet night gave way to a cloudy morning which turned into a glorious Derby Day. The good weather in the afternoon may be accounted for by the first appearance at the race of the Princess of Wales with her husband. Pretender, still the favourite, attended by Tom Dawson on his hack, was saddled at Tattenham Corner giving those around the paddock little chance to admire the brown colt's good looks.

71 *Sir Joseph Hawley's Pero Gomez, John Wells up (St Leger, 1869)*   Arthur Ackermann & Son Ltd.

The second favourite was Sir Joseph Hawley's Pero Gomez with Wells in the saddle. Pero Gomez had beaten Pretender in a race for two-year-olds. Belladrum was third favourite at 6 to 1 against, but fell back after the Corner, 'roaring'. Pretender overtook The Drummer at the distance and looked the certain winner. Pero Gomez had been accidentally interfered with at Tattenham Corner but Wells made him go again, bringing him right up to Pretender at the finish. Osborne hung on to win by a head (Plate 36), although from Wells's smiles as he rode back down the course to unsaddle, he obviously thought his was the prize. The northern turfites were delighted with the result as was Johnnie Osborne for whom this was his first, and only, Derby victory. Pretender remains the last northern-trained Derby winner to the present day.

There was a strange sequel to this Derby by which Sir Joseph Hawley temporarily made himself unpopular with the Jockey Club and turf alike. The rule that nominators must be alive the day 'their' horse runs was still in use. On settling day, 31 May 1869, Sir Joseph informed Messrs Weatherby that having heard a rumour that Mr Sadler, Pretender's nominator, died the day before the race was won, he claimed the race for Pero Gomez and asked them not to pay the stakes until the matter was cleared up. Despite witnesses saying they had seen Sadler at Epsom the Wednesday before, there was pandemonium for a time. It is possible that Hawley was the victim of a deliberate hoax, but it is surprising that a man of his calibre did not first establish whether the rumour, as he described it, was true before taking such drastic public action. He quickly withdrew once the truth was established but the damage was done and partly triggered another unfortunate incident a little time later. Sir Joseph scratched favourites from races on two occasions when he found himself forestalled in the betting market. The public were infuriated and a *Sporting Times* article written under the name of 'Caustic' described 'Sir Joseph Scratchawley' as being one of the most fortunate men of the turf, but:

> He casts a longing eye on the gate money, 'milk cans', and the corpses of the boiled, and the dead, that taint the atmosphere of the Ring.

Dr Shorthouse, the proprietor and editor of *The Sporting Times*, unaware of the piece until he read it in print, was horrified by the libel and immediately apologised to Sir Joseph. The Baronet, in the hope of revenging himself on Caustic, sued. By a combination of loyalty to his staff and the law being what it is, Dr Shorthouse found himself fined £50 and sent to prison for three months. Hawley did all that he could to have part of the sentence remitted since he never doubted Shorthouse's innocence in the matter, but he was unsuccessful. Sir Joseph was again not popular although everyone accepted that he was libelled abominably.

John Porter was critical of Wells's riding of Pero Gomez in the Derby but he acknowledged the incident at Tattenham Corner undoubtedly baulked the colt for a few strides. In the St Leger, for which Pretender was the 6 to 5 on favourite but came nowhere, Wells again rode an energetic and clever race driving Pero Gomez (Plate 71) to an easy win in front of Lord Calthorpe's Martyrdom with George Fordham up. The fickle public cheered Sir Joseph Hawley and Wells as the jockey weighed in. This was the last Classic victory for Wells. He was a tall man with the consequent problem of keeping his weight in check. He sorely tried Sir Joseph on one occasion when Blue Gown was disqualified because he failed to draw the weight after a race in 1867. Despite this and other incidents when he sailed close to the wind over his weight, his employer was always generous and loyal to the rather flashy 'Brusher' Wells.

In January 1869 Hawley made proposals to the Jockey Club regarding the racing of two-year-olds. He wanted them to start running later in the season than the rules then permitted, and that they should generally not be tried so hard while so young. Admiral Rous who had no liking for Hawley opposed him and a committee was formed to consider the proposals. The committee worked slowly and a year later Sir Joseph proposed even more radical reforms including the unspoken charge that the Jockey Club had lost its way in failing to promote the improvement of the thoroughbred stock and apparently endorsing heavy gambling as the raison d'etre for racing horses. There was some sympathy for Sir Joseph, but as others pointed out he himself raced two-year-olds for many years and had made considerable sums of money by betting. Another committee investigated Hawley's new suggestions while Rous was busy writing letters to *The Times* where the editorial staff were on Hawley's side. Some compromises, later repealed, were made on the running of two-year-olds and the Jockey Club committee considered they had no part to play in the matter of controlling gambling. Hawley was defeated. He continued to race, but became ill in 1873 and broke up the Leybourne Grange stud. Sir Joseph died on 20 April 1875, a somewhat disillusioned turfite.

— 1870 —

Mr James Merry remained a social outcast from the aristocratic ranks of the turf and his relationship with the Jockey Club was at best bleak. Outwardly Merry appeared unaffected by this ostracism but one suspects that at heart the wealthy ironmaster wished he was a little more acceptable, certainly in his position as a leading owner for more than twenty years. Merry was not an easy man to serve; he changed his trainer on at least four occasions. Starting with William Day, he moved to Mathew Dawson at Russley (who moved to Newmarket in 1866), followed by a period with James Waugh and finally, in late 1870, to Robert Peck. Another instance of Mr Merry's lack of faith in those who worked for him was that between 1855 and 1873, his six winners of seven Classic races were each ridden by a different jockey. Notwithstanding these uncomfortable relationships the public decided at an early stage that to bet on anything even moderately good with Merry's yellow jacket on its back was as sure a way to make money as any when following horses. The bookmakers naturally disliked the ease with which the public picked such winners making them favourites regardless of the Ring's intentions!

A Macaroni colt, Macgregor, showed considerable promise as a yearling in 1868, but he had a suspect foreleg. Merry, his owner, decided not to race him as a two-year-old but train him for a triumphant season in 1870. Another reason for holding Macgregor back may have been that James Merry did not want his filly Sunshine to be eclipsed in the succession of races she won as a two-year-old in 1869. Macgregor, described as one of the meanest and worst looking horses that ever raced, won the 2,000 Guineas in 1870 with ease, five lengths in front of Lord Stamford's Normanby and Lord Falmouth's Kingcraft. Mr Merry's success in financial terms was considerable and the victory contained the added sweetness of defeating Lord Stamford whom Merry detested as much as he did the Duke of Beaufort – an aversion probably reciprocated.

In 1867 Lord Falmouth moved his horses from John Scott whose health was failing (he died in October 1871) to William Boyce and the following year to Mathew Dawson who had taken over his older brother's training stables at Heath House, Newmarket, when he left Russley. Early in 1868 an already lanky Fred Archer, aged eleven, was apprenticed to the Heath House stables. Hurricane (1,000 Guineas, 1862) and Queen Bertha (Oaks, 1863), both trained by John Scott, had more than established Viscount Falmouth's name as a prominent owner. With the move to Newmarket his magpie colours of black, white sleeves and red cap were seen with increasing frequency flying past the posts of Classic and other courses. The association of Falmouth, Dawson and later Archer was one which dominated the turf in the 1870s and early 1880s. Kingcraft was among Lord Falmouth's yearlings who came to Newmarket in late 1868. As a two-year-old he ran in nine races winning

six, but towards the end of the 1869 season he was plainly exhausted. He recovered during the winter and was favourite for the following 2,000 Guineas, but only achieved third place as we have seen.

Macgregor was the 9 to 4 favourite for the Derby and Kingcraft fell back to 20 to 1 after his disappointing run in the Guineas. The public believed that Macgregor's victory was a certainty but George Fordham who was put up on the colt (ridden by John Daley in the 2,000 Guineas) was less enthusiastic. In the event, and to the horror of the betting public, Macgregor came fourth with Kingcraft (Plate 38) winning by four lengths from Stirling Crawfurd's Palmerston. Tom French, Dawson's first call jockey at the time rode Kingcraft. French, like Archer who succeeded him, was tall and wasted hard to keep his weight down. He was a skilful rider with a marvellous temperament to match. Honest, cheerful and respectful he quickly endeared himself to the quiet and unassuming Lord Falmouth. That very different character, James Merry:

> somewhat excited by the defeat of the crack, rushed onto the course, and was speedily relieved of his watch, fieldglass and umbrella.

The 1,000 Guineas had been won by Hester with James Grimshaw up. She ran in her trainer's name, Joseph Dawson. Joe Dawson was the second son of the trainer George Dawson and the older brother of Mathew. Coming down from Scotland, he first trained horses at Ilsley in Berkshire and then at Heath House until moving to new stabling at nearby Bedford Lodge. Like his younger brother, Joe was one of nature's gentlemen, correct in manner, dress and actions, to whom many owners now wished to send their horses. James Grimshaw was a clear-sighted brother of Harry who was shortly to be killed in a smash in a trap while returning from a race meeting on a dark night. The early loss of this 'character' of the turf saddened fellow jockeys and a great many owners and trainers alike. James Grimshaw was equally popular but not as good a rider as his brother.

Hester was last but one in the Oaks with reports that she was 'got at' before the race, (as there had been of Macgregor in the Derby, but this was thought impossible by his trainer). The winner was Gamos, owned by Mr W. Graham, giving her jockey Fordham some recompense for his recent Derby failure. James Merry's well-thought-of Sunshine was second in the race and it was his criticism of this performance and that of Macgregor which led to the split between Merry and James Waugh. The trainer had had enough of his master's suspicious nature and hoped that Robert Peck, who took his place, would fare better with such a difficult owner.

25 *Mr W. I'Anson's Blink Bonny, John Charlton up, with her owner (Derby, 1857)*   Schillay & Rehs Inc. USA

26 *Sir Joseph Hawley's Beadsman, John Wells up (Derby, 1858)*   Christie's

27 *Count Frederic de Lagrange's Black Prince, Quinton up, at Chantilly (French Derby, 1859)* Richard Green

28 *Mr W. I.' Anson's Caller Ou, Tom Challoner up (St Leger, 1861)* MacConnal-Mason

29 *Mr W. I'Anson's Blair Athol, Jim Snowden up (Derby and St Leger, 1864)*   Schillay & Reys Inc. USA

30 *Count Frederic de Lagrange's Gladiateur (Triple Crown, 1865)*   Christie's

31 *The Duke of Beaufort's Vauban, (2,000 Guineas, 1867) George Fordham up with Lady Hester*   Richard Green

32 *Mr H.Chaplin's Hermit, John Daley up (Derby, 1867)*   The National Trust, Northern Ireland

33 *A steeplechaser with jockey up and trainer, dated 1859*   Richard Green

34 *Lord Powlett's The Lamb, Mr Edwards (George Ede) up (Grand National, 1868 and 1871)*   Sotheby's

35 *Sir Joseph Hawley's Blue Gown, John Wells up (Derby, 1868)*   Richard Green

36 *Mr J. Johnstone's Pretender, John Osborne up (2,000 Guineas and Derby, 1869)*   York City Art Gallery

37 *Glenmasson* Richard Green

38 *Lord Falmouth's Kingcraft at stud, 1877 (Derby, 1870)* Private collection

39 *Mr Thelluson's Rataplan, Painted for The Sporting Magazine*   Richard Green

40 *Mr T.V. Morgan's Hawthornden (St Leger, 1870). Painted for The Sporting Magazine*   Richard Green

72 *Baron Meyer de Rothschild's Hannah (1,000 Guineas, Oaks and St Leger, 1871). Engraving by E.G. Hester*
Stirling and Francine Clark Art Institute, Williamstown, Massachusetts, USA

The attendance at the St Leger in 1870 was poor. This may have been because the race promised little excitement since Macgregor had broken down and, in reality, Kingcraft was not an outstanding horse. The early morning weather was fine but soon turned cloudy. By the afternoon it was bitterly cold keeping the less dedicated racegoers off the course and in the warmth of the many parlours of Doncaster's inns. There were half a dozen attempts at starting the nineteen runners for what became a slow race. A quarter of a mile from home Kingcraft looked the likely victor until James Grimshaw challenged on Hawthornden, winning by half a length. Hawthornden (Plate 40), belonging to Mr T. V. Morgan, was trained by Joe Dawson, providing an example of the friendly rivalry which existed between his stables and that of his brother Mathew for the next few years.

The Sporting Magazine stopped publication at the end of this year. Among its monthly numbers there were five engravings after paintings by Harry Hall: Vespasian, The Colonel, Kingcraft, Gamos, and Hawthornden. The gap in sporting literature left by the demise of the *Magazine* was already being filled by *Baily's Magazine of Sports and Pastimes* (first published in 1860) in which contributors writing about turf history re-used many of *The Sporting Magazine* plates, as did George Tattersall in his *Pictorial Gallery of English Race-Horses*. No doubt this made economic sense, but it also demonstrated the paucity of contemporary artists interested in painting racehorses. It was not long before these engravings gave way to photographs and an era of sporting illustration came to an end.

— 1871 —

In Classic-winning terms, 1871 was the annus mirabilis of Baron Meyer de Rothschild's racing career. He had been running horses for some years with less success than might have been expected from his great wealth and the resources he could deploy as a large-scale owner. He was made a member of the Jockey Club in 1864 in the year that his Tomato won the 1,000 Guineas. De Rothschild bred many of his horses from his favourite sire, King Tom, the father of Tomato and also of Hippia, the surprise winner of the Oaks in 1867. King Tom was also the sire of Hannah, named after de Rothschild's only daughter, the victor of three of the five Classic races of 1871 ensuring, with Favonius, that this racing season became 'The Baron's Year'.

The winter of 1870/71 was severe and late, making exercising in the early spring difficult. The form shown by runners early in the *Calendar* indicated their opportunities to train rather than their intrinsic merit. By the day of the 2,000 Guineas there had been only two or three weeks of reasonable weather. Bothwell, by Stockwell, was bred by a Mr Lamert, bought by Mr R. Jardine (later Sir Robert Jardine) and sent for training to Tom Dawson, the eldest son of George Dawson at Tupgill. As a two-year-old Bothwell met with mixed success. He was as fit as the rest of the field in the Guineas running in the name of Mr J. Johnstone, Jardine's racing partner. James Merry's King of the Forest was favourite followed by Sterling and Bothwell both at 11 to 2 against. De Rothschild had no entry. Tom Dawson put in Fisherman as pacemaker, a task he accomplished well before leaving the three at the shortest odds to battle out the finish. In the last fifty yards Johnnie Osborne with Bothwell stalled off Tom Cannon on Sterling to win by a length. King of the Forest with Jim Snowden was third.

One of de Rothschild's home-bred horses was a colt by Parmesan out of Zephyr and known as such (the Zephyr colt) until two days before the Derby when he was named Favonius. Some thought this chestnut the ugliest animal they had seen for many years; others found him good-looking! He did not run as a two-year-old but having performed well in a trial with Hannah shortly before the Derby he came to the race fourth in the betting. Bothwell was the 5 to 2 favourite but hardly featured at all. A quarter of a mile from the finish Mr Cartwright's Albert Victor ridden by Custance was going well but Tom French on Favonius drew away in the last two hundred yards to win comfortably by a length and a half. King of the Forest ran a dead heat with Albert Victor for second place. This was an immensely popular win both as a just reward for Baron Meyer's support of the turf and for the outstanding Tom French, for whom it was his second successive Derby victory. Sadly it also proved to be his last Classic win for he died of tuberculosis in 1873, possibly aggravated by too much wasting. He was twenty-nine.

Two days later, in front of a smaller crowd than usual, Charles Maidment only had to sit still on Hannah (trained by Joe Hayhoe at Newmarket), as he had done in the 1,000 Guineas, to win the Oaks by three lengths. Maidment started his career as a stable-boy with William Day before moving to Newmarket. At one time he tried the sisters Emblem and Emblematic, belonging to Lord Coventry, over hurdles and was able to advise George Stevens how to ride them in the Grand National. Stevens asked: 'Can I win on sisters?' 'Of course you can', Maidment is alleged to have replied. 'I could myself, and I'm not a steeplechase jockey.' Stevens rode them to victory in the Nationals of 1863 (Emblem) and 1864 (Emblematic). Harry Hall painted both horses and a number of other Grand National winners. Among them were Mr Hodgman's Emigrant (1857) (Plate 59) and the sixth Earl Powlett's The Lamb who won the race in 1868 with 'Mr Edwards' (George Ede) up (Plate 34), and again in 1871 when the horse was ridden by 'Mr Thomas' (Tommy Pickernell). Ede had been killed in a fall on the first day of the Aintree Meeting the year before. The Colonel was another steeplechaser painted by Hall on whom Stevens won the National in 1869 and 1870. This last painting was engraved and published privately at Cheltenham by a W. Stevens. Little is known of Maidment, the apparent Jack-of-all riding trades, but he was a successful jockey during the 1870s.

In 1871 the crowd at Doncaster for the St Leger was larger than the year before but the weather was not much better. A new saddling paddock allowed the spectators a better chance of seeing the runners before the race, which was much appreciated by the students of fitness and form. As well as Bothwell, Mr J. Johnstone had no less than three horses running in his name in the small field of ten starters. They did not include de Rothschild's Favonius. This was the first year that the extra weight carried by colts over fillies was reduced from five pounds to three pounds, since it appeared the original penalty to colts was allowing an exceptional number of St Legers to be won by the fairer sex. This change of weights made little difference to the result in which Hannah, again ridden by Maidment, easily beat Albert Victor, with Ringwood third and Général fourth. Hannah, as winner of the 1,000 Guineas, Oaks and St Leger (Plate 72) was an outstanding filly of whom de Rothschild was justifiably proud. She was, however, his last Classic winner and some of his previous luck deserted him in the following seasons.

In 1851 Baron Meyer de Rothschild had commissioned Joseph Paxton, the designer of the Crystal Palace for the Great Exhibition, to build him a large house at Mentmore. This vast and not particularly beautiful English Renaissance style mansion contained the Baron's considerable collection of good and not so good works of art. His daughter, Hannah, was the sole heiress of Mentmore on the death of the Baron in 1874. Three years later she married the politician, the fifth Earl of Rosebery, who later won the Derby on no less than three occasions and held the office of Prime Minister in 1894 and 1895. After the death of the sixth Earl in 1974, the family was forced to sell Mentmore and its contents to avoid the heaviest of the inevitable death duties. Among the pictures sold in May 1977, there were five portraits of the Baron Meyer's horses by Harry Hall: Hippia, King of the Vale, Restitution, Suffolk, and Hannah.

— 1872 —

Mr Jones, a farmer from Ely, owned a tall, dark chestnut with two white forelegs which he thought should win any race in which he ran if properly trained. He was not far from the mark in this speculation. Jones took the horse, Prince Charlie, to Joseph Dawson at Newmarket, who also recognised the colt's potential despite discovering that his respiratory system was slightly damaged and he 'roared'. As a two-year-old Prince Charlie won both his races and, surviving an exceptionally cold winter well, he was at very short odds for the 2,000 Guineas. To the alarm of the bookmakers this large, good-looking horse with the sweetest temper became the darling of the racing public who backed him with all the money on which they could lay their hands. Attempts by the Ring to nobble Prince Charlie were discovered quite by chance and a member of Joe Dawson's stable was sacked. Despite Maidment's best efforts on Mr Savile's Cremorne, Johnnie Osborne on Prince Charlie (running in Dawson's name) won easily, although only by a neck.

Mr Henry Savile was a popular member of the Jockey Club racing for many years with only moderate success. He was a kind-hearted sportsman who was always loyal to his trainer and jockeys, accepting with genial tolerance that the few good horses he owned were outnumbered by some very bad ones. His trainer was William Gilbert whose understanding of Cremorne was as considerate as that of Savile for his employees. Cremorne, by Parmesan (Favonius's sire) was an idle and greedy horse while in his box but a different animal once unrugged and roused. He ran well as a two-year-old and came to the Derby as second favourite at 3 to 1 with Prince Charlie ahead of him at 5 to 2 against.

The weather at Epsom was as glorious as it had been at Newmarket for the 2,000 Guineas, but in both places there were clouds of dust to irritate the large crowds. There were now almost as many race-goers travelling by train as there were arriving by road, the former method having become more reliable and faster than joining the melée of carriages and carts on the turnpike. The field of twenty-three was delayed in arriving at the start on time, which was twenty minutes late. This may have been the result of a slight change in the geography but not the length of the Derby course introduced this year. The crowd admired Prince Charlie who looked particularly fit and in whom Joe Dawson was completely confident. Pell Mell (then known as brother of Flurry), owned by Mr J. N. Astley and trained by Alec Taylor, also appeared in good form as did Cremorne in his lugubrious way. They were away well at the first attempt. Prince Charlie challenged the leaders at Tattenham Corner but then faded quickly while Maidment took Cremorne to the front pursued by Tom Challoner on Pell Mell, finishing in that order. As in the Guineas, Lord Falmouth's Queen's Messenger with Tom French was third.

The friendly rivalry between owners and trainers of two such splendid horses, Prince Charlie and Cremorne, was soured later by an allegation by Tom Jennings of an irregularity in the former's registration. Jennings kept his mouth shut at the time of the 2,000 Guineas but he knew that Eastern Princess, Prince Charlie's dam, had been sent to France to visit Monarque at stud. While abroad Prince Charlie (by Blair Athol) was born, but the certificate to this effect was never properly lodged as the rules of racing required. Before a race later in the year, when Prince Charlie was to run against one of Jenning's horses, the trainer objected to him and Joe Dawson scratched Prince Charlie. Henry Savile was annoyed that Jennings had not mentioned the irregularity before the 2,000 Guineas. Subsequently in 1872 Cremorne ran well and even better as a four-year-old until he injured himself halfway through the season. He was kept at stud by Mr Savile, being sold on the owner's death to a Mr Lumley for 5,400 guineas. Despite the advice of his old trainer, Gilbert, the stallion was not given much exercise, grew fat and dropped dead from heart failure a short time later.

At the outbreak of the war between France and Prussia in 1870, Count Frederic de Lagrange remained in Paris or stayed for short periods at his chateau near Gisors which was occupied by the Germans. He gave up racing until 1874, sending his whole stud to Tom Jennings at Newmarket and leasing his horses to M. Charles Lefèvre for a period of three years. Lefèvre, who raced in the name of T. Lombard in 1870 and 1871, was looked upon with some suspicion by Englishmen since his compatriots were not beyond spreading rumours born of jealousy about his successful

73 *The Duke of Hamilton's Barbillon, H. Custance up (Prix Gladiateur, 1873)* Arthur Ackermann & Son Ltd.

dealings on the Stock Exchange. However, with his usual courtesy, Mr George Payne soon befriended Lefèvre and he was then quickly accepted as a staunch supporter of the turf and Newmarket in particular; support the home of racing badly needed. Reine, by Monarque out of Fille de L'Air, was one of the horses leased to Lefèvre. With Parry up, she won the 1872 1,000 Guineas (run this year for the last time over the Ditch Mile course) from an otherwise poor field. Again in the Oaks the other starters were not exceptional and after three-quarters of a mile George Fordham took Reine to the front where she was neither headed nor really challenged. This was Fordham's fourth Oaks win. M. Lefèvre named his infant daughter after the successful filly.

Lord Wilton's Wenlock ridden by Charles Maidment won the St Leger five lengths clear of Prince Charlie, who ran gallantly despite his breathing problems.

Harry Hall painted all the Classic winners of 1872 as well as many other horses, but it was probably the marriage of his son Sidney which gave him the greatest pleasure in that year. Sidney was now a well established portrait painter and had recently returned from the scene of the Franco-Prussian War where he was the special artist for The Graphic. In the following year Emma Hall, Sidney's wife, gave birth to a boy, Henry Reginald Holland; Harry Hall's first of only two grandsons.

— 1873 —

Alec Taylor was the son of the trainer, Thomas Taylor. Tom Taylor trained for Robert Ridsdale until that erratic sportsman had to sell his stud in 1835. Taylor later took on Lord Chesterfield's much reduced stables at Bretby Park where, training on a small budget with poor horses, his successes were few and far between. However, it was Lord Chesterfield who suggested to Sir Joseph Hawley that he should employ the 25-year-old Alec Taylor as his private trainer at Fyfield in 1848. Alec's skill was based on what he had learnt from his father. When Hawley temporarily withdrew from racing, Alec Taylor continued to train for J. Massey Stanley until this owner ran into financial difficulties in 1856. Taylor's fortunes also suffered until the Marquis of Ailesbury sent him some horses in 1858, among them St Albans. St Albans' success and the performance of Savernake brought more owners to Fyfield in the 1860s including the Duke of Beaufort, Mr George Payne and Mr W. Stirling Crawfurd. The last owner was persuaded by Alec Taylor to put up the money to build a magnificent training establishment at Manton across the Bath road from the old stables. Moslem (2,000 Guineas, 1868) was trained at Manton as was Gang Forward, by Stockwell, entered by Stirling Crawfurd for the 1873 2,000 Guineas.

The organisation of meetings at Newmarket continued to be haphazard. While the construction of stands, paddocks, rails and other restrictions were resisted, the crowds on the course were often in danger and an accident was expected unless something was done to control them. After one or two false starts Gang Forward ridden by Tom Challoner beat Henry Savile's Kaiser (Maidment) by a short head in a thrilling finish. In the 1,000 Guineas which followed, Mr James Merry's Marie Stuart ridden by Cannon was the favourite. Cecilia, a rank outsider owned by Lord Falmouth and ridden by Jack Morris won the race; Marie Stuart was fourth.

Robert Peck was now training at Russley for James Merry whose interest in racing was on the wane, due partly to ill-health. Merry was certainly not enthusiastic when Peck bought a fat yearling by Stockwell at a Sledmere sale. As soon as the purchase was made, Peck named the colt Doncaster. He proved almost untrainable as a two-year-old and did not race in 1872. There seemed no way to make this chestnut colt go until the cheerful and quite heavy Peck rode him at exercise one early morning in February 1873. Doncaster took off and Peck realised there was a potential winner of the Blue Riband beneath him. Doncaster did not improve quickly and ran badly in the 2,000 Guineas, but Peck thought his jockey, Tom Cannon, was partly to blame. Mr Merry wanted to scratch Doncaster from the Derby, saving him for a race at Ascot. Peck persuaded the owner to let him run at Epsom where he started as a 45 to 1 outsider. Gang Forward was the favourite. Jim Snowden was beginning to rely too much on the bottle to give himself an enthusiasm for riding and failed to turn up for a Derby morning gallop on Doncaster. Little Fred Webb, who happened to be available, was given Merry's jacket. At the two furlongs mark, Doncaster overtook Gang Forward and Kaiser to win by a length and a half. There was a dead heat for second place. The crowd watched the finish in stunned silence. Merry cursed himself for not backing his own horse, while a happy Robert Peck looked forward to picking up his considerable winnings at the long odds he had obtained on the same day that he rode Doncaster at exercise.

Marie Stuart improved after her disappointing effort in the 1,000 Guineas. She won the Oaks easily with Tom Cannon up. Both Marie Stuart and Doncaster were entered for the St Leger and Mr Merry ran them on their merits. Kaiser was the favourite on this occasion but could only run into third place behind

Marie Stuart who beat Doncaster by a head.

As a four and five-year-old Doncaster was successful in a number of races, among them the Goodwood Cup in 1874 and Ascot Gold Cup in 1875. On Merry's retirement from racing Robert Peck bought the horse for £10,000, selling him on to the Duke of Westminster for £14,000 shortly afterwards. The Duke put him to stud at Eaton where he sired Bend Or (Derby 1880) and a number of other successful foals before being exported to Austria for £5,000. Marie Stuart was bought by Mr Stirling Crawfurd but was not a success as a mare. Again Harry Hall painted the season's winners, but a portrait of Marie Stuart is so extremely ugly that it may account for it being seen in the salerooms so often at the time of writing.

1873 was James Merry's last good year on the turf. He was not well and, selling his horses in 1875, he died at his London home in Eaton Square two years later. He was in Parliament for the last eighteen years of his life, known to many as the Member for 'Thormanby'. This shrewd but in some matters other than racing, quite ignorant man must have had the determination of a dozen others put together. He forced his way through life, largely unloved, suspicious, making enemies quickly and being regarded askance by the turfites in whose lifestyles he so wanted to share. In a way a sad existence which cannot have been entirely compensated for by amassing wealth, although this second passion drove the first.

— 1874 —

When Tom French died in early 1873, Mathew Dawson made the sixteen-year-old Fred Archer the Heath House stable's first jockey. Archer was barely out of his apprenticeship which he started with Dawson in 1866. He came from Cheltenham where his father, a sometime inn-keeper, was also close to the less sophisticated world of steeplechasing, having himself been a useful rider for some years. Whether trotting to school on his pony or taking part in local donkey races, Fred Archer grew up in the saddle and it was only his increasing height which looked like defeating him in his ambition to be a successful 'flat' jockey. At nearly five feet nine inches, Archer was much taller than many of his profession, and in later years his efforts to lose weight by both purgatives and turkish baths were far fiercer than any other jockey could sensibly endure. He was a quiet young man whom Mathew Dawson, and particularly his wife, took in hand immediately he was apprenticed to the stables. They ensured he was both well educated and led a moral life based on the good Christian principles which were practised in the Dawson household. While these traits were inculcated into all the apprentices and lads who worked for Mathew Dawson, there arose a special relationship between the trainer and Archer. Apart from boyhood successes, Archer's first major victory was in the 1872 Cesarewitch when he rode Salvanos. From that year onward his progress was meteoric.

Archer's stoop, slightly rounded shoulders and cadaverous face provide an impression of a man less cheerful than many others of his fraternity, and this would be true. On his own two legs he looked awkward, but once in the saddle he became one with his mount and there was no greater contemporary example of man and beast in harmony. He was not an elegant horseman, but marvellously effective. He liked to bet, which at one period led to accusations of a conspiracy of jockeys, for there were others like him who, in cahoots with some bookmakers, were fixing the results of races. It is unlikely that Archer was a party to this, if such a Ring existed; Dawson would have sacked him instantly if he had been. Usually generous, but careful on occasions, Archer's nickname of 'The Tinman' was apt in regard to his interest in coins! Perhaps some of Dawson's Scottish thrift rubbed onto his apprentice who, in a very short time, became both a successful rider and affluent man, a combination rarely found among jockeys of the period.

Throughout the few years in which he rode with such success, Archer made clear to any enquiry the debts he owed to both Mathew Dawson and his frequent employer and admirer, Lord Falmouth. Of the latter, he once said:

> I owe most of my success to having been able to ride his horses with such confidence, knowing that if I did make a mistake coming a bit too soon or a bit too late, there would be no complaint, and his Lordship would be sure that I had ridden to the best of my ability.

This confidence was first established with Atlantic, one of Lord Falmouth's entries for the 2,000 Guineas of 1874. M. Lefèvre's Ecossais was the favourite although his trainer, Tom Jennings, was not as confident as the betting public appeared to be. The weather on Wednesday 6 May was enjoyable and Dawson had trained Atlantic to perfection, looking the best among what proved to be an unspectacular group of three-year-olds. At this time Archer was so slight in physique that he carried three stone dead weight in the race. There was only a slight delay at the start. Atlantic was a lazy horse by nature and Archer had to ride him hard the whole way, finally winning by a neck from Reverberation with Jeffery up. Ecossais (George Fordham) was a poor third in the race. This was the first meeting of Archer and Fordham, and it gave the Newmarket crowd a taste of things to come from Dawson's young ex-apprentice.

On the death of Colonel Nevile King in 1833, a number of his horses were entailed to his eldest son Clifford who died a bachelor eight years later. The stable then passed to the Reverend J. W. King, who felt bound to race those horses in training. He also bred some of his own and following the example of the late Colonel sent them for training to Ashgill. Manganese, trained by John Osborne Snr, won the 1,000 Guineas in 1856. In 1873 and 1874 the younger Osbornes, Robert the trainer and Johnnie the jockey, were aware of the promise of the two-year-olds belonging to the parson, Apology and Holy Friar. At this time, the Reverend King, who held two beneficiaries in Lincolnshire, one of which was Ashby-de-la-Launde, ran his horses in the name of 'Mr Launde', although he rarely attended a race meeting himself being now quite old. La Coureuse, who was heavily backed by all the Newmaket people, made most of the running in the 1,000 Guineas but was caught at the finish by Johnnie Osborne on Apology.

Mr W. S. Cartwright, who had mining interests in Wales, was plainly a loyal subject of the Queen since he named so many of his colts and fillies after members of the Royal family. Some years before, the veteran steeplechase jockey, Tom Oliver, in financial straits as usual, was made bankrupt and his goods and chattels were put up for sale to meet the demands of his creditors. Among his possessions due to come under the hammer was a favourite mare named The Bloomer. Tom liberally coated her with mud letting her out into a wet field with a shaggy donkey for company. Unsurprisingly there were no offers for The Bloomer and Tom was allowed to keep her for £1. A few days later Mr Cartwright bought The (cleaned up) Bloomer for £25 and installed Tom as his trainer at Wroughton near Swindon. The Bloomer dropped a foal named The Princess of Wales who in turn bore George Frederick in 1871, the year in which Cartwright's Albert Victor was second in the Derby and St Leger. Tom Oliver died in 1874 shortly after his position as trainer to Cartwright had been taken by Tom Leader. George Frederick was a heavy horse whom Leader worked extremely hard (Cartwright thought too hard) to bring him into the right shape for racing. As a two-year-old he won a few late season races including beating Apology at Doncaster. He grew fat again during the winter of 1873/4 and Leader again settled to the task of reducing his weight and improving his fitness. Recent rain laid the dust at Epsom which made the meeting for the large crowd more enjoyable than for many years. It was an omen perhaps that

Derby Day, 3 June, fell this year on the birthday of Prince George Frederick, but James Merry's Glenalmond was the favourite. After a good start at the second attempt an uninteresting race followed until Harry Custance sent George Frederick along at the beginning of the straight to win in a canter by two lengths. A few weeks later the name of the victor was given to Mr Cartwright's great-nephew who was born two days before the race. This was Custance's third Derby victory and his last Classic win before retiring from the turf a few years later. Lord Rosebery's Couronne de Feu (recently bought from Henry Padwick for £3,000) was second and Atlantic, on this occasion ridden by Tom Osborne, third. Apology won the Oaks convincingly and proved herself to be the best filly of the season by a large margin. The Osbornes were well pleased with her performance and started her preparation for the St Leger knowing she had a chance of winning, not least because George Frederick suffered a mishap after the Derby.

The bookmakers could find nothing good about the royally named colt who, shortly before the St Leger, was again lame and after much speculation was quite rightly scratched the day before the race. In the meantime, Apology was seen to stumble at her morning gallop at Doncaster which led to rumours that she too would not run. The betting was therefore in some turmoil. Lame or not, Apology won the race very comfortably from Sir Richard Bulkeley's Leolinus and Mr Marshall's Trent. This was the first time for ten years that a northern horse had won the St Leger. Apology and the Osbornes were given a tremendous cheer by the crowd as they returned to weigh in.

A sequel to Apology's St Leger was the correspondence between the Bishop of Lincoln, Christopher Wordsworth, and the Reverend John King. Earlier in the season the Bishop had written to the parson remonstrating with him and suggesting quite forcefully that running horses in races did not befit the position of a clergyman, however quietly he went about pursuing this extra-ecclesiastical interest. King replied that he was sending the Bishop's letter to his solicitor to discover if the latter had any legal jurisdiction in this matter; and so the problem seemed to rest until the St Leger when Apology appeared to cock-a-snook, as it were, at the Bishop. Wordsworth immediately wrote again to King using the correspondence columns of The Times as a vehicle to give weight to his disapproval while demonstrating his compassion by pleading with the parson to desist.

It is with very great regret that I see from the public papers describing the races at Doncaster ... that my former remonstrance to you has been of no avail. I had hoped that you might have been induced . . . by regard for your own spiritual welfare as well as that of others, to listen to my earnest expostulations. I perceive you have shown no signs of remorse for your offence in bringing discredit on your sacred profession . . . by training racehorses for the turf instead of devoting yourself entirely to the work to which you pledged yourself at your ordination.

and much more in the same tone, followed by:

I now entreat you once more, solemnly and affectionately . . . either resign your pastoral cures or else to relinquish a course . . . at variance with the sacred obligations by which you are bound as a clergyman of the Church of England.

Bearing in mind that the Reverend King was aged eighty-one, had recently broken a thigh, was ill and by no stretch of the imagination could be numbered among the fast and loose element of owners or turfites, the letter was pretty heavy stuff, even from his diocesan.

King replied firmly that he had bred horses for fifty years improving the strain inherited from his brother, and that racing was almost incidental to this interest. He also wrote again that the Bishop had little standing in law either to order him to stop racing or remove him from his livings.

If, therefore, I resign the livings which I hold within your Lordship's diocese, it will not be from any consciousness of wrong, or from fear of any consequences which might ensue in the ecclesiastical Courts, but simply because I desire to live the remainder of my days in peace and charity with all men, and to save your Lordship the annoyance, and the Church the scandal of futile proceedings being taken against one who has retired for some time from parochial ministrations, and is lying on the bed of sickness at this moment.

King resigned his livings a month before he died on 9 May 1875.

Apology met with mixed fortunes as a four and five-year-old (Ascot Gold Cup, 1876) running in the name of Mr Seabrooke, but owned by King's widow. This 'Mr Seabrooke' was in fact C. Brook (Charles Brook, a son of W.H. Brook), an old friend of the parson and executor of his will. The horse was finally sold to Mr Vinet.

— 1875 —

Mr Clare Vyner was a very popular sportsman from Yorkshire; cheerful, kind-hearted and considerate to all with whom he came in contact. He kept a few

horses with John Osborne Snr and later, to be based at Newmarket, others were trained by Mathew Dawson and usually ridden by Johnnie Osborne. His only Classic victory was in the 1875 2,000 Guineas with Camballo. As a two-year-old Camballo won a number of races and came to the Guineas as the 7 to 2 favourite. Craig Millar, owned by Mr Stirling Crawfurd, was second favourite at 5 to 1 against with Balfe (who later beat Camballo), in third place in the betting. In the race Johnnie Osborne had little difficulty in bringing his horse to the front, heading off a challenge by M. Lefèvre's Picnic ridden by George Fordman. Lord Fitzwilliam's Breechloader was third; Craig Millar came in sixth.

Mathew Dawson was not only the most successful trainer of his day but probably the most highly respected. He was always in good spirits and thought the training and racing of horses was a sport and occupation to be enjoyed. He was also a self-educated, cultured man with a very strong belief in his Church which he also imbued in those who worked for him. Polite, with an even temperament, Dawson knew his position exactly both as an employee and friend of those owners who entrusted their horses to his care. His relationship with Lord Falmouth over a period of years suffered only one brief spasm of disagreement which was quickly resolved by Mathew's brother Joseph acting as a mediator. Each loved horses in their own way which was the bond between them. There are a number of references to show that Dawson and Harry Hall were great friends and many of his paintings of Falmouth's horses were on the walls of Heath House and later at Exning.

Lord Falmouth's filly Spinaway won the 1,000 Guineas and the Oaks in 1875 with Fred Archer in the saddle on both occasions. In the Oaks, Falmouth also owned Ladylove (ridden by Constable) who was the runner-up three lengths behind Spinaway. Attempts were made by some members of the Jockey Club to stop the practice of allowing jockeys deliberately to pull up a horse entered in a race as a pacemaker or for any other reason. This often led to ill-feeling and sometimes doubts over the real instructions of an owner if his declared horse ran badly and, perchance, he pulled off a betting coup elsewhere in the race! Strangely, the majority of the members of the Club threw out this proposal as interfering with the rights of owners to run horses as they pleased. In the Oaks, Lord Falmouth declared both his fillies would run on their merits.

Count Gustavus Batthyany came to England from Hungary when a young man and soon assimilated so many English habits and interests that to all intents and purposes he was regarded as a citizen of his adopted country. He was not a gambler and his interest in racing was based on a love of horses and the sports in which they were involved. He was also a keen amateur jockey but, being not much good, his offers to ride others' horses were rarely taken up! He lived for most of the year at Newmarket where his kindness to the poor and less fortunate inhabitants of the town became legendary. Batthyany started racing with a small stud in 1843 but had little success for the next twenty years; however, his enthusiasm and popularity were recognised by his election to membership of the Jockey Club in 1859. In 1870 he succeeded to the title of an older brother who died, becoming Prince Batthyany. The responsibilities of his elevation removed him from the English turf for a year or two, but no longer. In 1873, Batthyany bought a yearling named Galopin for 520 guineas. The colt was by Vedette (a son of Voltigeur) out of Flying Duchess (by The Flying Dutchman) and much was expected of him. Galopin went well in trials as a youngster and was successful as a two-year-old as well. Some weeks before the Derby the colt won a £500-a-side Match against Mr Henry Chaplin's very good filly, Stray Shot, which made Galopin the favourite for the Derby. At Epsom Camballo was unsound and Holy Friar who might well have been favourite was out of the race due to his owner's recent death.

Galopin, trained by John Dawson (yet another son of George Dawson of Gullane), did not appear in the paddock since his temper was suspect and he had to be kept calm and quiet before the start. The race itself was unspectacular with the colt an easy winner ridden by Jack Morris. Morris was very deaf and the story goes that at one stage in the race George Fordham on Lagrange's Gilbert, knowing he had no hope himself, shouted to Morris: 'Go on, Deafie', when he saw Maidment on Claremont creeping up on Galopin. Claremont was second and a colt belonging to Lord Falmouth third. The crowd gave Prince Batthyany an immense cheer to show their affection for this true sportsman and generous supporter of the turf. Galopin was put to stud at the end of the season to save him from punishment, this being Batthyany's wish. His fondness for Galopin extended to the stallion's progeny among whom was a fine colt named Galliard, the favourite for the 1883 2,000 Guineas, owned by Falmouth. The Prince's heart was always weak and

after animatedly discussing Galliard's prospects he was making his way to the stand luncheon room when he collapsed and died instantly. His death in ordinary circumstances would have been regretted by a wide circle of friends; as it was, this dramatic departure became something of a sensation, with the public deploring the sudden removal from their midst of a friendly and familiar figure.

There were 'poor cattle in this year's Leger field'. Claremont, Camballo and a well-fancied French horse named Salvator were scratched through mishaps in training; and Spinaway and Galopin were not entered. The way was therefore left open for Craig Millar, ridden by Tom Challoner, to provide a very popular win for Mr Stirling Crawfurd who was now racing on a much larger scale but without commensurate success.

Harry Hall continued to exhibit paintings at the Royal Society of British Artists and in this year the Ipswich Fine Art Club held its first of many annual exhibitions. Hall sent in two paintings: 'Mares and Foals', the property of Lord Falmouth; and 'Happy Joe', which were very favourably noted in the *Suffolk Chronicle* on 23 January 1875:

Mr Harry Hall's Mares and Foals, No. 4, and Happy Joe, No. 247, are, of course, excellent. Joe looks happy enough, and the donkey as though he knew that Joe meant him to go. Possibly Joe grew after he mounted his charger; to look at, he is rather long in the barrel.

The low regard in which the turf was still held by many people was illustrated by the experience of the Reverend J. W. King at the hands of his Bishop. Quite apart from the need to express the new Victorian morals and dictate changes in the behaviour expected of the country's churchmen, few of whom still rode to hounds, there was no doubt a hope in some hearts that the turf was on its last legs. However, with the financial state of the Jockey Club now much sounder due to the efforts of Admiral Rous, the Stewards and Committees were better able to direct improvements countrywide, preventing just a few of the evil practices of the bookmakers who previously had nearly everything going their way. Even so, progress was extremely slow.

CHAPTER 8

1876—1881

When Hope herself might well despair,
When Time had not a breath to spare,
With bird-like dash shoots clean away
And by a neck has gained the day.

IN JANUARY 1876 turfites were surprised but delighted to discover that Mr W. Stirling Crawfurd had married Caroline, Duchess of Montrose, the widow of the fourth Duke of Montrose. The surprise lay in the very different characters of the two now joined together. Crawfurd was reticent to say the very least while the Duchess was an extremely outspoken extrovert. The bond between them was racing. The Duke of Montrose had not been interested in the turf but Caroline Beresford (her maiden name) was a member of a family well known for its sporting activities, of which racing was the principal pastime. The joint interest made Stirling Crawfurd's few remaining years all that more enjoyable when his health was beginning to deteriorate. Mrs Stirling Crawfurd immediately gave a new impetus to his stables by her vigorous management which produced a string of good results. He died in 1883. Mrs Crawfurd then took over her late husband's colours (all scarlet), his horses and trainer, Alec Taylor, and raced in the name of 'Mr Manton'.

George Robert Hay was the eldest son of the twelfth Earl of Kinnoull; he was styled Viscount Dupplin at the age of eighteen. After a short period in the Life Guards, Lord Dupplin settled down to enjoy himself on the turf. His horses were trained by John Dawson and in 1875, in conjunction with Colonels Oliphant and Farquharson, he bought the successful two-year-old Petrarch from a Mr Spencer for the sum of £10,000. Being a headstrong young man, Dupplin insisted that the unfit Petrarch be tried against another of his colts, Kaleidoscope, in the early spring of 1876. Dawson advised against this and his views were partly justified by Kaleidoscope's easy win. Lord Dupplin then backed Kaleidoscope for the 2,000 Guineas, perhaps to cover bets he had made earlier on Petrarch in the same race. The Guineas was run on 3 May before a good crowd at Newmarket. In the race,

Petrarch ridden by his stable lad H. Luke, quietly slaughtered the opposition in the form of Robert Peck's Julius Caesar and Kaleidoscope, third. Lord Dupplin's initial faith in Petrarch was rewarded by the long odds which he had obtained. He made a considerable coup despite the losses on his other colt. He now looked forward with enthusiastic anticipation to the Derby in which Petrarch was the favourite.

With the Franco-Prussian War well behind them, Count Frederic de Lagrange and his confederates again raced horses on the English turf until the Count ran into financial difficulties in 1883. Tom Jennings continued to be Lagrange's trainer at Newmarket. The 1,000 Guineas of 1876 was a triumph for the French who took the first three places. The Count's Camelia, ridden by T. Glover (known as Tommy Clover) was first, and his Allumette with Morris up was second. In the other fillies' Classic, the Oaks, Enguerrande owned by M. Auguste Lupin and ridden by Hudson crept up on Camelia at the post and made a dead heat of the race. The stake was divided and Enguerrande walked-over, disappointing many of the Epsom crowd who would have preferred to see a run-off between the French horses.

The brothers Alexander, Hector and Aristides Baltazzi were of 'Levantine' Greek origin. The first two formed a stud in England in the mid-1870s and were immediately successful. Their few horses were trained by Joseph Hayhoe at Newmarket and ran in Alexander's name, for Hector enjoyed the hunting field more than the racecourse, although he was also an amateur rider of note. There was some suspicion of the Baltazzis' gambling activities which were on a large scale, but just as Mr George Payne had helped M. Lefèvre to enter the turf, so did Sir George Chetwynd sponsor the Baltazzi brothers. They bought a yearling from the Hungarian Imperial Stud at Kisber

74 *Lord Falmouth's Silvio (Derby and St Leger, 1877). Engraving by E.G. Hester* Sterling and Francine Clark Art Institute, Williamstown, Massachusetts, USA

and gave the colt the name from whence he came. The horse was in fact entirely English in that his sire was Buccaneer and dam Mineral, a daughter of Manganese bred by the late Reverend John King of Ashby-de-la-Launde. Kisber thrived on his work and came to the Derby as second favourite to Petrarch.

The weather was pleasant and the crowd at Epsom as numerous as ever. After a good start and some hard riding by Morris, Petrarch came to Tattenham Corner well in front and was looking a comfortable winner. However, below the distance Robert Peck's Forerunner and Julius Caesar challenged, as did Kisber. Petrarch fell back and Maidment on Kisber ran on to win by five lengths. Lord Dupplin's horse was fourth. For the second year running the Blue Riband was won by a foreigner which, for some reason, was now a less bitter pill for English turfites to swallow.

The Baltazzi brothers won between £60,000 and £100,000 on the race. Kisber went on to win the Grand Prix de Paris a few days later but inexplicably, if one disregards nobbling, ran a bad fourth in the St Leger when his jockey, Johnnie Osborne, considered him beaten before he started. The colt did not run again and was a moderate success at stud.

Between the Derby and St Leger, Petrarch's performance continued to be erratic, but he was second favourite to Kisber at Doncaster. Both horses were reported to be looking supremely fit in the saddling enclosure although Petrarch was fractious at the start. The race produced a most exciting struggle ending in victory for Petrach a neck in front of the Duke of Hamilton's Wild Tommy. On this occasion Petrarch was ridden by the accomplished jockey James Goater, who normally rode Count Frederic's horses. The steady Julius Caesar was third and everybody wished that Robert Peck could be rewarded with a Classic win as he approached the end of his career as a trainer and owner. Viscount Dupplin continued to race but never again quite reached the heights won for him by Petrarch. In 1886 he died very suddenly at Monte Carlo aged only thirty-six.

Harry Hall painted a number of portraits of Kisber, one of which was engraved by E. G. Hester and published by Baily Brothers in their now intermittent series of Derby winners. Earlier in the year he painted a portrait of Regal, Captain Machell's 1876 Grand National winner. The background in this painting includes trees and rather rougher country than that seen in his portraits of 'flat' horses. This difference provides a useful starting point if one is searching for the identity of a racehorse whose name has been lost. Among the four paintings which Hall exhibited at the Ipswich Fine Art Club this year there was a rare landscape; 'Sketch of Stand and Stables on Bunbury Mile, Newmarket', which formed the back-cloth of many of his racehorse portraits.

— 1877 —

The general public resented French, German and later American horses winning important races and stakes in England as an affront to their pride. The English owners were more specific in their complaint since the French did not allow them to run their horses in France except in the Grand Prix de Paris. This lack of reciprocity rankled and Lord Falmouth discussed the subject with other members of the Jockey Club in 1874. Admiral Rous was keen to maintain harmonious relations with France and wrote to the Société d'Encouragement, the French racing authority, explaining the irritation caused by the one-sided rules which allowed foreign horses to carry off English stakes but not vice versa. Also germane to the matter were the facts that French racing was in part the child of Englishmen's enthusiasm, and the blood of nearly every French horse came from English thoroughbreds. The Société's President, Vicomte Daru, was politely evasive in his reply saying that the Société had little influence over the conditions of races made by towns, railway companies and individuals who donated their prizes. The lack of progress in the matter led Lord Falmouth to put down a motion on the subject in 1877 for consideration of the Jockey Club. In summary, he proposed to close many English races to foreign horses unless their country of origin opened theirs on equal terms to British horses. The excitement which this proposition raised was almost as much as that engendered by Sir Joseph Hawley's earlier 'reforms'. Admiral Rous was in a quandary since he considered all races should be open to everybody, letting 'the best horse win'. Also he was not a substantial owner and was less hurt by the sight of valuable stakes disappearing abroad instead of being used to maintain and improve British studs. The Admiral now wrote to his friend M. Auguste Lupin declaring, among other arguments:

> A feeling exists in England that you take advantage of our free-trade policy; and that you deny us privileges which we freely accord. Such an imputation must disgust every true Frenchman!

Well, not as many as he hoped, for nothing happened! In the meantime, the unassuming Falmouth did not press his motion since he had no wish to be in conflict with the ageing Admiral. In the end the torch he lit fizzled out and reciprocity remained as sore a point as ever; a point sharpened by the result of the 1877 2,000 Guineas.

Lord Falmouth bred Silvio himself. The colt was a competent but not outstanding two-year-old, but in the spring of 1877 easily won a good trial among other horses owned by Falmouth and trained by Mat Dawson. In the Guineas, Silvio was seen to be in trouble within the distance and began giving way to the American horse Brown Prince who in turn failed to overtake Count Frederic de Lagrange's magnificent bay, Chamant. James Goater on the French horse held on to win comfortably by a length. This was one of the early occasions when the English public also realised that they could no longer totally despise American horses who were beginning to make an impact on the turf.

Belphoebe, ridden by H. Jeffery won the 1,000 Guineas. The filly belonged to Lord Hartington who earlier in his life raced in the name of Mr J. C. Stuart. The Marquis of Hartington, before succeeding the seventh Duke of Devonshire in 1891, was a politician who spent many years occupying the highest offices of State between rejecting offers of the Premiership. He is dealt with so unkindly in 'Men and Members of Parliament, 1874' as a:

> hardworking, conscientious, stolid man, wearing all the polish he is capable of receiving from high education and social intercourse, but withal slightly surly in manner, greatly impressed with the vast gulf that is fixed between Marquis and man, . . . innocent of the slightest spark of humour,

that one is bound to warm to his interest in racing, which remained throughout his life whenever he could spare a moment to pursue it.

The favourite for the Derby was Rob Roy, a Blair Athol colt owned by Mr J. T. Mackenzie. Chamant was second in the betting at 4 to 1 with Silvio well down the list at 100 to 9 against. There were fewer spectators at Epsom than usual, perhaps due to there being no really outstanding horse or the promise of an exciting race. Fred Archer was still comparatively unknown and his presence was not to act as a magnet in drawing crowds for another year or so. Tom Jennings led Chamant in the saddling paddock; the horse looked fit and only the owner and trainer were aware of the slight accident he had met with shortly before the race. Silvio was plainly in good form but Archer with his drooping shoulders and languid air gave no hint of how the outsider might run. The seventeen were away to a good start at the first attempt. At the distance Rob Roy went to the front and by the cheering of the crowd was assumed to have the race for the asking. A few strides on and Archer brought Silvio (Plate 74) up with a rush on the lower ground to overhaul Mr Mackenzie's colt, and also Glen Arthur, winning by half a length. The victory was warmly received by the crowd who were beginning to follow the Falmouth-Archer combination with increasing interest. An attraction, but also a difficulty for gamblers, was that Falmouth never laid a proper bet (which others could follow) in his life, resulting in his horses winning in a straightforward manner.

After the Derby, the weather changed for the worse and the Oaks was run in atrocious conditions. Part of the roof of Barnard's stand blew off and the enclosure and much of the course was in a very wet state on 1 June. Belphoebe made a great effort in the last hundred yards but could not catch Mr Pulteney's strong brown filly, Placida, with Jeffery up, who rode a clever race to establish himself as a sound if unexciting jockey.

Admiral Rous was at Epsom and attended the Prince of Wales's annual Derby night dinner which he gave to the members of the Jockey Club at Marlborough House, but the 82-year-old sailor appeared to have lost some of his usual high spirits. His health and strength faded quickly and he died in London on 20 June. His funeral was a quiet one, attended by the Prince of Wales and a few of his old friends, among them his boon companion, Mr George Payne. The Admiral's decisions on both the rules of racing and handicapping were sometimes questioned in his later years; questioned gently since nobody wished directly to confront a man whose life's work had been to improve racing in every way he thought possible. The oracle, dictator and true sportsman left a gap in the hierarchy of the turf which has not since been filled in quite the same way, with such devotion and effort as that given to it by Admiral Rous.

Silvio, with Archer up, was favourite for the St Leger, winning in a canter from his stable companion Lady Golightly (fourth in the Oaks) ridden by Jack Morris. Falmouth called upon Harry Hall to paint his two horses together, a formula employed on other occasions when the Viscount owned both the winner and the runner-up in a Classic race.

There is a note in the *Illustrated London News* this year of the Prince of Wales taking delivery of a portrait of Stockwell, by Harry Hall, but this painting seems to have disappeared from the Royal Collections. However, in 1877 Queen Victoria commissioned Hall to paint Springfield in a stall with his trainer James Ryan. This picture is now at Windsor Castle. In 1876/7, the Prince of Wales asked Harry Hall to paint the Grand National Winner Regal and also a favourite hunter, Paddy. The latter is shown saddled and standing outside a wood held by the stud groom J. W. Prince. The painting, signed: 'Harry Hall, Newmarket, 1877,' is at Buckingham Palace and a small sketch of it dated 9 April 1877 is at Sandringham. This Royal patronage gave a seal of approval to Hall's standing in society as much as to his painting skill.

— 1878 —

Crucifix pulled off the remarkable double of winning the 2,000 and 1,000 Guineas in 1840. This feat was not repeated until 1878 when Pilgrimage won both races outright; a performance of slightly greater merit than that of Formosa who ran a dead heat in the Guineas ten years before, conceding a walk-over to Moslem to save the filly for the second race which she won. Pilgrimage was bred by Mr Cookson who sold her to Mr Gerard (later Lord Gerard) in 1876; she was then bought by Captain Machell on behalf of the young fourth Earl of Lonsdale in September 1877. The Lonsdale title had passed in quick succession from the second Earl to his nephew and then to the latter's son between 1872 and 1876. The fourth Earl, who was styled Viscount Lowther during this period, died at the age of twenty-six in February 1882. The only previous 'Lowther' or Lonsdale Classic victory was with Spaniel in the 1831 Derby, owned by the son of the first Earl, himself a noted turfite in his day.

Pilgrimage had a suspicious leg but the going was good at Newmarket when overnight rain softened the hard ground. Tom Cannon rode a clever race to win from Count Frederic de Lagrange's Insulaire; Mr Stirling Crawfurd's Sefton was third and Lord Falmouth's Childeric fourth. In the 1,000 Guineas Pilgrimage beat Falmouth's charming little filly Jannette. Lord Lonsdale's filly was not entered for the Derby and Crawfurd took his first Blue Riband with Sefton. Insulaire was second and Childeric third which, with the absence of Pilgrimage, almost repeated the 2,000 Guineas placings. In the Oaks Jannette took her revenge on Pilgrimage who ran gallantly but finished very lame. Finally, in the St Leger, Jannette beat her stable companion Childeric by four lengths; the two horses were recorded in one painting by Harry Hall.

None of these animals was outstanding. However the five races provided the public with the enjoyment of seeing four respected owners, one with a longstanding turf background and three with considerable recent experience and success vying with each other for the honour of leading in their winners, (only the Frenchman failed in this respect!), and a demonstration of the skills of the best jockeys of the period.

Cannon rode Pilgrimage in the 2,000, 1,000 and Oaks; Jim Goater was on Insulaire and Harry Constable on Sefton for the Guineas and Derby; Archer on Jannette in the 1,000, Oaks and St Leger, and on Childeric in the Derby; while Harry Custance rode Childeric in the St Leger. All five were honest and straightforward men riding to the best of their abilities. Although bookmakers and other scoundrels went on attempting to fix races for their own ends, the occasions when they could influence a result with the help of a jockey became fewer and fewer. There were still instances when it was thought a rider, even Fred Archer, might have pulled his horse for some devious reason. At a later date these accusations were often seen to have been false when it became clear a horse could not stay, was no good on certain going or had been over-trained, however fit the appearance of the animal in the paddock. It would be wrong to say that blackguards were disappearing completely from racing in the late 1870s, but there was certainly a long awaited improvement in the standards and practices of those involved. The wish to reduce the elements of chance in gambling will always lead to malpractices, but some of the more desperate and crude methods of achieving such aims were on the wane.

Just a year after a small group of friends laid Admiral Rous to rest by his wife at Kensal Green Cemetery, a larger assembly, again led by the Prince of Wales, returned to the same place for the burial of Mr George Payne. When he came of age in 1824 (his father died of a wound received in a duel in 1810), George Payne inherited £300,000 and estates in Northamptonshire, including the family home at Sulby Hall, which brought in an income of £17,000 a year. It did not take him very long to lose this fortune. High living and, most of all gambling, both at cards and on the turf, saw his money slip away in tranches of tens of thousands. Two other fortunes went much the same way until he had to sell Sulby and partly reform his ways. From the 1840s George Payne led a quieter life which temporarily gathered pace when Lord Glasgow left him £25,000 and half his racing stud. Despite his ruinous ways, Payne was a charming, kind-hearted and popular gentleman who was a cheerful and true companion to such diverse turfites as Charles Greville and Lord George Bentinck. As an owner he had little luck, winning only one Classic race, the 1847 1,000 Guineas with Clementina ridden by his favourite jockey, Nat Flatman.

While unsuccessful himself, his opinion and advice on other people's horses or about the rules of racing were highly respected. In this way, combined with his indomitable humour, he always supported his intimate friend Admiral Rous. It is interesting to note that in Hall's large picture of The Great Match of 1851 (Plate 23), the central portraits of the painting are of Rous and Payne. When the Admiral's wife died they became inseparable friends whether at Newmarket or in London; Payne still playing cards while Rous, who disliked such games, played billiards for smaller stakes. Those who attended the two funerals must have wondered if the turf could ever be quite the same again without those two colossi of the Jockey Club. No doubt it was.

— 1879 —

The death of General Peel in February 1879 robbed the turf of not only one of its most distinguished patrons, but also the running of his promising colt Peter, who was entered for the 2,000 Guineas and the Derby that year. Jonathan Peel was commissioned into the Army three days before the Battle of Waterloo. The comparatively peaceful years which followed denied him opportunities to serve abroad and the distinctions which, by his character and resolve, he must otherwise have gained. He progressed steadily through the ranks from Ensign to General, partly by purchase, while spending much of his time on the turf, a passion which developed early in his life. Captain Peel won a few races in the 1820s, but it was not until 1832 that as Colonel Peel, in partnership with General Yates, he secured his first Classic victory with Archibald in the 2,000 Guineas. Twelve years later he won the Derby with Orlando when Running Rein was disqualified. Thereafter, General Peel, as he became, had little success despite the best efforts of his trainer Robert Peck at Russley. He was a tall, commanding figure who, while looking austere, had the kindest nature and far more humour and fun than his statesman eldest brother, Sir Robert Peel. His death at the age of eighty sounded the knell of the giants of old personified by Admiral Rous, George Payne and Lords Exeter and Glasgow, all of whom were firm friends. Lord Glasgow was known to his companions as 'Peter', the name given by Peel to his horse, reciprocating Glasgow's naming his best horse General Peel, (2,000 Guineas, 1864). Without Peter the 1879 crop of three-year-olds was very mediocre.

The racing trio comprising Lord Falmouth, Mathew Dawson and Fred Archer now provided the winners of so many races that Lord Rosebery printed a special form on which to send his congratulations after each success. It was therefore surprising that Falmouth's Charibert should start for the 2,000 Guineas at 25 to 1 against. The public were at a loss to know where to put their money having examined the relatively poor quality of the field; the bookmakers were in much the same fix. Charibert with Archer up went into a clear lead from Lord Douglas Gordon's Cadogan at the distance and won by a length and a half. Count Frederic de Lagrange's Rayon D'Or was a poor third. Two days later Wheel of Fortune, a filly of exceptional merit, also belonging to Falmouth and ridden by Archer, won the 1,000 Guineas from an undistinguished field of eight. As in 1878, the Guineas 'double' was won by the same owner, but this year with different horses.

Baron Meyer de Rothschild died in 1874. The family name temporarily disappeared from the lists of owners of Classic winners until resurfacing again in 1876 in the guise of 'Mr Acton'. The horses of Lionel Nathan de Rothschild, Baron Meyer's eldest brother, were trained at Acton, then on the edge of London, and were managed and entered for races by his youngest son, Mr Leopold de Rothschild.

Two Rothschild horses ran in the Derby: Sir Bevys and Squirrel. Sir Bevys won a race as a two-year-old but showed little form in trials before Epsom. However, the colt was ridden by George Fordham and there was no keener jockey than he to win the elusive Blue Riband of the turf. 'The Demon's' first Classic victory was on Mr Stirling Crawfurd's Mayonaise in the 1,000 Guineas in 1859, since which year he rode the winners of a further four 1,000 Guineas, two 2,000 Guineas (one of which was a dead heat on Formosa) and four Oaks. Fordham had left racing in 1876, ill with depression, but after a financial crash managed to pull himself together and was persuaded to ride again. The racing public was delighted by his return in 1878 for there was no more honest rider in the business, although there were many more elegant in the saddle! When Fordham nursed the moderate Sir Bevys through a sea of mud in the 1879 Derby, the crowd cheered as much for the fact that The Demon had won a Derby at last, as for the race falling to the popular Mr Leopold de Rothschild. Archer rode Charibert again in the Derby and came nowhere. The Tinman was a great admirer of Fordham and while he hated not winning a race, the hurt was less when inflicted by The Demon. Harry Hall painted Sir Bevys at Epsom and this picture was exhibited at the Ipswich Fine Art Club the following year.

For the Oaks, Lord Falmouth's Wheel of Fortune appeared in the paddock looking the fittest of yet another moderate lot. It was noted however that her trainer Mathew Dawson was not present as might have been expected. The evening before the race Tom Jennings called on Dawson to while away an hour or two discussing turf matters with his longstanding friend. Robert Peck was also present. The talk turned, as it often did, to the running of French horses in England. Peck said they should all be packed off back to France and prevailed on Dawson to take his side. Jennings, loyal to his French masters, naturally disagreed and decided to leave. A short fracas then ensued in which Jennings landed a punch on Dawson's eye. The following morning a very contrite but busy Tom Jennings sent his son to apologise sincerely to Mathew Dawson. The latter immediately sent messages of goodwill to Tom, blaming Peck for stirring up the trouble in the first place. However, Dawson did not feel he could quite face going onto the course with a bandage over his eye and a rather lame tale of being in a fight. Notwithstanding his absence, Wheel of Fortune won the Oaks in convincing style.

Lionel Nathan de Rothschild died on 3 June 1879 and there was speculation whether Sir Bevys would be able to complete his future engagements, including the St Leger. As mentioned already, the horse's nominator was in fact Leopold de Rothschild, or Mr Acton. In the event Sir Bevys proved a 'roarer' and ran miserably at Doncaster. Wheel of Fortune was also lame and unable to run leaving the way clear for Count Frederic de Lagrange's Rayon D'Or. The colt, ridden by James Goater, went straight to the front once the field had settled down, was never headed, hardly challenged and became the winner by five lengths giving Count Frederic his second St Leger and last English Classic victory.

Harry Hall portrayed nearly all Viscount Falmouth's Classic winners up to the end of this year, and no doubt would have continued to do so if there had been any more to paint before his own death in 1882, but there were not. Falmouth was Hall's most consistent patron and it seems certain that it was the artist's friend Mathew Dawson (who himself commissioned a number of paintings from Hall) who recommended that Falmouth employ Harry Hall to record his brilliant procession of colts and fillies. As well as these portraits, including one of Lady Coventry shown at Ipswich in 1879, Lord Falmouth asked Hall to paint groups of his mares and foals at Mereworth Castle: paintings which show the artist at his best, both in general composition and the conformation of horses.

— 1880 —

The eighth Duke of Beaufort, called The Blue Duke after the colour of the Beaufort Hunt uniform, was the best known sporting figure of his day. As well as owning racehorses he was a fine shot, fisherman and above all the Master of the Beaufort which was the best found hunt with the best bred foxhounds in the country. Sport was provided on six days a week in Gloucestershire during the season. In the summer the Duke turned his mind to racing, when he was not smothering the scandals surrounding his two younger sons which ended in their both having to go abroad, the first in 1879. In 1880 the Duke's horses were under the able management of Captain Machell. His Grace's three earlier Classic winners (Siberia, 1,000 Guineas, 1865; Vauban, 2,000 Guineas, 1867; and Scottish Queen, 1,000 Guineas, 1869) were all ridden by George Fordham. It was The Demon again who rode Petronel to victory in the 2,000 Guineas wearing the now familiar blue and white hoops with red cap.

Mr T. E. Walker's Elizabeth, ridden by Charles Wood, won the 1,000 Guineas on a day which was described as 'one of the worst programmes ever presented to the public at Newmarket'. There was still the argument put forward by some members of the Jockey Club that the Heath was for training, trials and private Matches, rather than the venue to which the public should flock to enjoy a full card of races with large fields. What the same members did not seem to appreciate was that the prestige of their Club was diminished by the unsatisfactory standard of racing at their own headquarters.

The wealth of the Grosvenor family was significantly increased when the second Marquis of Westminster married a daughter of the immensely rich Duke and Duchess-Countess of Sutherland. Their son, Hugh Lupus Grosvenor, born in 1825, became the third Marquis in 1869. He married his cousin, a daughter of the second Duke of Sutherland. It was suggested that such money and the power which it attracted could no longer be ignored, quite apart from the Grosvenors probably being more wealthy than the Queen. Gladstone, the Prime Minister, therefore included the Marquis's name in his 1874 dissolution honours:

> My dear Westminster, [he wrote] I have received authority from the Queen to place a Dukedom at your disposal and I hope you may accept it, for both you and Lady Westminster will wear it right nobly.

followed somewhat dramatically by:

> With my dying breath, Yours sincerely, W. E. Gladstone.

The Duke appeared to those who did not know him as an austere and uncommunicative man, and much the same impression was made upon his friends! He was an outstanding horseman who loved hunting but at first seemed to have little time for or interest in racing. The stud at Eaton in Cheshire had languished with poor quality animals and no racing successes since the death of the first Marquis in 1845. Lord Rosebery persuaded the Duke to engage Robert Peck as his trainer. Peck, a determined man, although suffering ill health, set about rejuvenating the names of Grosvenor and Westminster on the turf. An impediment to progress was the Duke's well known inability to make up his mind quickly and his opposite facility to change what he had recently decided. This sometimes led Peck to take an initiative upon himself

75 *The Duke of Westminster's Bend Or, Fred Archer up (Derby, 1880)*   Arthur Ackermann & Son Ltd.

to improve his master's racing fortunes. In 1874 the trainer had bought Mr James Merry's 1873 Derby winner, Doncaster, whom he now persuaded the Duke to buy from him for £14,000, a considerable sum to anybody but Westminster. A number of high class mares were also bought and sent to Eaton, but it was not until 1880 that the first significant results were achieved and the Duke's enthusiasm for breeding and racing thoroughly aroused. Bend Or was one of Doncaster's first crop of foals. His dam, Rouge Rose, bought from General Pearson, was a half-sister of the dam of Lord Lyon (Triple Crown, 1866) and Achievement (1,000 Guineas and St Leger, 1867). Bend Or, trained at Russley by Peck, won a number of good races as a two-year-old and was the 2 to 1 favourite for the Derby in which he was ridden by Archer.

On 1 May 1880, Archer was exercising a four-year-old belonging to Lord Falmouth, Muley Edris, whom the jockey had punished severely some time before. The horse had not forgotten, and when Archer dismounted he suddenly grabbed his arm and lifting him off the ground started to carry the struggling Tinman across Newmarket Heath. Muley Edris then dropped him and kneeling on his body was determined to kill the man who had thrashed him. Fortunately one of the horse's hind legs slipped to one side and he fell over. Probably startled by the fall, Muley Edris bolted away while Archer was lifted to his feet badly shaken and with a severely lacerated arm. Lord Falmouth arranged for the best surgeons to attend to his jockey who feared he might never have the strength to ride again. After three weeks in plaster the limb was partly healed but by that time the jockey's weight had shot up. Although hardly able to use his arm, Archer thought himself sufficiently fit to ride Bend Or, despite having to weaken himself further by losing a stone in weight during the few days which remained before the Derby on 26 May.

Mr McGeorge, still the official Starter, made a good job of sending the nineteen runners away together, if a little late. The third favourite, Robert the Devil owned by Mr Charles Brewer and ridden by a jockey named Rossiter, seemed to be in a commanding and unassailable lead from the halfway mark. In the straight The Tinman, riding with only one effective hand, crept up inch by inch with Bend Or to narrow the gap, cheered on by a wildly excited crowd. Two strides from the post they were level, and at the finish Bend Or won by a head. Prince Soltykoff's Mask was third and Lord Falmouth's Apollo ridden by Charles Wood fourth. Two weeks after the race, Brewer objected to the winner on the grounds that Bend Or was in fact a horse named Tadcaster, and that a mix-up of the two had occurred when the Duke

of Westminster's yearlings were sent from Eaton Hall to Russley. After taking evidence the Stewards of the Jockey Club decided unanimously that Bend Or was Bend Or. A few years later however, after Brewer had died, some new information came to light which cast doubt on the Stewards' decision and it is possible that it was Tadcaster who won the 1880 Derby and a number of subsequent races.

Jim Snowden, on one of his more sober days, rode Mr Charles Perkin's filly Jenny Howlet to victory in the Oaks. The field of thirteen, slightly larger than in recent years, was of very poor quality.

The 1880 St Leger took place in a blinding storm on 15 September, with the result that when the 'Umbrellas down' was shouted as the horses left the paddock few heeded it, until the demand was backed up by some unseemly struggling. The start was an excellent one at 4 p.m. precisely. Bend Or, the favourite, took up the running half a mile from home but was soon in trouble. Robert the Devil, ridden by Tom Cannon in this race, shot out to take a clear lead and won by three lengths from Lord Rosebery's filly Cipollata. Bend Or was unplaced. These two horses, Robert the Devil and Bend Or, met in three more races in which the former beat the Duke's horse on two occasions. At stud, Bend Or proved the better stallion, being twice second and twice third in the list of winning sires. When Charles Brewer died, Robert the Devil was sold to Mr John Bowes who was still racing in absentia (in Paris) from Streatlam in Durham.

Harry Hall painted the season's winners. Bend Or with Archer up (Plate 75) is an excellent example of his later style where more landscape improves the composition. Unfortunately I have not been able to locate the painting of Robert the Devil which is mentioned in a short obituary to Hall in the *Illustrated London News*:

> We were seldom at Newmarket without paying a visit to his studio, and, last spring, had the pleasure of seeing what is, perhaps, his best piece of work — a large picture of Robert the Devil, with Cannon up, the likeness of both horse and jockey being marvellously successful.

In 1880, Hall continued his brief association with the Ipswich Fine Art Club exhibiting two pictures: The Governor's Hack, and, as I have already mentioned, Sir Bevys at Epsom (The Property of Leopold de Rothschild Esq.).

— 1881 —

The Duchess of Westminster died in December 1880.

76 *Mr P. Lorillard's Iroquois, Fred Archer up (Derby and St Leger, 1881)* Private collection

She suffered from Bright's disease, a debilitating condition of the kidneys, which, during the last six months of her life prevented her from following as much racing as she would have liked; however, she saw Bend Or win the Derby. Because of her death, the Duke's Peregrine ran in the name of their son, the Hon Richard Grosvenor, in the 1881 2,000 Guineas. Peregrine with Fred Webb up had the race well in hand three furlongs from home and, striding along, won in a canter. Two American horses, Iroquois and Don Fulano were second and third.

A chestnut filly named Thebais belonging to Stirling Crawfurd was entered for the 1,000 Guineas and Oaks, to be ridden on both occasions by George Fordham. In the race at Newmarket, where Thebais was the favourite, she apparently struggled to gain a neck victory over Thora. The Demon, who never stretched a horse more than absolutely necessary, probably had plenty in hand for in the Oaks Thebais won in a canter. The fillies were always Fordham's 'speciality' and in 1883 he won the 1,000 Guineas for the seventh time, having won the Oaks on five occasions. Mr W. Stirling Crawfurd's death in 1883 coincided with Fordham's second retirement from racing. The Demon was having problems with his weight which, with age creeping up on him, he found more and more difficult to contain. It was said that he only made two mistakes in his life. One was to turn in Lord Clifden's saddle to look at Macaroni in the 1863 Derby, and the other was to trust a French financier. This honest and highly respected jockey died at the age of fifty in 1887.

Mr Pierre Lorillard's family was originally of German stock but two generations had been engaged in the manufacture of snuff and tobacco in America at the time of his birth in New York in 1833. As a young man Lorillard's interests lay in shooting and yachting, and later he turned to driving trotting horses. In 1873 he bought 1,200 acres of land in New Jersey and established a racing stud known as Rancocas. Five years later he started to ship horses to England. Iroquois was among a draft of yearlings sent to Newmarket in 1879 with Lorillard's trainer, Jacob Pincus. Iroquois was successful four out of the twelve times that he raced as a two-year-old in England, but the English trainers were sceptical of Pincus's stop-watch methods. A year later not much notice was taken of the colt's second place in the 2,000 Guineas, but Archer had seen the horse run and asked Pincus if he could ride Iroquois in the Derby; a request which was quickly met.

The weather at Epsom on 1 June was excessively hot and the large crowd sweltered on the Downs waiting for the race to start. Peregrine was favourite at the very short odds of 6 to 5, with Iroquois at 11 to 2.

The field of fifteen was away at the second attempt and in the last furlong Iroquois overtook Peregrine to win by half a length. Lord Rosebery's Town Moor was third. The colt (Plate 76) was the first American horse to win the Blue Riband and he and Archer received a tremendous cheer from the spectators who included many Americans, Mrs Lorillard among them. The colt went on to win the St Leger and in 1884 returned to America to stud in Tennessee.

Harry Hall painted Iroquois and another imported horse, Foxhall, owned by the American Mr James R. Keene. Foxhall was trained by William Day and, had he been entered for the Classics, might well have beaten Iroquois since he was considered to be a far better horse. Foxhall won the Cesarewitch and the Cambridgeshire as a three-year-old and the Ascot gold Cup a year later in 1882. The strong position of American horses on the English turf was established by these two colts who signalled that breeding in the United States, usually from English stock, was as effective as that practised in Britain.

Among his twenty-one Classic victories, Iroquois gave Fred Archer his third Derby and St Leger. In 1886 The Tinman won his last Derby and St Leger on the legendary Ormonde. The Duke of Westminster's colt was by Bend Or out of Lily Agnes by Macaroni. The Duke sent the yearling to John Porter at Kingsclere who became his trainer when Robert Peck retired in 1881. From Kingsclere the colt won the Triple Crown in 1886 ridden by George Barrett in the 2,000 Guineas and Archer in the other two races. In the late autumn of the same year Archer became ill, possibly brought on by severe wasting. His spirits were anyway pretty low since the loss of his wife (Helen Rose, a daughter of John Dawson) in childbirth two years before. On 8 November, in a fit of delirium, he shot himself. He was champion jockey for thirteen years of his brief racing career from 1869 to his death. Hall painted 'Archer up' on a string of winners stretching from Atlantic in 1874 to Iroquois in 1881. Portraits by Hall of Atlantic, Silvio (two), Spinaway and Iroquois hung on the walls of Archer's house at Newmarket. His sudden disappearance from the racing scene brought great sadness to everyone involved in the English turf and the general public alike, who had followed his exciting career in every newspaper. Lord Falmouth was deeply shocked at Archer's death which he survived by only three years, almost to the day. The triumvirate of Falmouth, Mathew Dawson and Archer ended when the owner suddenly sold his horses in 1884. The type of men they were and their regard for each other is demonstrated by the inscription on a piece of silver given to Falmouth by Dawson and Archer:

Offered for the acceptance of the Right Honourable the Viscount Falmouth by his trainer and jockey, Mathew Dawson and Frederick J. Archer, as a token of gratitude and esteem to the best, kindest, and most generous of masters on his retirement from the Turf, January 1884.

Lord Falmouth died in 1889. His death was keenly felt by the racing world and all those whom he employed and knew in Kent and Cornwall.

Harry Hall died before the first Classic race of 1882. For the sake of completeness I have taken the story of a few racing men by whom he was employed to the year they left racing, one way or another. Neither their deaths nor his can be described as the end of an era, except in so far that apart from Emil Adam and perhaps Alfred Havell there was no successor to Hall. The many owners, trainers and jockeys who followed Stirling Crawfurd, Lord Falmouth, the Duke of Westminster, the Osbornes, the Dawsons, Fordham and Archer provide a continuity in racing which stretches to the present day. With the exception of the paintings by Sir Alfred Munnings, their exploits and racehorses are recorded on canvas with far less panache.

CHAPTER 9

1882

But that the creatures of today
Are cast in quite a different mould
From what he recollects of old.

ON FRIDAY 21 APRIL, Harry Hall, feeling slightly off colour as he had been for the past few weeks, was walking from his Newmarket Church Lane studio to Audley Cottage, Upper Station Road (to which the family had moved the year before). In the High Street he experienced the agonising pain of a stroke, stumbled and fell. He was carried home where he died the following day, paralysed and without regaining consciousness. After a service in the Parish Church of All Saints his body was borne to the little cemetery at the top of the hill which overlooks the town and the Heath. Here he was buried with his son Frederick who had died twenty years before. The inscription on the stone over the grave is simple: 'Henry Hall. Born 18 August 1815. Died 22 April 1882.' His widow, Ellen, survived him by twenty-three years, dying in London in 1905.

The obituaries of the day do not say much about his painting ability, except *The Field*, but provide some insight into the character of the man, particularly in the *Cambridge Independent Press*, *Bell's Life* and *Baily's Magazine*.

The Times, Wednesday 26 April 1882

Mr Henry Hall, the animal painter, of Newmarket, died very suddenly last Saturday. In early life he was for a short time at Mr Pavis's School of Art, in London, Lowes Dickenson being among his fellow students. This constituted the whole of his schooling in art. Returning to Cambridge, his native place, he set up his studio as a portrait painter. The chance of work took him to Newmarket, where for 43 consecutive years he painted the winners of the Derby. He had considerable natural ability, not only for animal painting but for portraiture and landscape.

The Suffolk Chronicle, Saturday, 29 April 1882

Mr Harry Hall, the well known painter of racehorses, died at Newmarket on Saturday, of paralysis. His studio in that town was well known to all racing visitors, for Mr Hall painted nearly all the famous horses which have run during the last thirty or forty years. He had obtained so much celebrity in his line that he has often been sent for by owners of horses in various parts of Europe to paint their favourite racers. The exhibition of the Ipswich Fine Art Club has upon more than one occasion been enriched by works from his easel.

The Cambridge Independent Press and University Herald, Saturday, 29 April 1882

Newmarket. – The late Mr Harry Hall. – This famous artist and well-known inhabitant died somewhat suddenly on Saturday morning last, after only a few hours' illness. His friends had noticed evident signs of failing health for some time past, and about noon on Friday he was taken with an apoplectic seizure, to which he succumbed on Saturday without having regained consciousness. For nearly forty years the deceased gentleman had been well known as an artist, and was engaged by owners of famous racehorses in delineating the forms of the most celebrated performers of the day. So great was his fame that in the practice of his art he visited for this purpose France, Germany, Austria and even Russia. Were it possible to compile a list of the celebrities he has committed to canvas during his lengthened and honourable career, it would embrace nearly all the principal horses – not only of England but of other countries. He was a kind master and a genial man, much respected by all who knew him, and an excellent father to his family. His sons were indebted to him for a splendid education, and he lived to see most of them occupying distinguished and honourable positions, while the younger bid fair to attain distinction. All the principal houses in the High-street showed tokens of respect to the deceased during the passage on Tuesday of the funeral cortege through the town to the cemetery; and, notwithstanding the inclemency of the weather, a large number visited the cemetery during the ceremony.

Bell's Life of London and Sport, Saturday, 29 April 1882

Earlier in this melancholy morning the remains of Harry Hall, the well known artist, had been carried to their last resting place. News of his end came very unexpectedly to most of his friends and acquaintances, but to me he did not seem in his usual health when I talked to him in the Birdcage during the Craven week, and his rather dry, pungent criticisms of horses and men were quite wanting. I have had many a pleasant half hour in his studio, and heard many a sound opinion from his lips as to the result of some impending race of importance, and regret that his familiar form will be seen no more by the easel or sauntering among the cracks in the Birdcage before a Two Thousand or Cesarewitch.

Illustrated London News, 29 April 1882

A very large circle of friends and acquaintances will hear with deep regret of the somewhat sudden death of Mr Harry Hall, the well-known painter, which took place last Saturday. We were seldom at Newmarket without paying a visit to his studio, and, last spring, had the pleasure of seeing what is, perhaps, his best piece of work — a large picture of Robert the Devil, with Cannon up, the likeness of both horse and jockey being marvellously successful. A self-taught artist in the first instance, Mr Hall has for many years stood quite alone in his own particular line; indeed, he has enjoyed a complete monopoly of painting the portraits of famous winners, and his death has left a gap that it will be difficult indeed to fill up. He died at Newmarket, and was buried in the little cemetery at the 'top of the town'.

Baily's Magazine of Sports and Pastimes, May 1882

It is with deep regret that we refer to the sudden death of Mr Henry Hall, or 'Harry Hall', as he was familiarly called by his many friends and acquaintances. We were talking to him during the Craven week, and remarked that he looked ill and jaded, and appeared to us to walk with difficulty; but, in answer to our enquiries, he said he was very well. He was seized with paralysis on the 21st ult., and died the following day. We need scarcely say his loss is, in a certain sense, a public one, for he was without a rival in his special branch of art, and, so far as we know, there is no successor to take his place. His eldest son, Mr Sidney Hall, is a very talented artist, as we need scarcely say, but he does not follow in his father's steps. Mr Hall will be much missed by all Newmarket habitués, for he was a capital judge of a horse, was of course fond of racing, and his opinions thereon were freely given and worth listening to. To mention all the horses he has painted for the last five-and-twenty or thirty years would be to enumerate a list of Derby, Oaks and Leger winners, with many of the most celebrated horses in France, Austria and Germany. The proprietor of 'Baily's Magazine' will feel not only the loss of the clever artist who so faithfully put on canvas the counterfeit presentments of so many Derby winners, but he has to deplore the loss of a kind and genial friend. He was as beloved as he will be deeply mourned by his family, and his memory will long be respected in the town with which his name is identified.

The Field, or Country Gentleman's Newspaper, 29 April 1882

The obituary in *The Field* is very long and much of it is an essay on sporting painters of the past, and a complaint that no artist was able to paint a racehorse satisfactorily, least of all in motion.

Into his [George Stubbs] pictures of the Godolphin Arabian, of Eclipse, or of Highflyer, no soul and no inspiration entered; nor have they, in our judgement, much value, except in so far as they show what the race-horse of the last century was at his best.

To repeat the whole obituary would be tedious, so I have selected extracts which are directly relevant to Harry Hall.

The field is still open for a great master in this line, and the death of Mr Harry Hall — unquestionably the most accomplished of his fraternity at the moment when he was struck down by paralysis upon Thursday last week — leaves it more open than ever.

Born in 1814, Harry Hall took up his residence at

Newmarket just about the time when J. F. Herring, his predecessor, was on the decline. With the exception perhaps of Ben Marshall, Mr Hall was the only artist of his kind who gave himself up exclusively to the delineation of racehorses, and, almost without exception, to racehorses in condition. His predecessors had wandered over the whole range of equine portraiture; but it is doubtful whether any of them loved the crack three-year-old of his year with half the intensity that Harry Hall brought to bear upon his studies of the long series of Derby, Oaks and St Leger winners that he painted for Messrs A. H. Baily and Co., the sporting publishers of Cornhill. With the exception of a hunter or two in a stationary position, and of a sketch of the old and now dismantled stand at the end of the Bunbury mile, which its author called 'The Last Bit of Charles II that Newmarket contained', we can remember no picture by Harry Hall which was not the portrait of a racehorse pure and simple. ... A. Cooper's 'Oxygen' took the town by storm in 1831, but was in no degree superior to J. F. Herring's 'St Giles' in the following year, both pictures being in exactly the same style as that which Harry Hall subsequently adopted. We have said enough to show that, despite the many meritorious artists that have given themselves up to horse painting, the man of real genius in this line has not yet appeared ... The first winner that Harry Hall ever painted was Cossack, in 1847, and from that day, until Iroquois was led last year into the well-known studio to sit for his portrait to the artist who has just passed away. The likenesses were taken, almost without exception, for the owners of the victorious animals, although occasionally painted for sporting book-sellers, or for the editors of sporting magazines. A gallery of Derby, Oaks and St Leger winners, stretching from 1847 to 1881, sufficiently attests the lifelong devotion paid by Mr Hall to his art, and he is deserving of the highest praise that can be bestowed upon a workman who stuck to his easel conscientiously, and it may be added enthusiastically, from January to December, for so many successive years. His absences from Newmarket were few and far between, until, within the last decade, he was occasionally tempted abroad to paint some foreign crack. It was upon Newmarket, however, that his affections were centered, and no figure habitually seen in the little town's streets was more familiar than his. He had seen many changes and improvements during forty years of residence in the town of his adoption, which was greatly out of favour as a training centre when he first knew it, in about 1844, and then was looked down upon with scorn by the patrons of the great public stables in

Yorkshire and Hampshire, no less than by fierce Lord George Bentinck, who believed there was no such exercise ground upon earth as the Halnaker gallop at Goodwood. Mr Harry Hall lived, however, to see Newmarket acknowledged to be the turf metropolis in a far higher sense than that which our fathers attached to the word. Ever since the Derby of 1863 was won by Mr Naylor's Macaroni, Newmarket has carried away far more than its just share of the turf's great prizes. The result was that Mr Hall's brush has never been at rest, and it is difficult at this early date to pronounce which of the many pictures from his brush will ultimately be looked on as his chef d'oeuvre. The likeness of Bend Or is understood to have obtained the Duke of Westminster's hearty commendation; while that of Foxhall, sent to New York, has not found such unqualified favour in the critical eyes of Mr J.R. Keene. But we doubt whether this prolific artist was ever happier than in his representation of Silvio for Lord Falmouth, whose large gallery of pictures from the same brush speaks volumes for the astonishing success which has followed the magpie colours of Tregothnan during the last dozen years. Mr Hall's forte was undoubtedly a racehorse stripped and standing in his box. Portrayed in the open air, or standing upon the heath, his horses gave less satisfaction to critics, from the artist's inability to paint landscape adequately. Without claiming for him the title of a great artist, we may at least express the confident opinion that he will hereafter hold his own with Ferneley, Hancock, and J. F. Herring, the best of his predecessors; that his pictures will pass through the ordeal of criticism more successfully than those of the many rivals who have taken, without holding, the field against him during the last few years; and finally, that the works of his hand will fetch higher prices a century hence than those of Herring and Ferneley are commanding now. The pre-eminent position in his craft occupied by Mr Harry Hall is attested, indeed, by the difficulty of indicating who his successor will be. But for the early and lamented death of Mr Sheldon Williams, we think it probable that upon his shoulders Mr Hall's mantle would worthily have descended. Be this, however, as it may, the loss of England's best horse-painter will be widely regretted, not alone at Newmarket, where he was best known, but also in the many country houses scattered through the length and breadth of these islands, wherein his name has long been a familiar word.

When commenting on Hall's painting activity these obituaries concentrate quite naturally on his portraits of three-year-olds. While these commissions formed the major part of his work, Hall also painted steeple-chasers (more than a dozen Grand National winners, often the property of Classic-winning owners) and hunting portraits. As with his racing pictures, nearly all are painted in a static pose. There is more action in the many small genre paintings which he exhibited at the Royal Society of British Artists and the British Institution. These pictures of horses, dogs and donkeys were not always signed and, like his portraits, their identity is often lost. From time to time one comes across a delightful scene, usually with an element of humour in it, of some sporting or country activity which Hall must have experienced himself to be able to paint it with such conviction. They are not great works of art but exercises in relaxation, reflecting the kind of life which Harry Hall and his sons enjoyed near Newmarket in the mid-nineteenth century.

Hall's style of painting changed very little during the forty or so years that he portrayed racehorses. His smooth, early paintings of Bloomsbury and Crucifix with their windswept and featureless backgrounds gave way to more alert horses, better proportioned jockeys, with stands and ditches to show their locations. The differences are the same as those found when comparing the work of Abraham Cooper with that of J.F. Herring; the similarity of some of Hall's pictures to those of the latter is disappointing. Some of the charm of Hall's first paintings was lost in this first change in style. The requirements of publishers inevitably led him to adopt a formula for quickly catching a

likeness, the salient features and colouring of an animal, and the pose of a jockey which, once established, was often repeated. Such devices were skilfully interpreted by the engravers whose major contribution in the process of making a print is still under-rated. Once fluent in putting a picture together quickly, Hall probably found it quite difficult to return to a more careful and considered approach when he had time, which was not often. However, in the 1870s, when the pressures of publication were greatly reduced, his animals and their riders seem to be much more part of their surroundings. Previously they stood in front of a convenient landscape back-cloth; later they were integrated into the composition.

His contribution to the general field of British sporting painting is small and specialised, and is not of the same quality as the work of Marshall, Ferneley or J.F. Herring at his best. He was, however, a very successful journalist in paint providing a valuable and decorative record of thoroughbreds, some of whose names remain famous today; without his paintings we would have no idea what they looked like. His successors were more anatomically accurate in their portrayal of animals but they somehow lack the atmosphere and colour of the turf which is no less exciting now than during Hall's lifetime. The reason for this may have been the increasing use of photographs which give very little idea of the characters of the horses, owners or trainers portrayed. Hall's death coincided with and signalled the end of a style of sporting painting which had lasted for well over a hundred years.

HARRY HALL OF NEWMARKET

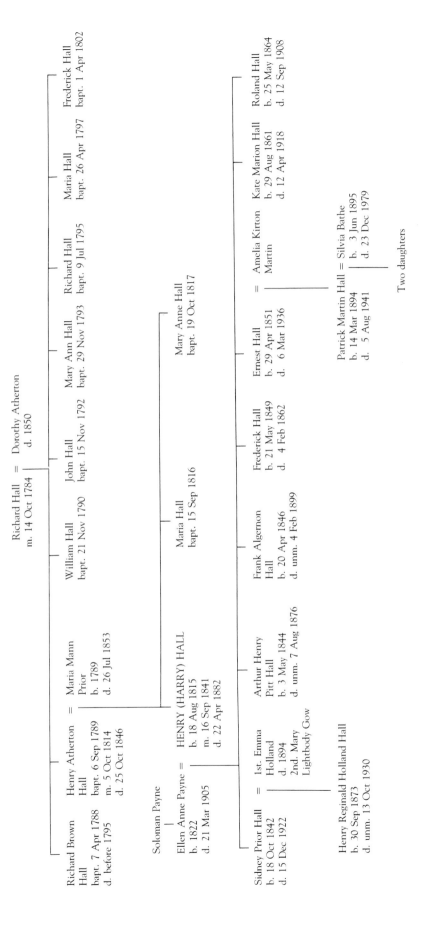

Richard Hall = Dorothy Atherton
m. 14 Oct 1784 | d. 1850

Richard Brown Hall
bapt. 7 Apr 1788
d. before 1795

Henry Atherton Hall
bapt. 6 Sep 1789
m. 5 Oct 1814
d. 25 Oct 1846
= Maria Mann Prior
b. 1789
d. 26 Jul 1853

William Hall
bapt. 21 Nov 1790

John Hall
bapt. 15 Nov 1792

Mary Ann Hall
bapt. 29 Nov 1793

Richard Hall
bapt. 9 Jul 1795

Maria Hall
bapt. 26 Apr 1797

Frederick Hall
bapt. 1 Apr 1802

Soloman Payne

Ellen Anne Payne =
b. 1822
d. 21 Mar 1905

HENRY (HARRY) HALL
b. 18 Aug 1815
m. 16 Sep 1841
d. 22 Apr 1882

Maria Hall
bapt. 15 Sep 1816

Mary Anne Hall
bapt. 19 Oct 1817

Sidney Prior Hall
b. 18 Oct 1842
d. 15 Dec 1922
= 1st. Emma Holland
d. 1894
2nd. Mary Lightbody Gow

Arthur Henry Pitt Hall
b. 3 May 1844
d. unm. 7 Aug 1876

Frank Algernon Hall
b. 20 Apr 1846
d. unm. 4 Feb 1899

Frederick Hall
b. 21 May 1849
d. 4 Feb 1862

Ernest Hall
b. 29 Apr 1851
d. 6 Mar 1936
= Amelia Kirton Martin

Kate Marion Hall
b. 29 Aug 1861
d. 12 Apr 1918

Roland Hall
b. 25 May 1864
d. 12 Sep 1908

Henry Reginald Holland Hall
b. 30 Sep 1873
d. unm. 13 Oct 1930

Patrick Martin Hall = Silvia Bathe
b. 14 Mar 1894 | b. 3 Jun 1895
d. 5 Aug 1941 | d. 23 Dec 1979

Two daughters

EXHIBITED WORK

Harry Hall's paintings were exhibited at the Royal Academy from 1838 to 1863 (7 pictures); the Royal Society of British Artists, 1839 to 1875 (26); the British Institution, 1847 to 1866 (17); and, at the end of his life, at the Ipswich Fine Art Club from its first exhibition in 1875 until 1880 (12). As well as a number of expected racehorse portraits, many of these exhibits illustrate Hall's interest and ability as a painter of human portraits and of genre scenes, of which very few of the latter are recognised as his work today.

Royal Academy

1838	235.	Edward Weatherby Esq.
1844	593.	William Pigott Esq., of Dullingham,
1845	659.	Newmarket.
		A Suffolk Cob, the property of the Revd Martin Lloyd, Branches Park, Newmarket.
1846	1331.	Thoroughbred Mares and Foal (Coranna's dam).
1851	694.	Hunters, the property of F. L. Popham Esq.
1852	1099.	'To him lads! Another blank'.
1863	248.	Favourite Hunters, the property of S. H. Arkwright Esq., Hampton Court.

Royal Society of British Artists

1839	13.	A Brood Mare.
1840	538.	The portrait of Bloomsbury, winner of the Derby 1839, and his jockey S. Templeman, with the portrait of Mr Wm. Ridsdale, his owner and trainer.
1844	97.	Portrait of the late Mrs Fairlie.
	109.	Portrait of John Fairlie Esq., of Cheveley Park, Newmarket.
1846	243.	Portrait of Mrs Hall Snr.
1847	482.	The Gipsy Girl.
1848	145.	The Children of R. W. King Esq.
	309.	Portraits of 'War Eagle', Marson and John Robinson.
1849	78.	Portraits of 'Surplice', John Kent Jnr, and Templeman, winner of the Derby and St Leger 1848, painted for the late Lord George Bentinck.

1851	134.	Portrait of Rhedycinz, ridden by F. Butler, winner of the Oaks at Epsom.
1854	58.	Old Pals.
	187.	The Gipsy's Haunt — Making a Move.
	287.	The Condemned.
1855	552.	The Keeper's Companion.
1857	186.	The Poachers Disturbed.
1858	213.	The Rendezvous.
1859	104.	The Cock o'the Walk.
1860	63.	A Patron of the Leash.
	553.	The Batthyany Arabian.
1861	204.	Magpie, a favourite Hunter, the property of John Fairman Esq.
	473.	Weatherbound, winner of the Cambridgeshire Stakes 1860.
1863	650.	Rufus, a Hunter, the property of John Manners Thorp Esq.
1864	246.	Portrait of Lord Clifden, winner of the Great St Leger Stakes 1863.
1874	152.	Portrait of a favourite Hunter, the property of J. M. Thorp Esq. of Chippenham.
1875	56.	Disputed Possession.
	435.	The 'Set To' for the St Leger by Lord Lyon and Savernake.

British Institution

1847	436.	The Interior of a Stable with Cart Horses.
	452.	Horses Frightened by a Dog.
1848	34.	The Gleaner.
1849	319.	Interior of a Bale Stable.
1852	257.	The Governor's Cob.
1853	355.	Shooting Companions.
1854	316.	Marking the Covey.
1855	542.	The First of September, a Welcome arrival.
1856	252.	Rabbit Ferreting. Look out Sir! They're running.
1857	147.	Happy Joe.
1858	473.	Government wins easy.
1859	374.	Thoroughbreds.
1860	190.	Down for the Season.
1861	119.	The Broken Fold.
1864	413.	Victory Proclaimed.
1865	163.	Desperate Poachers.
1866	315.	Rough and Ready.

Ipswich Fine Art Club

1875   4.   Mares and Foals, the property of Lord
                Falmouth.
       247.   'Happy Joe'.
1876   75.   A Favourite Cob.
       91.   My Hack.
       292.   Sketch of Stand and Stables on Bunbury Mile,
                Newmarket.
       308.   Queen of the Harem.
1879   224.   Midlothian (the property of His Grace the Duke
of Hamilton).

       229.   Lady Coventry (the property of the Hon.
                Viscount Falmouth).
       429.   Lily (the property of Mr W. C. Robertson,
                Dullingham Park, Newmarket).
       464.   Coomasie, winner of the Waterloo Cup 1877
                and 1878, painted for His Grace the Duke of
                Hamilton.
1880   98.   The Governor's Hack.
       210.   Sir Bevys at Epsom 1879 (The property of
                Leopold de Rotheschild Esq.).

ENGRAVINGS

Engraved plates of celebrated racehorses provided a widespread and interested public with the portraits of winners of Classic and other races from the late eighteenth to nineteenth centuries. Their comparative cheapness gave those who could not afford an original painting a memento of a success with which they might have some connection, if only to applaud a local hero. Because of their ephemeral interest it is very difficult to find such prints in good condition today. It is disappointing to report that neither the British Museum nor the Victoria and Albert Museum have a single example of the eighty or so aquatint engravings after the work of Harry Hall. Because of their scarcity, I have not been able to see every plate, let alone discover what comprises a 'complete list' of Hall engravings. The temptation is to continue searching but a line has to be drawn somewhere, and my line is drawn after fully recording more than sixty engravings. I have missed some, and should any readers be able to supply me with the details of such engravings, I would be most grateful to hear from them.

In a number of reference books it is said that Harry Hall painted forty-three consecutive Derby winners from 1838 to 1881. This may be so, but in terms of engravings there are certainly some gaps in the later years, the 1860s and 1870s.

In 1841 J. F. Herring gave up painting the racehorse portraits for the outstanding series of aquatint plates of St Leger winners (published by Herring and W. Sheardown at Doncaster from 1815 until being taken over by S. & J. Fuller of Rathbone Place, London in 1827), and Derby winners started by Messrs Fuller in 1827. Herring's last portrait was of Coronation (Derby, 1841). G.B. Spalding painted Satirist (St Leger, 1841) and Abraham Cooper portrayed Attila (Derby, 1842) for the Fullers. Harry Hall then painted the victors for both races until the Fullers stopped publication in 1846.

Another publisher, John Moore of St Martin's Lane, London, started a series of Oaks winners in 1836 which were painted by Herring from 1837 to 1841. In 1842 Abraham Cooper painted a very fine portrait of the Oaks winner, Our Nell; thereafter Hall provided for Moore a number of portraits of Derby, Oaks and St Leger winners between 1843 and 1847.

Finally, J. F. Herring was engaged by Baily Brothers of Cornhill, London, to paint their Derby, Oaks and St Leger winners from 1843 to 1847, (Abraham Cooper painted the Derby winner of 1847); after which Harry Hall portrayed a string of Derby, St Leger and other winners for Baily Brothers and later A. H. Baily & Co. until publication appears to have stopped at the time of the artist's death in 1882.

Goupil & Cie of Paris, with offices in The Strand in London, also published a number of plates of French racehorses after the paintings of Harry Hall between 1857 and 1880.

This complicated progression shows Hall working on series of engravings first for the Fullers, then the Fullers and Moore, and finally for the Bailys. Like his predecessors, Hall also painted a number of single plates used by these publishers, Goupil & Cie. and Thomas Maclean. Messrs Fores bought a number of Baily's plates and continue to re-issue them to the present day. The 'Hall' plates published by the Fullers, Moore, Baily and Goupil were engraved by George Hunt, Charles Hunt, C. N. Smith, John Harris (sometimes with Charles Quentery and William Summers), Summers alone, and Edward Gilbert Hester. These engravers served Hall and the publishers well, as did the army of colourists who, by their skill, brought the prints to life.

I have recorded the important detail from the titles of the plates; the sizes which I give are of the engraved surface excluding the titling. Where I have not seen an engraving and perhaps doubt that one exists I have, for the sake of completeness, included the name only of the Derby or St Leger winner for that year.

S. & J. Fuller

1842

St Leger
BLUE BONNET
Winner of the Great St Leger Stakes at Doncaster, 1842. 133 subscribers − 17 started. Rode by T. Lye. Bred by the Earl of

Eglinton, by Touchstone out of Maid of Melrose. The property of the Right Hon. The Earl of Eglinton.
Engraved by C. Hunt. Published 1 Nov 1842.
12¼ × 16¾ inches.

Jockey up, on a racecourse.

1843

Derby
COTHERSTONE
Winner of the Derby Stakes at Epsom, 1843. 153 subscribers — 23 started. Rode by Wm. Scott. By Touchstone out of Emma. The property of J. Bowes Esq.
Engraved by C. Hunt. Published 1 Jul 1843.
12¼ × 17 inches.

Jockey up, on racecourse.

St Leger
NUTWITH
Winner of the Great St Leger Stakes at Doncaster, 1843. 127 subscribers — 9 started. Rode by Marson. Bred by the late Captain Wrather, by Tomboy out of Comus Mare. The property of S. Wrather Esq.
Engraved by C. Hunt. Published 1 Nov 1843.
12¼ × 16¾ inches.

1844

Derby
ORLANDO
Winner of the Derby Stakes at Epsom, 1844. 155 subscribers — 29 started. Rode by N. Flatman. By Touchstone out of Vulture. The property of Colonel Peel.
Engraved by C. Hunt. Published Aug 1844.
12¼ × 17 inches.

Jockey up, in a landscape.

St Leger
FOIG-A-BALLAGH
Winner of the Great St Leger Stakes at Doncaster, 1844. 108 subscribers — 11 started. Rode by Henry Bell. Bred by George Knox Esq., by Sir Hercules out of Guiccioli. The property of E.H. Irwin Esq.
Engraved by C. Hunt. Published 1 Nov 1844.
12¼ × 17 inches.

Jockey up, on a racecourse.

1845

Derby
THE MERRY MONARCH
Winner of the Derby Stakes at Epsom, 1845. 138 subscribers — 31 started. Rode by F. Bell. Bred by Mr Gratwicke, by Colonel Peel's Slane out of Margravine. The property of Mr Gratwicke.
Engraved by C. Hunt. Published Jul 1845.
12¼ × 16¾ inches.

Jockey up, on a racecourse.

St Leger
THE BARON
Winner of the Great St Leger Stakes at Doncaster, 1845. 101 subscribers — 15 started. Rode by F. Butler. Bred by Mr Watts, by Birdcatcher out of Echidne. The property of George Watts Esq.

Engraved by C. Hunt. Published 20 Oct 1845.
12 × 16 inches.

Jockey up, by the rails of a course.

1846

Derby
PYRRHUS THE FIRST
Winner of the Derby Stakes at Epsom, 1846. 193 subscribers — 27 started. Trained by John Day, Rode by Saml Day. By Epirus out of Fortress. The property of John Gully Esq.
Engraved by C. Hunt. Published 10 Jul 1846.
15½ × 19¾ inches.

In a loosebox.

J. Moore

1842

2,000 Gns
METEOR
Winner of the Two Thousand Guineas at Newmarket, 1842. 24 subscribers — 8 started. Rode by W. Scott. Bred by Mr Burton, by Velocipede out of Dido. The property of J. Bowes Esq. of Streatlam Castle, Durham.
Engraved by C. Hunt. Published 20 Jun 1842.
12¼ × 16½ inches.

Jockey up, on a racecourse.

1846

Oaks
MENDICANT
Winner of the Oaks Stakes at Epsom, 1846, value £3,800. 138 subscribers — 24 started. Trained by J. Day Jnr, ridden by S. Day. Bred by Mr Witworth, by Touchstone out of Lady Moore Carew. The property of John Gully Esq.
Engraved by C. Hunt. Published 20 Jul 1846.
14¾ × 19½ inches.

Jockey up, in a landscape.

St Leger
SIR TATTON SYKES
Winner of the Great St Leger Stakes at Doncaster, 1846, value nett £3,975. 151 subscribers — 12 started. Trained by Wm Scott, Ridden by Wm Scott. Bred by Mr Hudson, by Melbourne out of Vitellius's dam. The property of Wm Scott.
Engraved by C. Hunt. Published 13 Nov 1846.
14¾ × 19½ inches.
Jockey up, being led off the course by Sir Tatton Sykes. Plate 45.

1847

Derby
COSSACK
Winner of the Derby Stakes at Epsom, 1847, value £5,500. 188 subscribers — 32 started. Trained by John Day, ridden by S. Templeman. By Hetmann Platoff out of Joannina. The property of T. Pedley Esq.
Engraved by C. Hunt. Published 1847.
15 × 19½ inches.

Jockey up, on a racecourse.

Goodwood Cup
THE HERO
Winner of the Goodwood Cup, 1847. By Chesterfield out of
Grace Darling. The joint property of Mr John Powney of
Lansdown, near Bath and Mr John Day of Danebury.
Engraved by C. Hunt. Published 31 Aug 1847.

14½ × 19½ inches.
Performance in other races also described. In a loosebox.

St Leger
VAN TROMP
Winner of the Great St Leger Stakes at Doncaster, 1847,
value £3,400. 148 subscribers — 8 started. Trained by J.
Fobert, ridden by J. Marson. Bred by Mr Vansittart, by
Lanercost out of Barbelle. The property of Lord Eglinton.
Engraved by C.N. Smith. Published 20 Oct 1847.

14½ × 19¼ inches.
Performance in other races also described. In a loosebox.
Reissued with the same publication date, recording winning
the 300 Sov. Stakes and Goodwood Cup in 1848, and the
Emperor's Plate at Ascot in 1849.

Cambridgeshire
THE WIDOW
Winner of the Cambridgeshire Stakes, 1847, value £1,800.
149 subscribers — 37 ran (the largest field ever started).
Trained by Lumley, ridden by R. Pettit. Bred by Lord
Westminster, by Abba Mirza out of Isabel. The property of
Lord Westminster.
Engraved by C. N. Smith. Published 13 Jan 1848.

14½ × 19¾ inches.
In a loosebox.

Goodwood Plate
CHANTICLEER
Winner of the Goodwood Plate, 1848.

Baily Brothers and, from 1862, A.H. Baily & Co.

1848

1,000 Gns
CANEZOU
Winner of the One Thousand Guineas Stakes at Newmarket,
1848. Ridden by Frank Butler. By Melbourne out of Madame
Pelerine. The property of Lord Stanley.
Engraved by C. Hunt.   15 × 20 inches.
Jockey up, on a racecourse.

Derby
SURPLICE
Winner of the Derby Stakes at Epsom, 1848. 215 subscribers —
17 started. Trained by J. Kent, ridden by S. Templeman. Bred
by Lord George Bentinck, by Touchstone out of Crucifix. The
property of Lord Clifden.
Engraved by C. Hunt. Published 15 Jun 1848.

15½ × 20¼ inches.
In a loosebox.

St Leger
SURPLICE
As above, with additional title: Winner of the Derby and St
Leger, 1848. Details of subscribers etc. deleted.

1849

Derby
THE FLYING DUTCHMAN
Winner of the Derby Stakes at Epsom, 1849. 237 subscribers —
26 started. Trained by J. Fobert, ridden by C. Marlow. By Bay
Middleton out of Barbelle. The property of the Earl of
Eglinton.
Engraved by C. Hunt.   15½ × 20¼ inches.
In a loosebox.

St Leger
THE FLYING DUTCHMAN
As above, with additional title: Winner of the Derby and St
Leger, 1849. Details of subscribers etc. deleted.

1850

Derby
VOLTIGEUR
Winner of the Derby Stakes at Epsom, 1850. 204 subscribers —
24 started. Trained by R. Hill, ridden by J. Marson. By
Voltaire out of Martha Lynn. The property of the Earl of
Zetland.
Engraved by C. Hunt.   15½ × 19¾ inches.
In a stable with Hill and Marson. Plate 49.

St Leger
VOLTIGEUR
As above, with additional title: Winner of the Derby and St
Leger, 1850. Details of subscribers etc. deleted.

Derby, St Leger & Doncaster Cup
VOLTIGEUR
R. Hill and Job Marson. Winner of the Derby Stakes at
Epsom, the Doncaster Great St Leger and the Doncaster Cup,
1850. Trained by R. Hill. By Voltaire out of Martha Lynn.
The property of the Earl of Zetland.
Engraved by J. Harris.   16 × 20 inches.
Unsaddled, on a racecourse, held by the trainer talking to the
jockey.

1851

The Great Match
The Great Match, between the Flying Dutchman 5 yrs & 8 st
8½ lb the property of the Earl of Eglinton and Voltigeur 4 yrs
8 st the property of the Earl of Zetland. Run at York, 13 May
1851; distance 2 miles for one thousand pounds. Won by the
Flying Dutchman by a length.
Engraved by C. Hunt. Published 1 May 1854.

21 × 42½ inches.
Scene of both horses with attendant owners, trainers, jockeys
and lads, with Admiral Rous and Mr George Payne, on York
Racecourse.

Derby
TEDDINGTON
Winner of the Derby Stakes at Epsom, 1851. 195 subscribers —
33 started. Trained by A. Taylor, ridden by Job Marson. By
Orlando out of Miss Twickenham. The property of Sir Joseph
Hawley Bart.
Engraved by C. Hunt.   19½ × 26½ inches.
Jockey up, on a racecourse, with other horses in the distance.

Goodwood Cup
NANCY
Winner of the Goodwood Cup, 1851. The property of Mr Martinson of Hull. By Pompey out of Hawise. Ridden by Job Marson.
Engraved by C. Hunt. Published 1 Oct 1851.
19½ × 26 inches.
Jockey up, on a racecourse, with owner and trainer.

St Leger
NEWMINSTER
Winner of the Great St Leger at Doncaster, 1851. Trained by J. Scott, ridden by S. Templeman. By Touchstone out of Bee's Wing. The property of A. Nichol Esq.
Engraved by J. Harris. Published 1 Nov 1851.
19½ × 26 inches.
Jockey up, on a racecourse, with John Scott and his grey hack.

1852

Derby
DANIEL O'ROURKE
Winner of the Derby Stakes at Epsom, 1852. Value of Stakes £3,050. 27 started. Trained by John Scott, ridden by Frank Butler. By Irish Birdcatcher out of Forget Me Not. The property of John Bowes Esq.
Engraved by C. Hunt.   19½ × 26 inches.
Jockey up, on a racecourse, with two other horses in the distance.

DANIEL O'ROURKE
Winner of the Derby Stakes at Epsom, 1852. 181 subscribers — 27 started. Trained by John Scott, ridden by Frank Butler. By Irish Birdcatcher out of Forget Me Not. The property of John Bowes Esq.
Engraved by J. Harris. Published 20 Jul 1852.
19½ × 25½ inches.
Jockey up, on a racecourse, with Mr Markwell.

St Leger
STOCKWELL
Winner of the Doncaster St Leger, 1852. 120 subscribers — 6 started. Trained by J. Harlock, ridden by Norman. By The Baron out of Pocahontas. The property of the Marquis of Exeter.
Engraved by J. Harris. Published 1 Nov 1852.
19½ × 26¼ inches.
Jockey up, on a racecourse with other horses in the distance. Plate 52.

1853

IRISH BIRDCATCHER
By Sir Hercules out of Guicioli. (Twice Champion Sire).
Engraved by J. Harris. Published 1 Jul 1853.
20 × 26 inches.

2,000 Gns, Derby & St Leger
WEST AUSTRALIAN
Winner of the 2,000 Guineas, Derby and St Leger, 1853. Trained by John Scott, ridden by Frank Butler. By Melbourne out of Mowerina. The property of John B. Bowes Esq.
Engraved by J. Harris. Published 21 Sep 1853.
19½ × 26 inches.
Jockey up, in a landscape, with the racehorse Sittingbourne.

1854

Derby
ANDOVER
Winner of the Derby Stakes at Epsom, 1854. 217 subscribers — 27 started. Trained by J. Day Jnr, rode by A. Day. By Bay Middleton out of Sister of Aegis. The joint property of John Gully and Henry Padwick Esqs.
Engraved by J. Harris & C. Quentery. Published 15 Aug 1854.
15 × 20 inches.
Jockey up, on a racecourse.

St Leger
KNIGHT OF St GEORGE
Winner of the Doncaster St Leger, 1854. Ridden by R. Basham. By Birdcatcher and dam of Hetmann Platoff. The property of and trained by J. Morris Esq.
Engraved by J. Harris & W. Summers.   19 × 26¾ inches.
Jockey up, on a racecourse.

1855

Derby
WILD DAYRELL
Winner of the Derby Stakes at Epsom, 1855. 191 subscribers — 12 started. Trained by Rickaby, ridden by Robert Sherwood. By Ion out of Ellen Middleton. The property of F.L. Popham Esq.
Engraved by J. Harris & C. Quentery. Published 1 Jul 1855.
18¾ × 26 inches.
Jockey up, in a landscape.

St Leger
SAUCEBOX

1856

RATAPLAN
By The Baron out of Pocahontas. The property of Mr Seymour Thelluson.
Engraved by J. Harris & C. Quentery. Published 1 Mar 1856.
18½ × 26 inches.
Held by his trainer, in a landscape.

MELBOURNE
Bred in 1834, by Humphrey Clinker, dam by Cervantes.
Engraved by J. Harris & W. Summers. Published 1 Mar 1856.
18½ × 26 inches.
In a loosebox, with a cat and groom.

Derby
ELLINGTON
Winner of the Derby Stakes at Epsom, 1856. Trained by T. Dawson, ridden by T. Aldcroft. By The Flying Dutchman out of Ellerdale. The property of Admiral Harcourt.
Engraved by J. Harris & C. Quentery. Published 1 Sep 1856.
19 × 26 inches.
Jockey up, on a racecourse.

St Leger
WARLOCK

1857

Derby & Oaks
BLINK BONNY
Winner of the Derby and Oaks Stakes at Epsom, 1857. Derby, 202 subscribers – 30 started. Oaks, 130 subscribers – 13 started. Ridden by J. Charlton. By Melbourne out of Queen Mary. The property of and bred and trained by Mr William I'Anson.
Engraved by J. Harris & W. Summers. Published 6 Jul 1857.
15 × 20 inches.
Jockey up, on a racecourse with other horses in the distance.

St Leger
IMPERIEUSE

1858

Derby
BEADSMAN
Winner of the Derby Stakes at Epsom, 1858. Trained by G. Manning, ridden by J. Wells. By Weatherbit out of Mendicant. The property of Sir Joseph Hawley Bart.
Engraved by J. Harris. Published 1 Aug 1858.
19 × 26 inches.
Jockey up, entering an enclosure, with two racehorses following.

St Leger
SUNBEAM

1859

Derby
MUSJID
Winner of the Derby Stakes at Epsom, 1859. Trained by G. Manning, ridden by J. Wells. By Newminster out of Peggy. The property of Sir Joseph Hawley Bart.
Engraved by J. Harris   19 × 26 inches.
In a loosebox.

St Leger
GAMESTER

1860

Derby
THORMANBY
Winner of the Derby Stakes at Epsom, 1860. 224 subscribers – 30 started. Trained by M. Dawson, ridden by Custance. By Melbourne or Windhound out of Alice Hawthorn. The property of James Merry Esq. M.P.
Engraved by J. Harris. Published 20 Jun 1860.
15¼ × 20 inches.
In a loosebox.

St Leger
ST ALBANS
Winner of the Doncaster Great St Leger, 1860. Trained by Alec Taylor, ridden by L. Snowden. By Stockwell out of Bribery. The property of the Marquis of Ailesbury.
Engraved by J. Harris. Published 1 Dec 1860.
15 × 19¾ inches.
In a loosebox, with a groom in the background.

1861

Derby
KETTLEDRUM
Winner of the Derby Stakes at Epsom, 1861. Trained by W. Oates, ridden by R. Bullock. By Rataplan out of Hybla. The property of Colonel Towneley.
Engraved by J. Harris.   15 × 20 inches.
In a loosebox.

St Leger
CALLER OU

1862

Derby
CARACTACUS
Winner of the Derby Stakes at Epsom, 1862. Trained by Zachery, ridden by J. Parsons. By Kingston out of Defenceless. The property of C. Snewing Esq.
Engraved by J. Harris.   15 × 20 inches.
In a loosebox.

St Leger
THE MARQUIS

1863

Grand National Steeplechase
EMBLEM
Winner of the Grand National, 1863. Ridden by George Stevens. The property of Lord Coventry.
Engraved by J. Harris.   15 × 20 inches.
In a loosebox.

Derby
MACARONI
Winner of the Derby Stakes at Epsom, 1863. Trained by James Godding, ridden by T. Chaloner. By Sweetmeat out of Jocose. The property of R.C. Naylor Esq.
Engraved by J. Harris. Published 1863.   15 × 20 inches.
In a loosebox.

St Leger
LORD CLIFDEN
Winner of the Great St Leger Stakes at Doncaster, 1863. Trained by Mr Edwin Parr, ridden by John Osborne. By Newminster out of Slave. The property of Viscount St Vincent.
Engraved by J. Harris. Published 1 Mar 1864.
15 × 20 inches.
In a loosebox.

1864

Grand National Steeplechase
EMBLEMATIC
Winner of the Grand National, 1864. Ridden by George Stevens. The property of Lord Coventry.
Engraved by J. Harris.   15 × 20 inches.
In a loosebox.

Derby
BLAIR ATHOL
Winner of the Derby Stakes at Epsom, 1864. Trained by
William I'Anson Esq., ridden by J. Snowden. By Stockwell
out of Blink Bonny. The property of William I'Anson Esq.
Engraved by J. Harris. Published 12 Jul 1864.

15 × 19¾ inches.

St Leger
BLAIR ATHOL
As above, with additional title: Winner of the Derby Stakes at
Epsom, 1864 and of the Great St Leger Stakes at Doncaster,
1864.

1865

Derby
GLADIATEUR
Winner of the Derby Stakes at Epsom, 1865. Trained by T.
Jennings, ridden by H. Grimshaw. By Monarque out of Miss
Gladiator. The property of Count Frederic de Lagrange.
Engraved by W. Summers.   15 × 20 inches.
In a loosebox.

St Leger
GLADIATEUR
As above, with additional title: Winner of the 2000 Guineas
Stakes at Newmarket; the Derby Stakes at Epsom and the
Great St Leger at Doncaster, 1865.

1866

Derby
LORD LYON
Winner of the Derby Stakes at Epsom, 1866. Trained by James
Dover, ridden by H. Custance. By Stockwell out of Paradigm.
The property of Richard Sutton Esq.
Engraved by W. Summers. Published 10 Jul 1866.

15 × 20 inches.

In a loosebox, with a cat.

St Leger
LORD LYON
As above, with additional title: Winner of the 2000 Guineas
Stakes at Newmarket, the Derby Stakes at Epsom and the
Great St Leger at Doncaster, 1866.

1867

Derby
HERMIT
Winner of the Derby Stakes at Epsom, 1867. Trained by Bloss,
ridden by J. Daley. By Newminster out of Seclusion. The
property of H. Chaplin Esq.
Engraved by W. Summers.   15×19¾ inches.
In a loosebox.

St Leger
ACHIEVEMENT
Winner of the Great St Leger Stakes at Doncaster, 1867.
Trained by James Dover, ridden by T. Chaloner. By Stockwell
out of Paradigm. The property of Colonel Pearson.
Engraved by W. Summers. Published 1 Nov 1867.

15 × 20 inches.

Held by a groom on a training ground.

1868

Derby
BLUE GOWN
Winner of the Derby Stakes at Epsom, 1868. Trained by
J. Porter, ridden by J. Wells. By Beadsman out of Bas Bleu.
The property of Sir Joseph Hawley Bart.
Engraved by W. Summers. Published 19 Aug 1868.

15 × 20 inches.

In a loosebox.

St Leger
FORMOSA
Winner of the Great St Leger Stakes at Doncaster, 1868.
Trained by H. Woolcott, ridden by T. Chaloner. By
Buccaneer out of Ella. The property of W. Graham Esq.
Engraved by W. Summers.   15 × 20 inches.

1869

Derby
PRETENDER
Winner of the Derby Stakes at Epsom, 1869. Trained by
T. Dawson, ridden by J. Osborne. By Adventurer out of
Ferina. The property of J. Johnstone Esq.
Engraved by W. Summers.   15 × 20 inches.
In a loosebox.

St Leger
PERO GOMEZ
Winner of the Great St Leger Stakes at Doncaster, 1869.
Trained by J. Porter, ridden by J. Wells. By Beadsman out of
Salamanca. The property of Sir Joseph Hawley Bart.
Engraved by W. Summers.   15 × 20 inches.
Jockey up, on a racecourse with the trainer and his hack.

1870

Derby
KINGCRAFT

St Leger
HAWTHORNDEN

1871

Derby
FAVONIUS
Winner of the Derby Stakes at Epsom, 1871. Bred by the
owner, by Parmesan out of Zephyr. The property of Baron
Mayer de Rothschild.
Engraved by E. G. Hester. Published 31 Jul 1871.

14¾ × 19 inches.

In a loosebox.

Ascot Gold Cup
MORTIMER
Winner of the Ascot Gold Cup, 1871. Trained by
T. Jennings, ridden by George Fordham. The property of Mr
T. Lombard.
Engraved by E. G. Hester.   15 × 20 inches.
In a loosebox.

St Leger
HANNAH
Winner of the One Thousand Guineas at Newmarket, the
Oaks Stakes at Epsom and the Doncaster Great St Leger in
1871. By King Tom out of Mentmore Lass. The property of
Baron Mayer de Rothschild.
Engraved by E. G. Hester. Published 5 Jan 1872.

15 × 19¾ inches.

In a loosebox. Plate 72.

1872

Derby
CREMORNE
Winner of the Derby Stakes at Epsom, 1872. By Parmesan out
of Rigolboche. The property of Henry Saville Esq.
Engraved by E. G. Hester. Published 4 Oct 1872.

15 × 19¾ inches.

In a loosebox.

St Leger
WENLOCK

1873

Derby
DONCASTER
Winner of the Derby Stakes at Epsom, 1873. By Stockwell out
of Marigold. The property of James Merry Esq. M.P.
Engraved by E. G. Hester. Published 25 Aug 1873.

14¾ × 19½ inches.

In a loosebox.

St Leger
MARIE STUART

1874

Middle Park Plate & 2,000 Gns
PRINCE CHARLIE
Winner of the Middle Park Plate and 2,000 Guineas at
Newmarket. By Blair Athol out of Eastern Princess. The
property of Henry Jones Esq.
Engraved by E. G. Hester. Published 1 May 1874.

15 × 20 inches.

In a loosebox.

Derby
GEORGE FREDERICK

St Leger
APOLOGY
Winner of the One Thousand Guinea Stakes at Newmarket,
the Oaks at Epsom and the Doncaster Great St Leger in 1874.
By Adventurer out of Mandragova. The property of Mr.
Launde.
Engraved by E. G. Hester.   15 × 20 inches.
In a loosebox.

1875

Derby
GALOPIN
Winner of the Derby Stakes at Epsom, 1875. By Vedette out
of Flying Duchess. The property of Prince Batthyany.
Engraved by E. G. Hester.   15 × 20 inches.
In a loosebox.

St Leger
CRAIG MILLAR

1876

Derby
KISBER
Winner of the Derby Stakes at Epsom, 1876. By Buccaneer
out of Mineral. The property of Mr A. Baltazzi.
Engraved by E. G. Hester.   15 × 20 inches.
In a loosebox.

St Leger
PETRARCH

1877

Derby
SILVIO
Winner of the Derby Stakes at Epsom, 1877. Trained by
Mathew Dawson, ridden by F. Archer. By Blair Athol out of
Silverhair. The property of Lord Falmouth.
Engraved by E. G. Hester. Published 25 Aug 1877.

14¾ × 19½ inches.

In a loosebox. Plate 74.

St Leger
SILVIO
As above, with additional title: Winner of the Derby Stakes at
Epsom and of the Great St Leger Stakes at Doncaster, 1877.

1878

Derby
SEFTON

St Leger
JANETTE

1879

Derby
SIR BEVYS
Winner of the Derby Stakes at Epsom, 1879. Trained by
Joseph Hayhoe, ridden by George Fordham. By Favonius out
of Lady Langden. The property of Mr Acton.

St Leger
RAYON D'OR

1880

Derby
BEND OR
Winner of the Derby Stakes at Epsom, 1880. Trained by
R. Peck. ridden by F. Archer. By Doncaster out of Rouge
Rose. The property of the Duke of Westminster.
Engraved by E. G. Hester. Published 31 Jul 1880.

15 × 20 inches.

Jockey up, in a landscape.

St Leger
ROBERT THE DEVIL

1881

Derby
IROQUOIS
Winner of the Derby Stakes at Epsom, 1881. Trained by J.
Pincus, ridden by F. Archer. By Leamington out of Maggie
B.B. The property of Mr Pierre Lorillard.
Engraved by E. G. Hester.   15 × 20 inches.
Jockey up, on a racecourse, with other horses in the distance.

St Leger
IROQUOIS
As above, with additional title: Winner of the Derby Stakes at
Epsom and the St Leger Stakes at Doncaster, 1881.

Goupil & Cie

1858

MADEMOISELLE DE CHANTILLY
Prix de l'Empereur, Paris, 1857; Prix de Diane, Chantilly and
Suburban Handicap, Epsom, 1858. Entrainée par Thom.
Jennings. Monté par Spreoty. Par Gladiator et Maid of Mona.
Appartenant a M. Le Comte Frederic de Lagrange.
Engraved by J. Harris.   19 × 26¼ inches.
Jockey up, at Newmarket. Plate 60.

ETOILE DU NORD
Prix de Diane, Chantilly, 1858. Entrainée par Thom.
Jennings. Par The Baron et Maid of Hart. Appartenant a M. le
Comte Frederic de Lagrange.
Engraved by J. Harris.   19 × 26¼ inches.
In a stable, with a groom

VENTRE-SAINT-GRIS
Derby français, 1858. Entrainée par Thom. Jennings. Monté
par Kendall. Par Gladiator et Balle de Nuit. Appartenant a M.
le Comte Frederic de Lagrange.
Engraved by J. Harris.   19 × 26 inches.
Jockey up, at Chantilly.

1859

BLACK PRINCE
Prix de premier pas à Chantilly, 1858; Prix du Jockey Club
(Derby français) à Chantilly; Derby Continental, Gand;
Grand St Leger de France, Moulins; Prix Special, Paris
(Réunion d'automne), 1859. Entrainée par Thom. Jennings.
Monté par Quinton. Appartenant a M. le Comte Frederic de
Lagrange.
Engraved by J. Harris.   19 × 26¼ inches.
Jockey up, at Chantilly.

1863

LA TOUCQUES
Par The Baron, La Mère Tapestry par Melbourne. 1863.
Engraved by J. Harris.   19 × 26 inches.

1865

FILLE DE L'AIR
Criterion Stakes et 4 autres Prix en Angleterre, 1863; Prix de
Diane; Grand Prix du Prince Imperial; Oaks et 5 autres Prix en
Angleterre, 1864; Grand Prix de L'Imperatrice; Derby Trial;
Claret Stakes et plusiers autres Prix, 1865. Entrainée par
Thom. Jennings. Monté par A. Edwards. Par Faugh a Ballagh
et Pauline. Appartenant a M. le Comte F. de Lagrange.
Engraved by J. Harris   19 × 26 inches.
Jockey up, at Newmarket.

GLADIATEUR
Clearwell Stakes à Newmarket, 1864; 2,000 Guineas à
Newmarket; Derby à Epsom; Grand Prix de Paris; Gt St Leger
à Doncaster, 1865. Entrainée par Thom. Jennings. Monté par
H. Grimshaw. Par Monarque et Miss Gladiator. Appartenant
à M. le Comte Frederic de Lagrange.
Engraved by J. Harris.   19 × 26 inches.
In a loosebox.

1866

GLADIATEUR
2,000 Guineas; Derby à Epsom; St Leger à Doncaster; Grand
Prix de Paris, 1865; Grand Prix de l'Empereur et de plusiers
autres Prix, 1866. Entrainée par Thom. Jennings. Monté par
H. Grimshaw. Par Monarque et Miss Gladiator. Appartenant
à M. le Comte Frederic de Lagrange.
Engraved by W. Summers.   19 × 26 inches.
Jockey up, on racecourse.

1873

MONTARGIS
Cambridgeshire, 1873. Entrainée par Thom. Jennings. Monté
par J. Carratt.
Engraved by E.G. Hester.   19 × 26 inches.
In a loosebox.

1877

JONGLEUR
French Derby and St Leger, 1877. Cambridgeshire, 1877. By
Mars out of Juliette. The Property of Count de Juinge and
Prince Auguste d'Arenberg.
Engraved by W. Summers.   19 × 26 inches.
In a loosebox.

1879

RAYON D'OR
St Leger, 1879. Monté par J. Goater. Par Flagelot et
Auracaria. Appartenant à Monsieur le Comte Frederic de
Lagrange.
Engraved by W. Summers.   19 × 26 inches.
Jockey up, on racecourse.

W. Stevens, Cheltenham

1870

Grand National 1869 & 1870
THE COLONEL
Winner of the Liverpool Grand National Steeplechase in 1869
and 1870. Ridden by George Stevens.
Engraved by W. Stevens.   18¾ × 26½ inches.
Jockey up, in a landscape.

T. McLean

1880

Ascot Gold Cup 1879 & 1880
ISONOMY
Engraved by E.G. Hester. Published 1 Oct 1880.
                                           14 × 19 inches.
In a loosebox.

J. Watson

1848

THE MERRY BEAGLERS
(left to right) C. Phelips Esq. of Briggens Park, Hertfordshire;
the Revd. P.J. Honywood, Rector of Marks Hall, Essex; and
Tom Pitts, huntsman.
Engraved by J. Harris. Published 5 Aug 1848.
                                       16½ × 28¼ inches.
Figures in an Essex landscape, with numerous hounds.
3¾ inches were cut from the right side of the original copper
plate in about 1897, resulting in the loss of two hound
portraits and part of the cottage depicted.

Year Not Known

BACCHUS
                                           15 × 20 inches.
In a loosebox.

ENGRAVINGS IN PERIODICALS

The Sporting Magazine

The Sporting Magazine was first published in 1792. In 1848 this magazine absorbed the *Sporting Review* (first published in 1839) which in turn had absorbed the *Sportsman* (1833) and the *New Sporting Magazine* (1831) in 1845 and 1846 respectively. However, all four titles continued to be used with identical contents until 1870 when *The Sporting Magazine* ceased publication. Engravings after the work of Harry Hall were published in *The Sporting Magazine* from 1840 to 1870. The majority of these plates are from small paintings on board (approximately 10 × 13 inches) of portraits of race-horses (mostly engraved by E. Hacker) and jockeys (engraved by J. B. Hunt). A comparison between the paintings and the plates shows that the engravers interpreted the inevitable crudeness of the small oils with considerable skill. I have also found that these small plates have been invaluable in rediscovering the names of horses and jockeys in pictures which have lost their titles. As early as 1850, nine engravings of racehorse portraits were republished to illustrate George Tattersall's *Pictorial Gallery of English Race-Horses*, and many more were reproduced with articles in *Baily's Magazine of Sports and Pastimes* from 1860 to 1926.

Engravings after Harry Hall:

Year	Month	Volume	Page	Subject
1840	September	96	360	Crucifix
1847	June	110	14	Cossack
	July	110	92	Miami
1848	January	111	10	Van Tromp
	July	112	10	Surplice
	August	112	134	Cymba
	October	112	288	The Hero
1849	January	113	11	Surplice and Canezou
	March	113	176	St Laurence
	May	113	367	Chanticleer
	June	113	447	The Harrier Kennel
	July	114	21	The Flying Dutchman
	August	114	136	Lady Evelyn
1850	March	115	162	Collingwood
	July	116	14	Voltigeur
	August	116	118	Rhedicyna
	November	116	368	Mounseer
1851	February	117	124	Russborough
	April	117	252	Peep o'Day Boy
	July	118	65	Teddington
	August	118	120	Iris
	November	118	297	Newminster
1852	January	119	58	James Chapple, jockey
	February	119	96	Nancy
	July	120	67	Daniel O'Rourke
	August	120	97	Songstress
	November	120	357	Stockwell
1853	January	121	50	James Robinson, jockey
	February	121	141	Irish Birdcatcher
	April	121	202	Joe Miller
	July	122	10	E. 'Nat' Flatman, jockey
	July	122	65	West Australian
	August	122	86	Catherine Hayes
	November	122	315	Jouvence
1854	February	123	143	F. Butler, jockey
	April	123	231	Melbourne
	July	124	1	Andover
	August	124	75	Mincemeat
	November	124	309	The Knight of St George
1855	January	125	1	Job Marson, jockey
	February	125	75	Virago
	July	126	1	Wild Dayrell
	August	126	88	Marchioness
	September	126	153	Mr John Scott, trainer
	November	126	374	Saucebox
1856	January	127	36	Simeon Templeman, jockey
	February	127	132	Rataplan
	July	128	59	Ellington
	August	128	94	Mincepie
	November	128	320	Warlock
1857	January	129	1	Charles Marlow, jockey
	February	129	85	Fandango
	July	130	1	Blink Bonny
	August	130	87	Emigrant
	November	130	333	Imperieuse
1858	January	131	1	J. Bartholomew, jockey
	February	131	83	Queen Mary
	May	131	344	Fisherman
	July	132	63	Samuel Rogers, jockey
	July	132	65	Beadsman
	August	132	98	Governess
	November	132	336	Sunbeam

1859	January	133	15	J. Wells, jockey
	February	133	95	Saunterer
	July	134	15	Musjid
	August	134	90	Summerside
	November	134	375	Gamester
1860	April	135	226	Longbow
	July	136	15	Thormanby
	August	136	139	Butterfly
	September	136	198	Alfred Day, jockey
	November	136	357	St Albans
1861	February	137	97	Underhand
	May	137	329	Gemma di Vergy
	July	138	65	Kettledrum
	August	138	143	Brown Duchess
	November	138	381	Caller Ou
1862	April	139	289	The late Luke Snowden, jockey
	July	140	23	Caractacus
	August	140	105	Feu-de-Joie
	November	140	388	The Marquis
1863	March	141	199	Tim Whiffler
	March	141	203	The late Ralph Bullock, jockey
	July	142	65	Macaroni
	August	142	105	Queen Bertha
	November	142	340	Lord Clifden
1864	July	144	15	Blair Athol
	July	144	61	Thomas Chaloner, jockey
	August	144	89	Fille-de-l'Air
1865	January	145	15	John Osborne, jockey
	February	145	131	Asteroid
	July	146	63	Gladiateur
	August	146	106	Regalia
1866	June	147	431	Lord Lyon
	June	147	463	Repulse
	July	148	22	Tormentor
	September	148	170	George Osbaldeston Esq., as a jockey
1867	March	149	167	Achievement
	June	149	421	Vauban
	July	150	42	Hermit
	August	150	89	Hippia
	August	150	93	John Daley, jockey
1868	January	151	15	Julius
	June	151	408	Formosa
	July	152	15	Blue Gown
1869	January	153	31	The Earl
	June	153	449	The Pretender
	July	154	23	Brigantine
	November	154	341	Pero Gomez
1870	March	155	176	Vespasian
	May	155	323	The Colonel
	July	156	26	Kingcraft
	August	156	99	Gamos
	November	156	329	Hawthornden

A vignette after Harry Hall appears in Volume 112, July 1848.

The Field, or Country Gentleman's Newspaper

The Field was first published on Saturday, 1 January 1853. As well as current affairs and other 'intelligence', a large proportion of this weekly publication was devoted to field sports. Harry Hall joined John Leech, Richard Ansdell, Harrison Weir, H. K. Browne and others in illustrating the sporting activities during 1853 and 1854. By mid-1854 T. H. Wilson was providing the majority of the steel plate engravings, including horse portraits, perhaps as a staff illustrator. From January 1855 there were very few illustrations at all; a limited number in the 1860s, mostly by Ben Herring, and thereafter none to speak of through to the 1880s where my interest ends. Engravings by or after Harry Hall:

20 April 1853
    West Australian — the winner of the Two Thousand Guineas Stakes. From a drawing by Hall, of Newmarket.
28 April 1853
    West Australian and Sittingbourne. Drawn by Hall, of Newmarket.
4 June 1853
    Catherine Hayes.
11 June 1853
    Portrait of Rataplan — winner of the Queen's Vase. Drawn by Harry Hall, of Newmarket.
18 June 1853
    Teddington — the winner of the Emperor's Vase. Drawn by Harry Hall, of Newmarket.
18 June 1853
    Stockwell. Drawn by Harry Hall, of Newmarket.
2 July 1853
    Vanning the Favourite. Drawn by Harry Hall.
9 July 1853
    Marsyas — winner of the Newmarket July Stakes. Drawn by Harry Hall, of Newmarket.
23 July 1853
    The First Lesson. Drawn by Harry Hall.
30 July 1853
    Portrait of Adine — winner of the Goodwood stakes. Drawn by Harry Hall.
30 July 1853
    Horses on the Road to Goodwood. Drawn by Harry Hall.
30 July 1853
    Just in from Exercise — 'Dressing Over'. Drawn by Harry Hall.
6 August 1853
    Jouvence — winner of the Goodwood Cup, and French Derby and Oaks, 1853. Drawn by Harry Hall.
3 September 1853
    Going to Sweat. Drawn by Harry Hall.
17 September 1853
    The winner of the Champagne Stakes at Doncaster. Drawn by Harry Hall.
24 September 1853
    The Start for the St Leger. Drawn by Harry Hall, of Newmarket.

24 September 1853
  Portrait of Hungerford — winner of the Doncaster Cup. Drawn by Harry Hall, of Newmarket.
29 October 1853
  Backed for the First Time — 'Hold Tight, Boy'. Drawn by Harry Hall of Newmarket.
7 January 1854
  'Autocrat', the first favourite for the Derby, 1854. Drawn by H. Hall.
11 March 1854
  Coursing Cracks, No. V — Lord Stradbroke's Merry Maid and Mr Miller's Barabbas. Drawn by H. Hall.
1 April 1854
  Portrait of 'Melbourne'. Drawn by H. Hall.
6 May 1854
  'The Hermit', winner of the Two Thousand Guinea Stakes. Drawn by H. Hall.
3 June 1854
  'Andover', winner of the Derby. Drawn by H. Hall.
10 June 1854
  'Mince-Meat', winner of the Oaks. Drawn by H. Hall.

Illustrated London News

The *Illustrated London News* was first published in 1842. From the outset this weekly paper was profusely illustrated and for a short time in a humorous vein. A number of portraits of Derby, Oaks, Ascot Cup and St Leger winners, by or after drawings by J. F. Herring, Abraham Cooper, and predominantly by Ben Herring were published until the mid-1850s; a few were by Harrison Weir, J. F. Herring's so-in-law. These 'sketches' are crude line engravings, far less fine than those of the various race trophies of the period. Apart from a single sketch in 1844 the majority of winners by or after Harry Hall appear, with those of Ben Herring, between 1857 and 1867. After 1867 they are poorly drawn by Samuel Carter until John Sturgess comes on the scene with a few very good illustrations.

On 18 March 1854 there is an engraving after Harry Hall's 'Marking the Covey', a painting which had recently been exhibited at the British Institution. Each year, the editor selected four or five pictures from this exhibition, had them finely engraved (Plate 6) and commented on their merit.

'Marking the Covey'
Harry Hall's picture of 'Marking the Covey' will be admired and appreciated by the votaries of field sports as well as admirers of art. It is a capital sporting group, in a true sporting country; the old gamekeeper seated on his donkey, and pointing to the distant covey as they are about to settle, is true to life; the rough shooting pony and the boys in attendance indicate that the party are waiting on the setting out of the 'squire, heir master; to whom appearance promises a good day's sport.

Engravings by or after Harry Hall:

18 May 1844
  Portrait of Ratan.
3 January 1857
  Greyhounds 'Lady Clare' and 'Asylum' from the Newmarket Champion Meeting.
9 May 1857
  Lord Zetland's 'Vedette', the winner of the Two Thousand Guineas Stakes at Newmarket.
6 June 1857
  Blink Bonny, the winner of the Derby and Oaks.
26 September 1857
  'Imperieuse', the winner of the St Leger Stakes at Doncaster, 1857
24 October 1857
  The deciding heat for the Cesarewitch Stakes, 1855.
7 November 1857
  'Odd Trick', winner of the Cambridgeshire Stakes at Newmarket.
12 December 1857
  The celebrated racehorse 'Fisherman' (unsigned, but probably by Hall).
Supplement 1 May 1858
  'Fitzroland', winner of the 2,000 Stakes.
Supplement 1 May 1858
  'Governess', winner of the 1,000 Stakes.
29 May 1858
  'Beadsman', winner of the Derby.
21 May 1859
  Promised Land, winner of the 2,000 Guineas (unsigned, but probably by Hall).
24 September 1859
  Gamester.
11 May 1861
  Diophantus, winner of the 2,000 Guineas.
8 June 1861
  Brown Duchess, winner of the Oaks.
8 June 1861
  Kettledrum, winner of the Derby (unsigned, but probably by Hall).
22 June 1861
  Thormanby, winner of the Ascot Cup (unsigned, but probably by Hall).
10 August 1861
  Starke, winner of the Goodwood Cup.
28 September 1861
  Caller Ou, winner of the St Leger Stakes.
17 May 1862
  The Marquis, winner of the 2,000 Guineas.
14 June 1862
  Caractacus, winner of the Derby.
14 June 1862
  Feu de Joie, winner of the Oaks.
28 June 1862
  Asteroid, winner of the Ascot Cup.
9 August 1862
  Tim Whiffler, winner of the Goodwood Cup.
2 May 1863
  Macaroni, winner of the 2,000 Guineas.
30 May 1863
  Queen Bertha, winner of the Oaks.

13 June 1863
   Buckstone, winner of the Ascot Cup.
3 October 1863
   Lord Clifden, winner of the St Leger.
7 May 1864
   General Peel, winner of the 2,000 Guineas.
4 June 1864
   Blair Athol, winner of the Derby.
   'Our sketches are by Mr Harry Hall, of Newmarket, who recently had the honour of submitting his large portrait of Stockwell, the sire of Blair Athol, to his Royal Highness the Prince of Wales, at Marlborough House.'
4 June 1864
   Fille de L'Air, winner of the Oaks.
18 June 1864
   Scottish Chief, winner of the Ascot Cup.
6 August 1864
   Dollar, winner of the Goodwood Cup (unsigned, but probably by Hall).

13 May 1865
   Gladiateur, winner of the 2,000 Guineas.
24 June 1865
   Ely, winner of the Ascot Cup.
28 April 1866
   Lord Lyon, winner of the 2,000 Guineas.
26 May 1866
   Tormentor, winner of the Oaks.
11 August 1866
   The Duke, winner of the Goodwood and Brighton Cups.
4 May 1867
   Vauban, winner of the 2,000 Guineas.
1 June 1867
   Hermit, winner of the Derby.
1 June 1867
   Hippia, winner of the Oaks.
15 June 1867
   Lecturer, winner of the Ascot Cup.

INDEX

Racehorses